# Insanity, Psychiatry and Criminal Responsibility

Finbarr McAuley

THE ROUND HALL PRESS

The typesetting for this book was
produced by Reepro, Dublin
for The Round Hall Press,
Kill Lane, Blackrock, Co. Dublin.



A catalogue record for this book
is available from the British Library.

ISBN 1-85800-011-4

ACKNOWLEDGMENT

The author and publishers wish to acknowledge
a grant in aid towards the cost of publication of this book
from the Academic Publications Committee,
University College, Dublin.

Printed by
Betaprint, Dublin

To Francesca and Victoria

# Contents

# Preface

This book is about the way in which mental disorder affects criminal responsibility. Unlike the standard treatments of this subject which tend to concentrate on the jurisprudence on the insanity defence, the approach set out here also draws heavily on the scientific literature on mental illness. The result is an attempt—unique, as far as I am aware—to integrate the psychiatric understanding of mental illness into a conventional analysis of the knot of legal problems surrounding the insanity plea. Although I have tried to avoid the use of technical terms except where their employment is essential to the development of the argument and their meaning clearly explained, I have not sought to protect the reader from the difficulties of the subject; and there are parts of most chapters—particularly the sections on schizophrenia in chapters 2 and 3 and on neurophysiology in chapters 4 and 5—that are likely to prove taxing to the tyro. My hope is that these will yield to concentrated attention and, in the final analysis, enhance the reader's—and particularly the legal reader's—appreciation of the complexity of the issues involved in the proper management of the mentally disordered defendant at all stages of the criminal process.

In particular, I hope that the detailed critique of the notion of irresistible impulse in chapter 3 will help to convince the reader that, the stated position of the Irish Supreme Court to the contrary notwithstanding, serious mental disorder is better understood as a cognitive failing affecting the ability to make valid inferences from the relevant available data, rather than as a volitional disability affecting an agent's capacity to control his actions; and that this insight is essential to the development of a sound criterion of exculpatory insanity in the criminal law. Similarly, I hope that the book's emphasis on the neurophysiological basis of human behaviour will help to undermine the dogma that psychological evidence must be confined to the sphere of recognised mental disorders, and should not be admitted in respect of mental conditions and emotional states that do not answer to this description because they fall within the range of normal human variation. As I argue in chapter 5, there is no scientific basis for this rule or the policy considerations usually relied on to justify it.

Finally, I hope that what I have to say about the psychiatric assessment of dangerousness—in chapters 1 and 6—helps to dispel the myth that the discipline of psychiatry somehow guarantees its practitioners privileged access to the future. Given that the scientific evidence suggests that psychiatric prediction is a very poor guide to future conduct, it is submitted that we should be loathe to accept it as evidence of dangerousness or, *a fortiori*, as a reliable basis for the compulsory hospitalization or continued detention of mentally disordered defendants adjudged to be dangerous on foot of psychiatric evidence to that effect.

Again in contrast with the standard accounts of the insanity plea, the book also has a substantial comparative law component. Each chapter draws on material from other common-law jurisdictions and chapter 9 consists of a comprehensive survey of the relevant civilian material. Most readers will at least be familiar with the broad outlines of the former, but, for obvious reasons, will know very little about the latter. As chapter 9 illustrates, this constitutes a significant gap in our knowledge given the variety and sophistication of the solutions civilian systems generally—and German and Italian law particularly—bring to the entire spectrum of problems associated with the mentally disordered defendant. In addition, chapter 8 compares and contrasts the three leading models—the Scottish, English and Californian, respectively—of the plea of diminished responsibility, which typically caters for the mentally disordered but sane defendant and which is shortly to be introduced into Irish law.

# Acknowledgements

Largely because of its interdisciplinary and comparative character, I have incurred many debts in writing this book. My oldest debt is to Mr Justice Rory O'Hanlon, whose stimulating lectures on the insanity defence delivered at University College Dublin in 1964, first aroused my interest in the subject. The book's interdisciplinary emphasis stems from Professor Carstairs' and Professor (now Sheriff) Gordon's joint graduate seminars on mental disorder and the law which I was lucky enough to attend while studying criminology at Edinburgh University in 1969.

Several chapters of the book began life as conference papers and guest lectures delivered, in the main, to civilian audiences in Italy and Germany, and have benefited greatly from critical reactions to their original incarnations; indeed, these exchanges are directly responsible for the book's comparative law focus. Sections of chapter 4 were presented as a paper to the XVth International Congress on Law and Mental Health in Jerusalem in 1990 and subsequently published as part of the conference proceedings; I am grateful to the organisers and publishers for permission to re-use them here. Chapter 8 is a revised version of a paper given to a colloquium on diminished responsibility at the University of Malaya in 1991, and owes much to Professor Molly Cheung's penetrating criticisms of the original. A slightly altered version of chapter 9 was published in (1990) *24 Irish Jurist*; and I am grateful to the editor for permission to re-use it here.

My colleague John O'Dowd read the bulk of the manuscript and made valuable comments on it, thereby saving me from error on several points. My colleagues Tom Cooney and Jim Casey made helpful suggestions for the improvement of the argument in chapters 1 and 6, respectively. The argument of chapter 4 has benefited from conversations I had with Professor Thomas Szasz during his visit to the Law Faculty, University College Dublin, last Spring; and from long-running discussions with Dr John Lowry of the Institut de Chimie Physique at the University of Lausanne. Dr Margaret Grace of the Department of Psychiatry at St. James' Hospital kindly read chapters 2, 3 and 4 and drew my attention to a number of psychiatric sources that I would otherwise have missed. Professor Christine Van Den Wyngaert of the University of Antwerp kindly provided me with an English summary (from Flemish) of the section on insanity in her recently published book on Belgian criminal law. Professor Heine Kühne of the University of Trier helped me track down some of the German sources utilized in chapter 9. The Director of Public Prosecutions, Mr Eamonn Barnes, provided me with otherwise unavailable information on many of the issues raised in chapters 5, 6 and 7. The Director of the Central Mental Hospital, Dr Charles Smith, was similarly helpful with chapters 6 and 7.

I am grateful to all of the aforementioned, and to my publishers' referees, for their help and advice, although naturally none of them—and most especially Professor Szasz, for whom my basic thesis that insanity properly constitutes a good excuse in law is a serious mistake—should be blamed for any errors or defects that the book may still contain.

I owe a particular debt of gratitude to the Director, Professor Ramacci, and staff at the Istituto di Diritto Penale at the University of Rome for their hospitality when I was writing chapter 9 (and revising chapters 6 and 7) during my stay there as Visiting Erasmus Fellow last May. Apart from giving me the use of an air-conditioned office during the early summer heatwave, Professor Ramacci also provided me with easy access to the Institute's extensive civilian holdings. His practical assistance and scholarly comradeship helped to ease the sense of panic that stalks the researcher who ventures down the less well-lit avenues of a foreign (and particularly a foreign-language) legal system. It is not his fault that the book is no better than it is.

My debts to the published works of others are, I hope, acknowledged in the notes to the main text.

The book is dedicated to my wife, Francesca, and daughter, Victoria, to whom I owe so much.

# [1]

# Introduction

The defence of insanity in Irish law has undergone considerable development over the last fifty years. The process of development has occurred in two stages: the theoretical acceptance of the notion of irresistible impulse by the Court of Criminal Appeal in the 1930s[1] and the recognition of a full-blown defence of volitional insanity by the Supreme Court in 1974,[2] respectively. Both stages were made possible by the fact that, as early as the 1930s, Irish judges were unwilling to accept the dogma, which is still current in English law,[3] that the insanity defence is confined to the small class of insane delusions covered by the traditional interpretation of the M'Naghten Rules:[4] viz. those where the accused's condition prevented him from knowing either what he was doing in the physical sense or that he was acting contrary to law. That dogma, which had its origins in early modern concern with the problem of regicide (and was reinforced by Victorian worries about the vulnerability of public figures to would-be assassins),[5] is

1 In *AG v. O'Brien* [1936] IR 263 and *AG v. Boylan* [1937] IR 449; see also *AG v. Manning* [1954] 89 ILTR 155 and the unreported cases discussed by O'Hanlon in (1968) *3 Ir. Jur.* (n.s.) 61 at 71. On the concept of irresistible impulse see infra, ch. 3, n. 9.

2 In *Doyle v. Wicklow County Council* [1974] IR 55. Both stages are discussed in detail in ch. 3.

3 *R v. Sullivan* [1984] AC 156, [1983] 2 All ER 673.

4 Ch. 2.2; the Rules were formulated in 1843 and provide the basis of the insanity defence in the common-law tradition.

5 See the discussion of *Hadfield* [1800] 27 St. Tr. 1281, infra, ch. 2.1. George III, Hadfield's intended target, was the subject of two earlier assassination attempts in 1786 and 1790, respectively: Walker, *Crime and Insanity in England* (Edinburgh, 1968), pp. 185-6. Queen Victoria was the target of no fewer than seven assassination attempts: Walker, ibid., pp. 185-90. One of these was the subject of *R v. Oxford* [1840] 4 St Tr (n.s.) 497; 9 Car. and Payne 526: infra, ch. 2.1. See also *M'Naghten* [1843] 4 St. Tr., (n.s.), 817; 10 Cl. & F. 200; 8 Eng. Rep. 718; infra, ch. 2.2.

largely responsible for the anti-defendant bias that has shaped the insanity defence throughout the common-law world, and for the emergence of the damaging myth that the legal and psychiatric notions of insanity belong to two irreconcilable fields of discourse.[6]

By rejecting it outright in 1935, in *AG v. O'Brien*,[7] the Court of Criminal Appeal signalled that discussion of the insanity plea in Irish law would be firmly focused on the question of the defendant's responsibility for his actions and so would not be dominated by the issue of social protection that shaped the traditional interpretation of the M'Naghten Rules. Moreover, delivering the judgment of the Court in that case, Kennedy CJ drew attention to the importance of the findings of the medical and psychological sciences in this area,[8] thus opening the way for the kind of dialogue between law and psychiatry that has become a characteristic feature of the modern approach to the mentally disordered defendant, and that we shall argue is essential to the development of a satisfactory criterion of exculpatory insanity in the criminal law.[9]

## 1. EXCUSES AND DIAGNOSES

It should however be emphasised at the outset that, although heavily influenced by modern psychiatry, the test of insanity in Irish law is not co-extensive with the psychiatric conception of madness. There are several reasons for this. First, legal insanity is an excuse for wrongdoing, not a diagnosis of the accused's mental condition. We excuse the insane for the same reason we excuse the very young: because they lack the capacity to act rationally, i.e., to understand what they are doing and why they are doing it, and to act on the basis of that understanding.[10]

6 See, for example, Winslade and Ross, *The Insanity Plea* (London, 1983), p. 12; Morris, *Madness and the Criminal Law* (London, 1982), p. 54; Walker, op. cit., ch. 6. The alternative (compatibilist) position is presented and defended in chs. 2 and 3. The tension between legal and psychiatric reasoning has recently been explored in Brown, Farrier, Neal and Weisbrot, *Criminal Laws: Materials and Commentary on the Criminal Law and Process of New South Wales* (Sydney, 1990), pp. 681-4.

7 [1936] IR 263.

8 [1936] IR at 267.

9 See chs. 2 and 3. See also Finkel, *Insanity on Trial: Perspectives on Law and Psychology* (New York, 1988) p. xi; (generally) Simon and Aaronson, *The Insanity Defence: A Critical Assessment of Law and Policy in the Post-Hinkley Era* (New York, 1988).

10 1 Hale 30. Hence the close affinity between the test of criminal insanity and the criterion underlying the rebuttable presumption of *doli incapax*. Broadly speaking, both appeal to the accused's alleged incapacity to reason like a normal adult: see, Radden, *Madness and Reason* (London, 1985), ch. 10.

Thus insanity is not a defence because it is a disease, if indeed it is a disease,[11] but because it is a species of one of the excusing conditions traditionally recognized by the criminal law in a civilized society.[12]

This point is fundamental, as it underlines the fact that the question of the proper scope of the insanity defence is not an empirical matter that can be settled by psychiatrists. Psychiatrists may agree that a particular defendant is insane or that a particular mental disorder constitutes insanity. To the extent that they do agree on such matters,[13] the law should take cognizance of their views. But that still leaves the question of whether or not the relevant mental disorder should be regarded as an excuse; and that is a matter that can only be determined by assessing the effects of the disorder in the light of the general moral principle on which the insanity defence is based: namely, that an inability to act rationally precludes criminal responsibility. In the nature of things, that is an ethico-legal matter that must be settled by

11 This issue is discussed at length in ch. 4.2; 'Because the notion of a disease entity refers to underlying organic states of the person . . . drawing an analogy between the psychological manifestations or 'symptoms' of madness, on the one hand, and the symptoms of ordinary physical diseases on the other—as the disease model of madness does—presupposes that the 'disease' of schizophrenia, for example, refers not—or not only—to the psychological states making up its 'symptoms' (hallucinations, thought disorder, etc.), but also to unknown physical states of malfunction producing them . . . I [accordingly] shall adopt the more cautious convention of referring to the medical model as presupposing an analogy, not an identity, between madness and physical disease. Madness then is a 'disease'—not a disease—in my formulation of the disease model': Radden, ibid. at pp. 17-8.

12 Aristotle described the relevant genus as ignorance (which, with compulsion, he saw as exhausting the category of excusing conditions): *Nichomachean Ethics*, trans. Thompson (London, 1955), pp. 77-8. Modern writers on the criminal law usually refer to it as criminal (in)capacity: Williams, *Textbook of Criminal Law* (London, 1978) p. 587; Stuart, *Canadian Criminal Law* (Toronto, 1987), p. 311; Burchell et al, *South African Criminal Law and Procedure*, vol. 1 (Cape Town, 1983), p. 239.

13 Psychiatric diagnosis is notoriously unreliable: Ennis and Litwack, 'Psychiatry and the Presumption of Expertise: Flipping Coins in the Courtroom' (1974) *62 Cal. L. Rev.* 693; Ziskin, *Coping with Psychiatric Testimony*, 2nd ed. (New York, 1975). According to a recent study, diagnostic agreement between psychiatrists was only 43 per cent better than would be expected by chance alone: Haynes, 'The Predictive Value of Clinical Assessment for the Diagnosis, Prognosis and Treatment Response of Patients' in Webster, Aron and Hucker, eds. *Dangerousness, Probability and Prediction: Psychiatry and Public Policy* (New York, 1985), p. 55. The standardization of diagnostic criteria by the American Psychiatric Association has gone some way towards solving this problem: Martin, 'The Reliability of Psychiatric Diagnoses', ibid., p. 65. But serious difficulties remain: Bartholemew and Milte, 'The Reliability and Validity of Psychiatric Diagnoses in Courts of Law' (1976) *50 ALJ* 450 at 452; Cooke, 'Being an "expert" in Court' (1990) *The Psychologist* 216.

the courts when framing (and re-framing) the insanity defence; and by juries in the context of particular cases. But it is not a matter in which psychiatrists have any special competence, although their evidence may quite properly have a decisive influence on how judges and jurors actually determine it.[14]

## 2. MEDICAL AND LEGAL INSANITY

Second, the psychiatric conception of madness is bound up with the clinical problem of diagnosing and treating severe mental disorders. Thus while not itself a diagnosis, it is closely tied to the diagnostic categories of psychiatric nosology: schizophrenia, psychosis, paranoia, manic-depression and so on. Broadly speaking, modern psychiatry defines madness as a pervasive inability to hold and act upon sufficient reasons—i.e., beliefs and desires which have been acquired in accordance with the laws of logic and evidential reasoning.[15] Thus the psychiatric definition covers all forms of schizophrenia, both functional and organic, severe melancholia and classical or pure paranoia. Schizophrenics come within this definition because they have lost—however temporarily—the ability to 'test reality': to distinguish the private, idiosyncratic world of their own (hallucinatory) thoughts, feelings, fantasies and desires from the public, intersubjective world of shared experience and meaning.[16] Severe depressives qualify under it to the extent that their mood disorder leads to a radically unrealistic assessment of their objective circumstances[17] (e.g., a parent who kills his children in a state of unrealistic despair about the family's future prospects ). And paranoids are covered by it to the extent that their delusional system involves a radically biased assessment of the conflicts implicit in ordinary social intercourse.[18]

In contrast, in addition to the psychiatric disorders just mentioned,

14 '[The issue of legal insanity must] ultimately be decided by the judge and jury. This conclusion is consistent with the important legal principle that expert opinion, including medical and psychiatric opinion, should be used to assist the court in arriving at a finding, but that the responsibility of making this finding is, and must remain, in the hands of the [court]': Orchard, 'Insanity—A Psychiatrist's View of the Recent Rulings of the Supreme Court of Canada' (1981) *2 Supreme Court L Rev* 405 at 406-7; Hall, *General Principles of Criminal Law* (New York, 1962), p. 455-8.

15 The psychiatric conception of insanity is discussed in ch. 2.8.

16 Ibid.

17 Ibid.

18 Ibid.

the legal conception of insanity embraces a wide range of conditions or diseases that are only of incidental concern to psychiatrists—such as hypoglycaemia, arteriosclerosis, and hypertension, to name but a few. Indeed the legal definition covers any and every physical or mental condition that prevents a person from acquiring and holding justified beliefs and desires or from acting on them,[19] notwithstanding the fact that psychiatrists would not describe the person so affected as insane and that ordinary people would not think of them as such. Thus an epileptic[20] or someone suffering from arteriosclerosis[21] would be insane for legal purposes if their underlying physical condition interfered with their reasoning powers in the appropriate way, just as a kleptomaniac would have a good defence of insanity to a charge of larceny if his condition was such that he was 'debarred from refraining' from the act of stealing.[22] This follows from the fact that, unlike its psychiatric counterpart, the legal criterion of insanity is essentially a test of moral responsibility. The question is whether illness exonerates the defendant from blame for his actions, not whether he is suffering from a recognized mental illness.

### 3. INSANITY AND THE LEGAL PROCESS

Third, the difference between the legal and psychiatric definitions of insanity is complicated by the fact that both legal and medical insanity mean different things at different stages of the criminal process, and by the inherent limitations of psychiatric testimony at the trial and post-trial stages.[23] Thus when insanity is raised in connection with the accused's competence to stand trial, the issue is whether he is insane at the time of trial.[24] In this context the legal test of insanity is whether the accused is capable of understanding the proceedings, although evidence of certifiable insanity is normally accepted as conclusive proof that he is insane in the required sense. In other words, evidence

19 '[I]n a legal sense 'disease of the mind' embraces any illness, disorder or abnormal condition which impairs the human mind and its functioning, excluding however, self-induced states caused by alcohol or drugs, as well as transitory mental states such as hysteria and concussion': *Cooper* [1980] 51 CCC (2d) 129 at 144 (SCC); per Dickson J, for the majority; this point is examined in detail in ch. 4.1.

20 *Bratty* [1963] AC 386; *DPP v. Ellis* [1990] 2 IR 291.

21 *Kemp* [1957] 1 QB 399 (CA).

22 See ch. 3.1.

23 See generally, Morse, 'Crazy Behaviour, Morals and Science: An Analysis of Mental Health Law', (1978) *51 S Cal Law Rev*, 527-654.

24 See ch. 7.

that the accused has been diagnosed as psychotic is generally enough to convince the court that he should not be tried as charged.[25]

This practice can be defended on the grounds that evidence of certifiable insanity is normally given by psychiatrists who have clinically examined the accused while he was in custody awaiting trial, i.e., because such evidence is based on a psychiatric diagnosis in the strict sense, although it is open to the objection that a diagnosis that someone is certifiably insane does not necessarily mean that he is incapable of following the proceedings.[26] A defendant who kills his victim in the irrational belief that the Archangel Gabriel has ordered him to do so may well be psychotic, but it is submitted that he is entitled to be tried if he knows why he has been charged and is well enough to instruct counsel. If he is found to be unfit to plead, he will be detained in the Central Mental Hospital; and it is undesirable that defendants who have not had the benefit of a trial should be subjected to what is in effect automatic indeterminate detention in an asylum for the criminally insane.[27]

When insanity is raised as a defence to a criminal charge, the question is whether the accused was insane at the time of the act that forms the basis of the charge.[28] In the nature of things, this means that psychiatrists testifying on the issue of insanity as a defence are being asked to offer an opinion on the accused's state of mind at some time in the past. Such evaluations are difficult given that the memories of the participants may have faded or become distorted, and because the expert is being asked to reconstruct psychological states that typically existed under conditions of haste and pressure. As Morse has argued:

> These and other factors tend to compromise the reliability and validity of the expert's opinion and have led to claims that reconstructive opinions are inherently untrustworthy. In addition, the evaluating experts often spend very little time with the defendant and rarely seek extensive information from the accused's family, friends, co-workers, and other information that might aid in the production of more valid evaluations, further

25 Ch.7.5; Walker found that this is because judges do not like trying defendants who have been diagnosed as certifiably insane: op. cit., p. 225.

26 See Morse, 'The Role of the Mental Health Expert', *International Encyclopedia of Criminal Justice* (New York, 1983), p. 1041 at 1044.

27 This point is discussed in detail in ch. 7.

28 See ch. 5. The meaning of insanity at this stage of the criminal process is discussed in chs. 2-4.

> vitiating the probative value of the expert's opinion. In many ways, the opinions of lay persons who were able to observe the defendant at the crucial moment will be more helpful to the fact finder trying to piece together the defendant's past psychological state.[29]

In the context of the criminal trial, this difficulty can perhaps be overcome by inviting the jury to consider the psychiatric evidence in the light of the evidence as a whole, and by reminding them that psychiatric evidence relating to the accused's state of mind at the time of the alleged offence does not have the value of a diagnosis *stricto sensu,* since medical diagnosis is normally based on the more or less contemporaneous examination of the patient. Indeed, it is submitted that a direction along these lines is highly desirable where there is uncontradicted medical evidence of insanity, given that juries appear to be bound to accept 'unanimous medical evidence unless there is other evidence which can displace or throw doubt on [it]'.[30]

Similar difficulties arise when psychiatric testimony is used as a basis for the prediction of future behaviour—for example, when it is used at the post-trial stage to justify the continued detention of insanity acquittees on the grounds that they would be a danger to themselves and others if released from commitment.[31] Once again the problem is that evidence of this type is apt to be offered and accepted as diagnostically-driven, when in fact there is virtually no clinical basis for it. On the contrary, research has shown that psychiatric diagnosis is an extremely poor predictor of long-term future behaviour, and that psychiatrists generally tend to over-predict violence.[32] Indeed, the best-known study concludes that it is rare for psychiatrists to predict future violence with better than thirty three percent accuracy.[33]

Unfortunately, it is extremely difficult to counter the pseudo-diagnostic aspects of psychiatric testimony at this stage of the criminal process, given the essentially secret character of the review procedures governing applications for release from preventive detention. One way of doing so, it is submitted, might be to issue members of review

29 Op. cit. at 1043.
30 *R v. Matheson* [1958] 1 WLR 474 at 477.
31 See ch. 6.2-3.
32 See the references cited supra at n. 13.
33 See, Monaghan, *The Clinical Prediction of Violent Behaviour,* (Rockville, Md., 1981), p. 121 et seq. U.S. Department of Health and Human Services, Public Health Service, Alcohol, Drug Abuse, and Mental Health Administration.

committees established for this purpose with a clear warning about the unreliability of psychiatric predictions of dangerousness; and, given that a criminal record of interpersonal violence is the best predictor of future violence,[34] to invite them to consider the psychiatric evidence in the light of such ordinary actuarial data as the defendant's age, sex, and previous criminal record. In other words, review committees should be advised that it is unsafe to recommend continued detention unless the psychiatric testimony of mental illness is bolstered by evidence of violent recidivism.

## 4. THE CAUSAL FACTOR

Fourth, the legal criterion of insanity is typically concerned with the phenomena of mental disorder only to the extent that they can be shown to have caused the defendant's wrongdoing.[35] In the absence of a causal link of this kind, the courts will ignore evidence pertaining to these matters notwithstanding its cogency from a psychiatric point of view and the fact that it accords with the legal criterion of insanity as defined in the abstract. Since the moral impulse to excuse the insane arises if and only if their behaviour can be seen to be connected with the psychological states, and their effects, that constitute their madness, such evidence would quite properly be regarded as irrelevant for legal purposes.

Thus a paranoid schizophrenic charged with burglary would not be entitled to the defence of insanity if his actions were unrelated to the beliefs and desires making up his delusions—as would be the case, for example, if his fancied persecutors were members of the Catholic Hierarchy and the particulars of the charge against him were that he broke into a supermarket and stole cigarettes.[36] Similarly, a rapist would not be entitled to the defence on the grounds that he was a pyromaniac, since the compulsive disorder of pyromania does not interfere with the ability to control one's sexual impulses. Once again these conclusions follow from the fact that the defence of insanity

34 See Monaghan and Splane, 'Psychological Approaches to Criminal Behaviour' in Bittner and Messenger (eds.), *The Criminology Review Yearbook,* (Beverly Hills, 1980), pp. 17-47; and the references cited therein. See also Rabkin, 'The Criminal Behaviour of Discharged Mental Patients' (1979) *86 Psychological Bulletin,* 1-27.

35 *Washington v. United States* [1967] 390 F 2d 444 (USCADC).

36 This point is developed in the discussion of melancholia: infra, ch.3.4.

functions as an excuse for wrongdoing rather than a diagnosis of the accused's mental condition.

The issue of causation is more difficult to resolve in cases where the connection (or lack of it) between a defendant's illness and the wrongful act alleged against him is not obvious—for example, where there is psychiatric evidence of mental illness—say severe depression—coupled with evidence of a random, apparently motiveless killing. The difficulty in such cases is that there may be little to go on apart from the psychiatric evidence; and if this is disputed by expert witnesses called by the prosecution, the proceedings are apt to degenerate into the kind of 'battle of the experts' that often confuses juries and may well weaken public confidence in the efficacy of the criminal process. However, this danger can be avoided, or at least minimised, if juries are properly directed on the ultimately legal and common-sense character of the issue of causation. As Gordon has argued:

> The causal approach accepts that to succeed in a defence of insanity it is necessary to show that the criminal conduct was caused by mental illness: the mere co-existence of mental illness and criminal conduct is insufficient. Even persons who suffer from severe mental illness behave in certain ways and at certain times just as they would have behaved had they not been suffering from the illness, and in these situations their conduct is not caused by their illness even in terms of sine qua non causation. But where the illness is severe, conduct of this kind is likely to be restricted to trivial matters, such as eating, or dressing, or performing other routine operations. The law, however, is concerned with extraordinary and important types of behaviour, and it may be possible to say that certain illnesses are so extensive as to affect any important decisions the patient may make, or his ability to control his behaviour in all important matters. In such a case it could be said that any unusual behaviour should be ascribed to the illness. What is 'unusual' is a matter of fact in the circumstances of the case. If a thief developed a mental illness and continued to steal the stealing would not be ascribed to the illness, but if he began to indulge in serious violence after the onset of the illness it would be reasonable to ascribe that change in his behaviour to the illness. In any event, however difficult it may be in theory, the causal problem is not necessarily insurmountable in practice: the court will merely ask whether the mental illness was a cause of the criminal conduct, applying the same causal standards as are applied in other branches of

the law. These standards may not be free from difficulty, but the difficulty is no greater with regard to mental illness than in any other situation.[37]

## 5. THE PRODUCT TEST

Fifth, the insanity defence should not be confused with the doctrine—originally known as the Durham Rule—that an accused has a good defence to a criminal charge 'if his unlawful act was the product of mental disease or mental defect'.[38] For while this doctrine, which represents the high point of the influence of medical psychiatry on the insanity defence, might appear to be a straightforward application of the causal requirement discussed in the previous section, its effect is to subvert the operation of the defence as a test of an accused's responsibility for his actions. An example will help to illustrate this point.

Take the case of a defendant who kills his victim by acting on a violent impulse, and let us assume that there is clear medical evidence that the impulse was caused by a brain lesion which the defendant sustained in a car accident. If the insanity defence depended solely on proof of the existence of a causal link between the brain lesion and the killing, it follows that the defendant in this example would be entitled to the defence since the lesion caused the homicidal impulse which in turn caused the killing. Indeed the defendant would

37 Gordon, *The Criminal Law of Scotland*, 2nd. ed. (Edinburgh, 1978), p. 361-2.

38 *Durham v. United States* [1954] 214 F 2d 862 at 874 (DCCA). For a detailed analysis of *Durham* see Hall, op. cit. at 500-18; Becker, 'Durham Revisited: Psychiatry and the Problem of Crime: Part II' (1973) *Psychiatric Annals*, 1. The roots of the Durham Rule can probably be traced back to Isaac Ray's seminal work, *A Treatise on the Medical Jurisprudence of Insanity* (London, 1839), the first edition of which was published in the United States in 1838. Ray's views were based on contemporary French psychiatry and Article 10 of the Code Napoléon of 1810, which provided that: *'Il n'y a ni crime ni delit, lorsque le prévenu était en etat de démence au temps de l'action'*; infra, ch. 9.2. Ray modified this rule to the effect that 'the mental unsoundness, necessary to exempt from punishment [must be such as ] to have embraced the criminal act within its sphere of influence': op. cit. at 174. This added to the rule in Article 10 the requirement that there must be a causal link between the accused's mental disorder and his act, thus creating an academic precursor to the *Durham* doctrine of the following century. By and large, the civilian world has continued to eschew the causal approach to the issue of insanity; it is generally enough that the accused was suffering from a 'disease of the mind' at the time he committed the act. For example, Article 88 of the Italian Codice

be entitled to the defence on this reasoning even if he could have resisted the impulse, since—*ex hypothesi*—the unresisted homicidal impulse would still be a product of the underlying brain lesion! But this cannot be right, since it produces the unacceptable result that the accused would be acquitted of murder notwithstanding the fact that he could have controlled his impulse, in other words, even though he was responsible for his actions and, therefore, not entitled to be excused on moral grounds.[39]

The flaw in the *Durham* doctrine stems from a faulty analysis of the way in which diseases—whether physical or mental—affect action. Plainly diseases sometimes affect behaviour in the way the *Durham* doctrine imagines: by causing it to happen in the mechanical

Penale provides that: *'Non e imputabile chi, nel momento in cui ha commesso il fatto, era, per infirmità, in tale stato di mente da escludere la capacità d'intendere o di volere'*—there being no requirement that the accused's condition must be shown to have affected the specific conduct that forms the basis of the charge against him: Fiandaca and Musco, *Diritto Penale, Parte Generale* (Bologna, 1985), p. 164. It should however be noted that Article 88 provides that the accused must have been suffering from a condition that rendered him incapable of understanding what he was doing *(la capacità d'intendere)* or of controlling his actions *(la capacità di volere)*, thereby limiting the scope of the insanity defence to cases of severe mental disorder—something that the *Durham* test failed to do: see the text accompanying this note. Moreover, although most common-law tests require proof that the accused's derangement was causally responsible for his alleged misconduct, this is likely to be taken as read—both by judges and juries—in cases in which the accused was suffering from a pervasive want of reason, i.e., in most, if not all, cases of serious mental disorder: *Report of the Royal Commission on Capital Punishment, 1949-53*, Cmnd. 8932. Insistence that the causal element be strictly proved in such cases would be highly artificial: *Gordon*, op. cit.; and, in the event of no causal link being established, would result in the conviction of the seriously mentally disordered. Indeed, this consideration lies at the root of civilian doubts about the propriety of inquiring too deeply into the issue of causation in this connection: Fiandaca and Musco, op. cit.

39 This issue was thrown into sharp relief in *Blocker v. United States* [1961] 288 F 2d 853 (USCADC), where the question of the appellant's responsibility for his actions was held to be irrelevant on the grounds that the staff at the psychiatric hospital at which he had been treated had recently reclassified 'sociopathic personality'—the condition from which the appellant was said to be suffering—as a mental disease. The rule in *Durham* was pruned back in *McDonald v. United States* [1962] 312 F 2d 847 (USCADC), where it was held that the category of mental disease was limited to 'any abnormal condition of the mind which substantially affects mental or emotional processes and substantially impairs behaviour controls': ibid at 850-1; in *Washington v. United States* [1967] 390 F 2d 444 (USCADC), where the element of causation in the rule was restrictively defined; and finally abandoned in *United States v. Brawner* [1972] 471 F 2d 969 (USCADC) in favour of the test of responsibility proposed by the Model Penal Code: infra, ch. 3.6. The latter test was preferred to the alternative idea that the defence should be available to a defendant if he was

sense that one billiard ball causes another to move when played on to it, or in the sense that a particular pattern of behaviour is part of what it means to have the disease. Thus if an epileptic were to strike someone whilst having a spasm, we would say that his behaviour was caused by the epilepsy in this sense, and that he had a good defence (of automatism)[40] to a charge of assaulting his victim because his behaviour was caused by the epilepsy. Notice, however, that we are obliged to describe the movement of the defendant's arm in this example in morally neutral terms: as a bodily movement rather than an action. Since the defendant played no causal role in the production of the bodily movement, we cannot describe it as his action, any more than we could describe the forcible movement of his arm by a third party as his action. And since we cannot describe it as his action, it follows that there can be no question of his being responsible for it. *Inter alia,* responsibility presupposes agent causation.[41]

But diseases do not always affect behaviour in this way. Much more frequently, they do so through the medium of psychological states, such as thoughts, beliefs and desires. For example, Huntington's chorea and Pick's disease—both forms of genetically transmitted arteriosclerosis—typically affect the cerebral blood supply in a way that may lead to mental confusion and, consequently, to grossly anti-social behaviour on the part of those suffering from them. Similarly, victims of a functional disorder like paranoia sometimes have extremely violent reactions as a direct result of their condition.

But notice that a completely different type of causation is at work in these examples. Here the disease causes the defendant to *do* something by influencing the content and direction of his thoughts and feelings (paranoia) or by generally interfering with his thought processes (Huntington's chorea and Pick's disease). Thus what follows are actions, not mere movements of the defendant's body such as might occur in the course of an epileptic seizure or during an attack of St. Vitus' dance. In the result, the question of the defendant's responsibility for what happened arises in such cases in a way that it

suffering from mental disease to the extent that 'he ought not to be held responsible' for his actions. As Gordon has observed, adopting that test involves 'recourse to an unhelpful tautology', since the point of having a test of insanity at all is to decide the issue of responsibility: op. cit., p. 362.

40 In certain circumstances the appropriate defence might be insanity: infra, ch. 4.5.

41 McAuley, 'The Action Component of *Actus Reus*' (1989) *23 Ir Jur (n s)* 218 at 229 et seq.

does not arise in cases where the effects of the disease are not mediated by psychological states.

Given the element of agent causation in the mediated cases, i.e. given that they are genuine cases of action as opposed to mere bodily movement, our impulse to excuse the defendant depends on whether he can fairly be blamed for what he has done (whereas the question of blame is otiose in cases in which no action can be ascribed to the defendant, since there is quite literally nothing to blame the defendant for in such cases). And while that impulse clearly holds firm in cases in which the defendant's condition has undermined his capacity to act rationally, i.e. to understand what he was doing and why he was doing it, and to act in the light of that understanding, it plainly does not hold in cases—like the brain lesion example discussed above—in which he could have controlled his behaviour notwithstanding the fact that it was a causal product of an underlying medical condition.

This criticism of *Durham* has an analogue in everyday life, where we frequently disapprove of people's misbehaviour notwithstanding the fact that we recognize it as being entirely in character. We do not blame people for having the particular characters they happen to have, since the development of character, like the development of disease, is generally something over which we have no control. But we do blame them for acting in character, since we quite rightly assume that ordinary people are capable of holding the bad sides of their character in check unless and until we are given compelling evidence to the contrary. So, for example, we both blame and censure the unreliable and the aggressive for their failings if we feel they could have met their obligations or controlled their violent impulses, respectively, notwithstanding the fact that unreliability and aggressiveness are character traits for which the individual may not be responsible.

## 6. *DURHAM* IN IRELAND

Unfortunately, warnings about the faulty logic underlying the *Durham* doctrine are still apposite in Ireland, since a variant of the doctrine may actually be part of Irish law. In *AG v. Coughlan*, Kenny J left the issue of insanity to the jury in terms which seem indistinguishable from the wording of the Durham Rule: namely, 'Was the act caused by disease of the mind?'[42] Moreover, the judge went on to suggest that acts which were the product of insane delusions of the kind which prevent a person from knowing what he was doing or that he was acting contrary to law, on the one hand, and acts which result from severe affective disorders of the kind which prevent a person from controlling his actions, on the other, were merely examples of the sort of factual situation that would support the insanity defence.[43]

If this means that Kenny J's examples are to be regarded as paradigm cases of legal insanity, a direction along these lines is probably unexceptionable. But if the examples were intended (or might be understood) as mere illustrations of the requirement that the act for which the defendant hopes to be excused must merely be a causal product of a mental disease or defect, then Kenny J's direction—or one based on it—would be open to the criticisms outlined in the preceding paragraphs. Admittedly, *Coughlan* does not appear to have been followed; at all events, there is no reported case of a jury having been directed according to Kenny J's formula.

## 7. THE HEGEMONY OF LAW

The relationship between law and psychiatry as described above has recently been criticised as unduly hegemonic.[44] According to this view, the fact that the legal definition of insanity takes precedence over the psychiatric in the context of the criminal process is 'an example of the power [of] legal discourse to set itself above . . . psychology', thereby eschewing the challenge posed by a rigorously scientific account of human behaviour. The argument is that 'the epistemological and purposive foundations of the discipline of law are framed by the concepts of free will, moral choice, guilt and innocence', whereas 'psychiatry is informed by "scientific" understandings of determinism, degrees of cognitive and volitional control, classification of diseases, and definition of treatments'; and that the inevitable result of the resolution of this tension in favour of law has been to weaken the latter's credibility and efficacy when dealing with the mentally disordered defendant.[45]

This thesis contains a number of serious misconceptions. The most serious misconception is the imagined antinomy between law and

42 *Irish Times* 28 June 1968; O'Hanlon, op. cit. at 76.
43 Ibid.
44 Hunter and Bargen, 'Diminished Responsibility: 'Abnormal' Minds, Abnormal Murderers and What the Doctor Said', in Meng Heong Yeo (ed.), *Partial Excuses to Murder,* (Sydney, 1991), p. 128.
45 Ibid.

science (as embodied in psychiatry). The discipline of law certainly does proceed on the basis that individuals are moral agents, and that moral agents are responsible for their actions. Far from being unscientific, this postulate is essential to a scientific account of human behaviour, given the reciprocal assumption of moral agency that characterises ordinary social intercourse: viz., the fact that individuals see themselves as autonomous subjects and expect others to treat them as such. Since this assumption is part of the fabric of social intercourse, the law is obliged to build its regulatory mechanisms around it. In short, the law's refusal to abandon the language of moral responsibility is a reflection of its abiding commitment to the irreducible facts of human experience, not an ostrich-like posture in the face of scientific progress.

It is also a serious mistake to suppose that psychiatric explanation implies a form of behavioural determinism that leaves no room for purposive action. On the contrary, most forms of psychiatric disorder coincide with the ability to engage in purposive action, and this fact is widely acknowledged by psychiatrists. The psychotic who kills under the delusion that he is executing a divine command is obviously capable of purposive action, as is the depressive who kills his children to unite his family in heaven. The problem in cases of this kind is not that the killer is driven to behave as he did willy nilly, in the sense that he is a mere conduit for his homicidal beliefs and desires. The difficulty is rather that he is unable to understand the manifest irrationality of his beliefs and desires in the way that a sane person could; and, as already suggested, it is precisely this inability that informs the psychiatric explanation of serious mental disorder.[46] Moreover, given that a predisposition to violence is not one of the symptoms normally associated with psychosis, this conclusion holds notwithstanding the impressive scientific evidence that schizophrenia may be genetically determined.[47]

Finally, the hegemony argument completely misses the obvious point that the psychiatric approach to mental disorder is relatively

46 This problem is discussed at length in ch. 3.

47 This conclusion is based on the evidence from studies of twins, where it has been repeatedly found that if one twin has a history of schizophrenia, there is a higher than average chance that the other is similarly affected, and that this probability increases if the twins are monozygotic, i.e., twins that came from the same *ovum:* infra, ch. 4.2. See also Shields and Slater, 'Genetic Studies' in Eysenck (ed.), *Handbook of Abnormal Psychology,* (London, 1960), p. 124; Cowie and Slater, 'Genetic Studies of Schizophrenia' in Fleming (ed.), *Recent Progress in Psychiatry III* (London, 1959), p. 76.

new, whereas its legal counterpart has a lineage that dates back at least to the thirteenth century.[48] The antiquity of an approach may be no guarantee of its correctness, but it does make it harder to displace, particularly in the inately conservative ambience of the law. Moreover, the argument also seriously underestimates the degree to which the traditional legal approach to the issue of insanity has been transformed by psychiatry since the latter was put on a professional footing as a distinct branch of medicine in the nineteenth century. At a purely doctrinal level, it is true that modern legal systems have taken a long time to abandon pre-psychiatric assumptions about the nature of insanity: the M'Naghten Rules, formulated in 1843, still form the basis of the insanity defence in many common law jurisdictions;[49] and as we shall see in chapter 9,[50] the concept of *démence*, first introduced in article 10 of the Code Napoléon, continues to exert a similar influence in some civilian jurisdictions.

The influence of psychiatry on the criminal process is nevertheless pervasive. Evidence of insanity is universally supported by psychiatric testimony at all stages of the process, and is often not contested by the prosecution. In the result, the issue of insanity is frequently decided on the basis of psychiatric evidence alone; and this is likely to be an even more frequent occurrence in legal systems—such as our own—that recognise the so-called control test of insanity, given that that test is normally adopted in order to narrow the gap between the legal and medical conceptions of insanity.[51]

Moreover, it is important to realise that a finding of insanity automatically leads to the indeterminate detention of the accused in a hospital for the criminally insane, and that the decision to release someone from preventive detention, though technically an executive function, is effectively a matter for the psychiatric authorities to whose care he has been entrusted. In practice, this means that detainees can be kept in custody for periods in excess of the average term of imprisonment for the crime charged. Where the charge is murder, for example, this sometimes results in periods of detention of more than ten years.[52] It should also be remembered that preventive detention is frequently imposed on defendants who have been found unfit to plead on the grounds of insanity, and who have therefore

48 Ch. 2.1.
49 See the case law cited in ch. 2.
50 9.2.
51 See ch. 3.6.
52 See ch. 6.4; ch. 8.3, where this point is explored in relation to the defence of diminished responsibility.

never been tried for the offence for which they are being detained; and that the decision as to whether or not detention should be continued in these cases is also effectively in the hands of the psychiatric authorities supervising the detention.[53]

In other words, there are good grounds for arguing that the real problem is one of *psychiatric* rather than legal hegemony, and that there is an urgent need for legal systems to claw back some of the sweeping discretionary powers that have been vested in forensic psychiatrists over the last hundred years. As we shall see,[54] this process is already well advanced in some legal systems, although it has yet to get under way in Ireland.

53 See ch. 7.
54 In chs. 6, 7 and 9.

# [2]

# Cognitive Insanity

## 1. BEFORE *M'NAGHTEN*

The roots of the insanity defence can be traced back at least to the thirteenth century.[1] Bracton defined the insane person as 'one who does not know what he is doing, who is lacking in mind and reason, and who is not far removed from the brutes.'[2] In similar vein, Hale wrote that the insane are not criminally responsible 'for they have not the use of understanding, and act not as reasonable creatures, their actions are in effect in the condition of brutes.'[3] Hale's words were

1 See generally Crotty, 'The History of Insanity as a Defence to a Crime in English Criminal Law,' (1924) *12 Cal L Rev* 105. Walker has argued that there was no defence of insanity *stricto sensu* in pre-Norman English law because the contemporary 'practice in dealing with serious offences by the insane, such as homicide, was to make the offender's family pay [compensation to the victim's family] and look after him, and that this was done without presenting him formally for trial: local knowledge of his insanity settled the matter without the necessity for that': op. cit. p. 26.

2 6 Bracton DL 420. The development of a formal test of insanity was probably the result of the replacement of trial by ordeal by trial by jury. 'Since the petty jury consisted of local men, it was perfectly reasonable to ask them to declare to the king's justice or the coroner whether the accused had really been mad when he committed the offence; this was no breach with the ancient practice. But since they were now doing so at the extremely formal stage of trial', there was an obvious need for a rational criterion of insanity that would serve as a vehicle for a special verdict; hence Bracton's test: Walker, op. cit., pp. 26-7.

3 1 Hale PC 31-2. The word 'brutus' in Bracton's and Hale's formulations has often been understood as implying an unsympathetic comparison between the insane and wild beasts: Hall, op. cit., pp. 472-7. But it probably meant no more than 'dumb animal', i.e., a creature lacking rationality: Platt and Diamond, 'The Origins of the 'Right and Wrong' Test of Criminal Responsibility and its Subsequent Development in the United States: An Historical Survey', (1966) *54 Cal L Rev* 1227 at 1239. 'The comparison between the insane and animals was so influential in the course of the next six centuries that it would be interesting to trace it to its ultimate source. It is unlikely that it was Bracton's own inspiration,

clearly intended as a metaphor for the radical want of reason that distinguishes the insane defendant from the ordinary individual, not as a prosaic description of a sub-human species. This is clear from his suggestion that defendants who are not totally lacking in reason, such as those suffering from melancholia, should only be held accountable if they have sufficient understanding to defeat the presumption of *doli incapax,* i.e., if they were more like adults than children.[4]

Unfortunately, what was intended as a metaphor hardened into a rigid requirement in the hands of the judges. In a line of cases spanning

and not merely because he was not given to inspiration of this kind. He makes the comparison twice, in exactly the same words . . . which suggests that it was a traditional argument. Moreover, it can be found in Continental jurists who, though later than Bracton, are unlikely to have been influenced by him—for example, in Matthaeus *(De Criminibus* (Amsterdam,1644), ch. 8, n. 3)': Walker, op. cit., ch. 1, n. 23. Isaac Ray, writing in 1838, explained Hale's reliance on the comparison thus: [In Hale's time] the popular notions concerning [insanity] were derived from the observations of those wretched inmates of the madhouses whom chains and stripes, cold and filth, had reduced to the stupidity of the idiot, or exasperated to the fury of the demon. Those nice shades of the disease in which the mind, without being wholly driven from its propriety, pertinaciously clings to some absurd delusion, were either regarded as something very different from real madness, or were too far removed from the common gaze, and too soon converted by bad management into the more active forms of the disease, to enter much into the general idea entertained of madness. Could Lord Hale have contemplated the scenes presented by the lunatic asylums of our own times, we should undoubtedly have received from him a very different doctrine for the regulation of the decisions of after generations': supra, ch. 1, n. 38. But this observation had earlier been made by Haslam, *Medical Jurisprudence, as it relates to insanity, according to the Law of England,* (London, 1817), ch. 1. It was repeated by Alexander Cockburn in his celebrated defence of Daniel M'Naghten: infra, n. 9.

4 'The best measure that I can think of is this; such a person as labouring under melancholy tempers hath yet ordinarily as great an understanding, as ordinarily a child of fourteen hath, is such a person as may be guilty of treason or felony': op. cit. 30, 412. Bracton also drew a parallel between the insane and children: op. cit., 423. 'The fact that the madman tended to be compared to the child under the age of fourteen rather than the child under seven suggests that—at first at least—it was failure to appreciate the true nature and quality of his act that was supposed to be his defect.' Moreover, a child's appreciation of the nature and quality of his actions was assessed by whether he could count to twelve, 'or perform tasks in his father's occupation, such as measuring cloth': Walker, op. cit., p. 40. In other words, the emphasis was on knowing 'what was what' (rather than appreciating the physical character of his actions), 'and it was this sort of common sense that [was thought to be] lacking in children and the insane': ibid., p. 28. On this view, the inability to tell right from wrong, the so-called 'right-wrong' test of criminal responsibility—infra, 2.5—was a later accretion to the insanity defence, probably invented to justify acquitting the insane defendant who intended to kill his victim (and therefore knew the nature and quality of his act).

the eighteenth century, it was established that Hale's words meant that only those who were completely bereft of reason were entitled to the defense of insanity. In *R v. Arnold,*[5] decided in 1724, the jury were told that the defendant 'must be a man that is totally deprived of his understanding and memory.' Arnold had shot Lord Onslow in the insane belief that he had sent devils and goblins to persecute him. Not surprisingly, he was convicted, since he knew who he was, who Lord Onslow was and that he was firing at a human being. The direction was substantially the same in *R v. Earl Ferrers.*[6] In *R v. Hadfield,*[7] the test was whether the defendant was so deranged that he didn't know what he was doing and couldn't distinguish right from wrong. In *R v. Bellingham*[8] it was held that the crucial issue was whether the defendant could distinguish right from wrong, and this ruling was also applied in *R v. Oxford.*[9]

*Hadfield* is interesting as it is one of the first reported cases where someone suffering from what is now known as schizophrenia was acquitted on the grounds of insanity. The defendant was under the

5 16 St. Tr. 695, 764. The jury were also told that the accused must 'not know what he is doing, no more than an infant, than a brute or a wild beast' and that they should consider 'whether the condition this man was in . . . doth show a man, who knew what he was doing, and was able to distinguish whether he was doing good or evil, and understood what he did': ibid. Commenting on the differences between the summing-up and Bracton's criterion of insanity—supra, n. 2—Walker has remarked that, '[i]n the first place, 'brutus', which merely meant 'animal' as distinct from 'human', had become 'brute or wild beast'—a phrase which must have conjured up a rather different picture from the subdued figure in the dock. Secondly ... [the trial judge] does not make it clear whether inability *either* to know what he was doing *or* to know that it was wrong would have excused Arnold; he speaks as if the two went together. It was not until the nineteenth century that they became clearly separate alternative tests': Walker, op. cit., pp. 56-7.

6 19 St. Tr. 885. This is probably the first reported case in which psychiatric evidence was called by the defence. The expert witness was Dr John Munro, Physician Superintendent of Bethlehem. 'Ferrers was pronounced guilty ... At his hanging the newly devised mechanics of the drop failed to work properly, and the executioner had to resort to the old practice of jumping on the back of the slowly strangling man': Walker, op. cit., p. 63.

7 27 St. Tr. 1281.

8 Coll. Lun. 636. Bellingham, a paranoid schizophrenic, shot the Prime Minister, Spenser Perceval, in the lobby of the House of Commons.

9 4 St. Tr., (n.s.) 497; Oxford had fired a pistol at Queen Victoria. Incidentally, Cockburn, in his defence of M'Naghten, clearly understood Hale's metaphor; he described insanity as 'that disease . . . which deprives man of reason, and converts him into the similitude of the lower animal ... ': *R v. M'Naghten* [1843] 4 St. Tr. (n.s.) at 874.

delusion that he had been given a divine command to sacrifice his life in order to save the world, but couldn't bring himself to commit the mortal sin of suicide. His solution was to fire a shot at George III in the hope that he would be executed for the capital offence of (attempted) murder. O'Hanlon has suggested that his acquittal marked the emergence of a more enlightened attitude towards the insanity defence, on the basis that the trial judge, having heard the defence evidence, advised the Crown to accept the plea of insanity.[10] Yet it is submitted that the acquittal could not have been predicted from the trial judge's statement of the law, which was to the effect that insanity was an excuse only where it completely dethroned the ability to distinguish right from wrong:[11] in essence, the rigid version of the Hale test that had been applied since *Arnold*;[12] and since Hadfield admitted that he knew that suicide was a sin and killing a capital offence, he could scarcely be said to have lost all moral sense. The better view would seem to be that the outcome was rather the result of defence counsel Erskine's successful argument that the established test—the rigid version of the Hale formula—was so restrictive that no one but a congenital idiot could satisfy it; and that the jury should acquit the defendant if they were satisfied that he suffered from a delusion which prompted his act.[13]

It is submitted that the real doctrinal breakthrough came in *R v. M'Naghten,* where Tindal CJ told the jury that they should acquit the prisoner unless they were satisfied that he was 'capable of distinguishing right from wrong with respect to the act of which he stands charged.'[14] The problem with the established test was that it required that the defendant be completely incapable of distinguishing right from wrong, whereas this way of putting the matter left it open to the jury to acquit if they thought that the defendant did not have sufficient reason to apply the moral distinctions of which he may have been aware.

M'Naghten was accordingly acquitted of murdering the Prime Minister's secretary, Edward Drummond, whom he mistook for the

10 Op. cit. at 63. Walker—op. cit., ch. 3—has argued that successful insanity defences were a regular feature of Old Bailey trials for at least sixty years before *Hadfield* was decided. His survey does not disclose the extent to which success may have been achieved despite, rather than because of, the way the issue of insanity was left to juries. But it does demonstrate that the probability of success does not seem to have been affected by the decision in *Hadfield.*

11 27 St. Tr. 1281 at 1284.

12 16 St. Tr. 695.

13 27 St. Tr. 1281 at 1289. See the discussion of causation supra, ch. 1.4.

14 4 St. Tr. (n.s.) 817; 10 Cl. & F. 200; 8 Eng. Rep. 718.

Prime Minister, Sir Robert Peel, in the insane belief that he was being persecuted by the Tory Party and that his life had been endangered as a result.[15] Unfortunately, his acquittal revived early modern concern with the threat of regicide and generally aroused such controversy that the House of Lords (in its legislative capacity) put a series of questions to the judges regarding the proper scope of the insanity defence, the answers to which became known as the M'Naghten Rules. Despite the unusual circumstances of their enactment, the Rules quickly acquired quasi-statutory status in England, and were followed throughout the common-law world, including Ireland, where they still represent the core of the insanity defence.[16]

## 2. THE M'NAGHTEN RULES[17]

The relevant parts of the Rules are as follows:

> *Rule 1.* Persons who labour under partial delusions only, and are not in other respects insane, and who act under the influence of an insane delusion, of redressing or revenging some supposed

15 M'Naghten's mistake as to the identity of his victim appears to have been a result of the fact that he had frequently seen Drummond entering and leaving the Prime Minister's offices. On 20 January he followed Drummond up Whitehall to his bank and as he was returning shot him in the back. 'M'Naghten was pulling another loaded pistol from inside his coat when a constable threw his arms around him; the pistol went off in the struggle but did no further damage. Drummond was able to walk back to the bank and a doctor was summoned, but he died five days later in great pain': Walker, op. cit. at p. 91.

16 See generally Walker, op. cit., for a good account of the origin and reception of the Rules.

17 Several different spellings of M'Naghten's name occur in the literature: viz., 'M'Na*u*ghten': Kenny, *Select Cases on Criminal Law* (Cambridge,1919), p. 43; 'M*ac*na*u*ghton': *Archbold's Criminal Pleading Evidence and Practice,* 23rd edn., p. 25; 'M'Naghten'; 'M*ac*na*u*ghten'; 'M*ac*naghten': Diamond, (1964) *25 Ohio State LJ,* 1. Mr. Justice Frankfurter once complained to the editor of *The Times* of London about that paper's preference for the now standard spelling, which the editor replied was justified by a letter bearing the defendant's signature. Frankfurter rejoindered: 'To what extent is a lunatic's spelling, even of his own name, to be deemed an authority!': *US v. Freeman* [1966] 357 F (2d) 606 (USCA); per Kaufman J. In point of fact, the signature to which the editor referred—which could be McNa(u)ghten, McNa(u)ghton or McNa(u)ghtan—is doubtful authority for the standard spelling; as Walker has remarked, the latter 'has the distinction of being the only one that cannot be reconciled with the man's own signature': op. cit., p. 102, n.

grievance or injury, or producing some public benefit are nevertheless punishable if they knew at the time of committing the crime that they were acting contrary to the law of the land.[18]

*Rule 2.* Every man is presumed to be sane and to possess a sufficient degree of reason to be responsible for his crimes until the contrary be proved.

*Rule 3.* To establish a defence on the ground of insanity, it must be clearly proved that, at the time of the committing of the act, the party accused was labouring under such a defect of reason, from disease of the mind, as not to know the nature and quality of the act he was doing, or, if he did know it, that he did not know he was doing what was wrong. [With respect to the latter part of this rule], if the accused was conscious that the act was one that he ought not to do, and if that act was at the same time contrary to the law of the land, he is punishable.[19]

*Rule 4.* A person labouring under a partial delusion only and not in other respects insane must be considered in the same situation as to responsibility as if the facts with respect to which the delusion exists were real. For example, if under the influence of his delusion he supposes another man to be in the act of attempting to take away his life and he kills that man as he supposes in self-defence, he would be exempt from punishment. If his delusion was that the deceased had inflicted a serious injury to his character and fortune and he killed him in revenge for such supposed injury, he would be liable for punishment.[20]

The weakness of the Rules is obvious: they confine the insanity defence within extremely narrow limits. Daniel M'Naghten was acquitted at first instance because the jury evidently accepted that he was too deranged to understand the moral implications of what he was doing. But he would probably have been convicted under the Rules, given that he knew that he was killing a human being (rule 3) and would not have been entitled to a defence (of self-defence or necessity) had the facts on which his delusion was based—that a Tory conspiracy had endangered his life—been real (rule 4). Hadfield would also have been convicted under the Rules since he acted on the understanding that murder was a capital offence (rule 1) and morally wrong (rule 3).[21]

18 4 St. Tr. (n. s.) 930.
19 4 St. Tr. (n. s.) 931.
20 4 St. Tr. (n. s.) 932.
21 27 St. Tr. 1281.

*A fortiori,* the Rules afford no protection to the person suffering from melancholia who kills (usually a loved one and sometimes his whole family) in unrealistic despair at the hopelessness of his situation, since—as Hale conceded—the depressive defendant generally knows what he is doing and that he is acting contrary to law and common morality.[22] In other words, the effect of the Rules was to confine the insanity defence to the small class of cases where the accused's psychosis is marked by (severe hallucinations leading to) a loss of contact with physical reality or the total disintegration of his moral sense, thereby reinstating, albeit in a different guise, the old *Arnold* test equating insanity with the complete dethronement of reason.[23]

Rules 1 and 4 posit the existence of partial insanity, in the sense that they assume that a person can be insane with respect to one matter and yet perfectly sane with regard to everything else. As Gordon has observed, this requires us to believe 'that while a man's judgment may be so warped that he believes his neighbour is trying to make him impotent by black magic, he may yet be sane enough to be responsible for killing that neighbour.'[24] This assumption should not be confused with the view expressed by Tindal CJ, in *M'Naghten,*[25] that insanity does not necessarily exclude the ability to tell right from wrong, by which it may have been inspired. As we have seen, Tindal CJ's view is vindicated by cases like *Arnold,*[26] *Hadfield*[27] and *M'Naghten* itself—which demonstrate that this ability often co-exists with serious mental disorder.[28] However, these cases also demonstrate that there is a difference between being able to distinguish right from wrong and being able to choose between them. Hadfield knew that murder was wrong, yet choose to commit it in the delusional belief that it was the only alternative open to him if he was to abide by his divine instructions to sacrifice himself in order to save the world.[29] In other words, his delusion affected his reason and judgment and so cannot be regarded as an isolated psychological state that had no bearing on his subsequent actions.

Similarly, it seems equally wrong to regard Daniel M'Naghten's

22 1 Hale 30.

23 16 St. Tr. at 764.

24 The Criminal Law of Scotland, 2nd. ed. (Edinburgh, 1978), p. 355. Cf. Taylor, *Principles of Medical Jurisprudence,* vol. 1, 11th ed., (London, 1957), pp. 577-8.

25 4 St. Tr. (n. s.) 847.

26 16 St. Tr. 695.

27 27 St. Tr. 1281.

28 See supra, pp. 1-2.

29 Ibid.

delusion in these terms, or to deny a *M'Naghten*-type defendant the insanity defence on the grounds that he would have been guilty of murder had the facts on which his delusion was based been real (rule 4). M'Naghten knew that he was killing a human being and that murder was wrong, but insanely believed he had to take drastic action to prevent the Tories from destroying him.[30] Like Hadfield's, his actions were also governed by his delusions, so it seems entirely artificial to treat them separately or to suppose that he was in a position to evaluate them rationally. If it is unreasonable to expect a sane person to apply the standards of rational detachment when he believes his life has been threatened,[31] it cannot be right to expect a defendant to apply the same standards when the balance of his mind has been upset by insane delusions. Apart from being inherently unfair, this requirement seems to be in conflict with the common sense understanding of madness as a pervasive defect of reason,[32] and, it is submitted, is as likely as not to be ignored by juries—particularly modern juries—for that reason.[33]

## 3. RE-INVENTING THE RULES

These criticisms do not mean that the M'Naghten Rules should be completely abandoned. If the Rules did not exist, it would be necessary to invent something very like them. This follows from the inescapable fact that serious mental illness is a cognitive failing that radically affects an agent's capacity to act rationally, and that there is a strong moral impulse to exempt those who—like Arnold, Hadfield and M'Naghten—are manifestly incapable of acting rationally from criminal responsibility.[34] The problem is therefore to fashion a

30 Supra, p. 3 and accompanying notes.

31 *Beckford v. R.* [1987] 3 All ER 425 (PC).

32 Infra, 2.6-7.

33 See Pasewark, 'The Insanity Plea: a Review of the Research Literature', (1982) *9 J Psychiatry Law,* 357. 'The nature of the charge, the type of accused, prior criminal or psychiatric history, treatment suitability, psychiatric diagnosis, the nature of the disposition following the insanity verdict, the scope of relevant psychiatric evidence and the burden of proof are likely to have more relevance to the insanity plea outcome than the precise scope of the test': Ferguson, (1984) *3 Medicine and Law* 287 at 294. See also Steadman, 'Insanity Acquittals in New York State 1967-78' (1980) *Am. J Psychiat* 137; Petrila, 'The Insanity Defence and Other Mental Health Dispositions in Missouri' (1982) *5 Int. J Law & Psychiat* 5:81; Arafat, Mc Cahery 'The Insanity Defence and the Juror' (1973) *22 Drake Law Rev* 538, 548.

34 Infra, 2.4-5.

criterion of insanity that accords with the common perception of mental illness as a pervasive defect of reason, and that enables juries to acquit where it seems morally appropriate to do so. Given their overwhelmingly cognitive emphasis, it is submitted that this can best be done within the framework of the M'Naghten Rules, by amending the traditional interpretation of the knowledge requirement in rule 3.[35]

The alternative is to by-pass the Rules and create a separate insanity defence, capable of operating instead of or in addition to them. This has been done in several common-law jurisdictions, including Ireland, and the results have not been entirely satisfactory.[36] Once the umbilical link with the Rules is broken, the cognitive component of insanity tends to be neglected. And when that happens, the outcome is either an insanity test that depends on an unconvincing account of why serious mental disorder is regarded as a denial of responsibility for what would otherwise be a crime, and is therefore more likely to be a hindrance than a help to juries, or, what is worse, one that is so wide that it ceases to be a test of criminal responsibility altogether. The causal or product tests based on the Durham Rule, which have already been discussed, are examples of the second outcome.[37] The first is illustrated by the so-called control tests based on the concept of volitional insanity, which will be discussed in the next chapter.

## 4. KNOWLEDGE OF NATURE AND QUALITY

There are two limbs to the cognitive component of rule 3: the question is whether mental disorder prevented the accused from knowing (1) the 'nature and quality' of his act or (2) that it was 'wrong.' The notion of what it means not to 'know the nature and quality' of an act is not clarified in rule 3, and is usually explained[38] by appealing to the hypothetical examples given by Stephen[39] and Kenny:[40] the defendant who kills 'under the delusion that he is breaking a jar' and 'the madman

35 Supra, 2.2.
36 See ch 3.
37 Supra, ch. 1.5.
38 For example, see Smith and Hogan, *Criminal Law,* 7th edn. (London, 1992), p. 201; Cross and Jones, op. cit., p. 58.
39 *A History of the Criminal Law of England,* vol. II, (London, 1883), p. 166. Stephen also offers the example of someone who cuts off a sleeper's head because 'it would be great fun looking for it when he woke up': ibid.
40 *Outlines of Criminal Law,* 19th edn., (London, 1965), p. 76.

who cut a woman's throat under the idea that he was cutting a loaf of bread', respectively. These examples suggest that the defendant must be ignorant of the physical nature of what he is doing and this interpretation is confirmed by the leading case of *R v. Codère,*[41] where the Court of Appeal decided that the 'nature and quality' phrase denoted the 'physical character' of an action as distinct from its moral aspects.

However, the concept of the 'physical character' of an action is ambiguous. It could be taken to refer to the behavioural component of the defendant's conduct, in which case it would be confined to the surface features of an action—i.e., to the bodily movements or physical activity involved in shooting, stabbing, choking etc. Or it could be taken to refer to the accused's conduct as a whole, in which case it would include the consequences of his actions as well as their surface features. Nor is this a distinction without a difference, since the first interpretation would remove the insanity defence from a defendant who knew he was engaged in the physical activity of squeezing his victim's throat even if he was too ill to appreciate that that activity was likely to cause her death.[42]

Thus in *R v. Dickie*[43] it was held that the defendant did know the nature and quality of his actions despite the fact that there was medical evidence that he was in the manic phase of manic-depressive psychosis such that he did not appreciate that what he was doing was dangerous. The accused set fire to a wastepaper basket and sat watching a blank television screen while the basket and the carpet underneath it burned and smoke filled the room. In the opinion of the court, the medical evidence did not go to his ability to understand what he was doing. Since he knew he was setting fire to the basket, it was irrelevant that his psychosis prevented him from appreciating the dangers, including the risk to life and property, arising from his conduct![44]

On the other hand, if we opt for the second interpretation, the basis for the 'physical character' limitation seems doubtful. Apart from the fact that some crimes, like assault, are defined in terms of their *psychological* consequences for the victim, others are defined in terms

41 [1916] 12 Cr App Rep 21; *Sullivan* [1984] AC 156. The institutional writers had a much wider understanding of what it means to know the nature and quality of one's actions: supra, 2.1 and accompanying notes.

42 The facts of *Cooper,* infra, where the Supreme Court of Canada adopted the second interpretation.

43 [1984] 3 All ER 176.

44 The decision has been trenchantly criticised by Griew, 'Another Nail for M'Naghten's Coffin?' [1984] *NLJ* 935.

of non-physical circumstances such as whether or not the victim is consenting[45] or has attained a certain age.[46] And since knowledge of both consequences and circumstances is required by the ordinary principles of *mens rea*,[47] it cannot be right that the insane should be treated more harshly with respect to criminal liability than the ordinary individual. Indeed, this conclusion is bolstered by the provision in rule 4 that an insane defendant 'must be considered in the same situation as to responsibility as if the facts with respect to which his delusion exists were real.'[48] For on this reasoning, a defendant who insanely believed that his victim was consenting to sexual intercourse would be entitled to the insanity defence notwithstanding the fact that he was fully aware of the purely 'physical character' of his actions.

The artificiality of confining the first limb of the knowledge test to the 'physical character' of the defendant's actions has been acknowledged by the Canadian courts.[49] For example, in *O*,[50] there was evidence that the defendant had admitted to a neighbour that she had killed her children by hanging them. Yet the jury was asked to consider whether her subsequent claim that she wanted to return and look after them showed that she did not 'appreciate the nature and quality' of her actions. Similarly, in *Adamcik*,[51] the jury was allowed

45 For example, as in the case of rape, to sexual intercourse.

46 For example, section 17 of the Criminal Law (Amendment) Act 1935 defines statutory rape as sexual intercourse with a female between fifteen and seventeen years of age.

47 Smith and Hogan, op. cit., p. 59.

48 4 St. Tr. (n.s.) at 932; supra, 2.2.

49 In *Cooper* [1980] 51 CCC (2d) 129 (SCC) and *Barnier* [1980] 51 CCC (2d) 193 (SCC). In *Cooper* Mr. Justice Dickson, for the majority, held that there had to be 'real understanding of the nature, character and consequence of the act at the time of its commission . . . An ability to perceive the consequences, impact and results of a physical act'; and concluded that 'this is simply a restatement, specific to the defence of insanity, of the principle that mens rea, or intention as to the consequences of an act, is a requisite element in the commission of a crime': [1980] 51 CCC (2d) 129 at 146-7. In *Barnier* Mr. Justice Estey, for a unanimous Court of seven judges, held that appreciating (the term used in s. 16 (2) of the Canadian Criminal Code) the nature and quality of an act included knowing its nature and quality but that the converse was not true. 'The verb 'know' has a positive connotation requiring a bare awareness, the act of receiving information without more. The act of appreciating, on the other hand, is a second stage in the mental process requiring the analysis of knowledge or experience in one manner or another': [1980] 51 CCC (2d) 193 at 203. On this point see infra, 2.6. *Cooper* and *Barnier* are discussed by Braithwaite in (1981) *2 Supreme Court* (of Canada) *L Rev.* 177 at 191-3.

50 [1959] 3 CLQ 151 (Ont. HC).

51 [1977] 33 CCC (2d) 11 (BC. Co Ct).

to consider whether a defendant who tried to rob a bank (by using a toy gun) in order to obtain money to buy a crucifix which he believed was blasphemously displayed in a shop window was 'capable of appreciating the nature and quality of his actions.' Both defendants were acquitted notwithstanding that they knew what they were doing in the *Codère*[52] sense and had not claimed that they did not know that their actions were contrary to law (the form of the second limb of the knowledge test in the Canadian version of rule 3).[53]

Moreover, the Ontario Court of Appeal has recently held, in *Swain*,[54] that a defendant who scratched an 'X' on his wife's chest with a cleaver in the knowledge that bleeding would result did not know the nature and quality of his actions since he insanely believed he was protecting her from evil spirits—distinguishing the apparently contrary decisions of the Supreme Court of Canada in *Kjeldsen*[55] and *Abbey*[56] on the grounds that they were confined to the rejection of the proposition that a psychopathic[57] (as opposed to psychotic) defendant was entitled to rely on the claim that he was emotionally incapable of appreciating the consequences of his actions as evidence that he did not know what he was doing.[58]

Admittedly, the decision in *Swain*, like the probable outcome of the rape hypothetical just mentioned, can arguably be explained as a straightforward application of the provision in rule 4[59] that a defendant must be judged on the facts as he insanely believed them to be. But this provision cannot be invoked to explain the decisions in *Adamcik*[60] and *O*.[61] Since blasphemy is not a justification for bank robbery and as O was not in a position to claim any putative justification for killing her children, these decisions seem genuinely to turn on the defendant's inability to comprehend the motives or reasons for

52 [1916] 12 Cr App Rep 21.
53 *Schwartz* [1977] 34 CRNS 138 (SCC). See also Verdun-Jones, 'The Insanity Defence since Schwartz v. R.: First Steps Along the Road Towards the Rationalization of Canadian Policy? (1979) 6 CR (3d) 300 and 'The Evolution of the Defences of Insanity and Automatism in Canada from 1843 to 1979: A Saga of Judicial Reluctance to Sever the Umbilical Cord to the Mother Country' (1979) *14 BC L Rev* 1.
54 [1986] 50 CR (3d) 97 (Ont CA).
55 [1981] 24 CR (3d) 289 (SCC).
56 [1982] 29 CR (3d) 193 (SCC).
57 Infra, ch. 4.6.
58 [1986] 50 CR (3d) 97 at 128 (Ont CA).
59 Supra, 2.2.
60 [1977] 33 CCC(2d) 11 (BC Co Ct).
61 [1959] 3 CLQ 151 (Ont HC).

his actions *(Adamcik)* or the consequences normally associated with them *(O)*—notwithstanding the fact that the court in both cases was operating within the framework laid down by the M'Naghten Rules.

In other words, if the Rules are construed from the point of view of their implicit logical form, the first limb of the knowledge test can be seen to be much wider than has traditionally been supposed. Contrary to the interpretation that comes down from *Codère*,[62] it goes to the accused's ability to evaluate his actions, including his reasons or motives for committing them and the consequences normally associated with them, in the way that a sane person can. An accused who cannot do this may know what he is doing in a literal sense, but he does not know why he is doing it and cannot assess its true effects. He may be quite clear about the 'physical character' of his actions, as Arnold, Hadfield and M'Naghten were, or even about their immediate physical consequences, as O and Swain appear to have been. But since he cannot break out of the circle described by his insane delusions, he does not know what he is doing in any epistemologically significant sense. Unlike the sane person, he cannot measure the effects of his actions or assess the validity or propriety of his motives against the criteria by which they are ordinarily judged.[63] And, as the Canadian authorities demonstrate, it seems wrong to suppose that the insanity defence is tied to a conception of knowledge that cannot be defended on epistemological grounds.[64]

## 5. KNOWLEDGE OF WRONGNESS

It is clear that the second limb of rule 3 was intended to be read in the light of the *error juris* rule that everyone is presumed to know the law. Hence the rider to the rule to the effect that the insanity defence is unavailable 'if the accused was conscious that the act was one which he ought not to do, and if that act was at the same time contrary to the law of the land'[65]—a proposition which plainly entails the conclusion that the insanity defence is available where an accused was *not* conscious that the act was one which he ought not to do. This

62 [1916] 12 Cr App Rep 21.

63 Gordon cites the case of Straffen, who killed little girls in order to annoy the police, as an illustration of this point: op. cit., p. 355. See also, Fairfield and Fullbrook, *Trials of John Thomas Straffen* (London, 1954).

64 Infra, 2.6-7.

65 4 St. Tr. (n. s.) 931.

position has been complicated by *R v. Windle,*[66] where the English Court of Appeal said that the word 'wrong' as used in the Rules meant 'contrary to law'.[67] This dogmatic assertion is not easy to reconcile with the express terms of the rider, yet it has been repeated so often that it seems to represent the law in England,[68] and may well do so in Ireland.[69] To the extent that it does, it has made the task of transcending the limitations of the M'Naghten Rules more difficult. For its effect is to close off the possibility of expanding the interpretation of the word 'wrong' along the lines suggested by the trial judge in *M'Naghten*: namely, to include situations where the accused's mental disorder prevented him from realizing that his actions could not be rationally justified.[70] If mental disorder prevents an accused from knowing that something is wrong in this sense, it is at least plausible to argue that he was not 'conscious that the act was one that he ought not to do'; whereas this option disappears if we insist that all rule 3 requires is a bare awareness that the act contravenes a given legal (or even moral) norm.[71]

This point has long been accepted by the Australian courts. Thus in *R v. Porter,* Dixon J (as he then was) said that:

> The question is whether he was able to appreciate the wrongness of the particular act he was doing at the particular time. Could this man be said to know in this sense whether his act was wrong if through a disease or defect or disorder of the mind he could not think rationally of the reasons which to ordinary people make that act right or wrong? If through the disordered condition of the mind he could not reason about the matter with a moderate degree of sense and composure it may be said he could not know that what he was doing was wrong.[72]

66 [1952] 36 Cr App Rep 85 (CCA).

67 The Court of Criminal Appeal had reached a similar conclusion in *Codère* [1916] 12 Cr App Rep 21; supra, 2.4.

68 Smith & Hogan, op.cit., p. 202.

69 But *cf. Doyle v. Wicklow County Council* [1974] IR 55 at 70, where, albeit obiter and without discussion, the Supreme Court noticed the position in Australia: infra.

70. 4 St. Tr. (n. s.) 817 at 821.

71 The decision in *Windle* thus extinguished a line of English authority stretching back through the Rules and *M'Naghten's* case itself, to *Arnold*—supra, 2.1—according to which the proper criterion of insanity is whether the defendant knew right (good) from wrong (evil). In Walker's words, it was the final step in the judicial retreat from this principle and 'like most retreats . . . was dictated by expediency and carried out in confusion': op. cit., p. 115.

72 [1933] 55 CLR 182 at 189.

And in *Stapleton v. R*,[73] the High Court of Australia affirmed that the word 'wrong' meant 'wrong having regard to the everyday standards of reasonable people' and that the crucial question was whether the accused could 'think rationally' about the reasons that made his act 'right' or 'wrong' by those standards.

It is submitted that the Australian view of the second limb of rule 3 would secure the insanity defence for the type of defendant excluded by the traditional interpretation based on *Windle*.[74] Paranoid schizophrenics, like Arnold and M'Naghten, and psychotics, like Hadfield[75] and Adamcik,[76] who cannot claim any putative justification for their actions under the relevant provision in rule 4, would seem to be covered by it, as does the depressive who kills his children in order to end their earthly travail,[77] since in these cases the defendant's insane motives override or neutralize his awareness of the legal and moral considerations governing his actions. Admittedly, there is a risk that it would also embrace the psychopathic defendant who merely lacks appropriate moral feelings for his victim, since it might be argued that he too is incapable of giving due weight to the ethical considerations that constrain the ordinary individual. Indeed, this is one of the reasons why the Supreme Court of Canada,[78] in *Schwartz*,[79] recently declined to follow *Stapleton*[80] and upheld *Windle*,[81] notwithstanding the express recommendation of the McRuer Commission to the contrary.[82]

However, since psychopathy is a personality disorder that affects an agent's emotional responses,[83] as distinct from a psychosis that

73 [1952] 86 CLR 358.
74 [1952] 36 Cr App Rep 85 (CCA).
75 Supra, 2.1.
76 Supra, 2.4.
77 Infra, ch. 3.4.
78 By a majority of four to three.
79 [1977] 34 CRNS 138 (SCC). Mr Justice Dickson, in dissent, held that the word 'wrong' was 'not to be judged by the personal standards of the offender but by his awareness that society regards the act as wrong': [1977] 34 CRNS 138 at 151. Cf. Fingarette, *The Meaning of Criminal Insanity* (New York, 1972) p. 124 et seq., who argues for a subjective interpretation of the requirement that the accused must know that the act is 'wrong'. See also Mewett, 'Section 16 [of the Canadian Criminal Code] and 'Wrong' (1976) *18 CLQ* 413.
80 [1952] 86 CLR 358.
81 [1952] 36 Cr App Rep 85 (CCA).
82 *Report of the Royal Commission on the Law of Insanity as a Defence in Criminal Cases* (Toronto, 1956) at 160-1.
83 Infra, ch. 4.6.

undermines his capacity to act rationally, it is submitted that the Supreme Court of Canada should have confined itself to a declaration that psychopathy was not a 'disease of the mind' within the meaning of the M'Naghten Rules.[84] This would have achieved the desired result of insulating the insanity defence from defendants who simply do not care about their victims while at the same time preserving it for the deserving cases of psychosis we have been discussing. Indeed, the flexibility of the Rules in this regard is a further reason for seeking to accommodate the insanity defence within the framework they provide.

Moreover, given that the issue of insanity need only be proved on the balance of probabilities and that the prosecution must disprove it beyond all reasonable doubt,[85] it seems appropriate that juries should be able to consider all of the evidence bearing on the accused's knowledge of the legal status of his actions, even if that evidence does not disclose a putative justification for them. This point was accepted by the Alberta Court of Appeal in *R v. Budic*.[86] The defendant shot the deceased, a physician, in the insane belief that he was part of a conspiracy to withhold medical treatment from him. He was convicted of murder on the grounds that the psychiatric evidence that he knew that killing was legally wrong precluded him from relying on the defence of insanity. The Court of Appeal reversed the conviction, arguing that the jury should have been allowed to consider the fact that the appellant told a witness not to touch the gun used in the killing as it would be needed in evidence and then waited for the police in order to help them with their inquiries. Delivering the judgment of the Court of Appeal, Mc Gillivray CJ said that this evidence was 'consistent with a belief [on the part of the appellant] that he had done nothing wrong, just as a householder who shoots an intruder would, in calling the police and waiting for them, not be assumed to be thinking that he had committed a crime.'[87]

*Budic* has recently been approved by the Ontario Court of Appeal in *R v. Kirkby*,[88] which suggests that the provincial courts may be unwilling to apply the decision of the Supreme Court of Canada in *Schwartz*,[89] to the effect that 'wrong' meant contrary to law, in cases where there is a strong moral impulse to acquit the defendant on the

84 Ibid.
85 Infra, ch. 5.1.
86 (No. 3) [1978] 43 CCC (2d) 419 (ACA).
87 [1978] 43 CCC (2d) 419 at 432-3.
88 [1985] 21 CCC (3d) 31 at 49-50.
89 [1977] 34 CRNS 138 (SCC).

grounds of insanity. And since there is empirical evidence that juries are in any event inclined to acquit in such cases,[90] it seems right that they should not have to ignore a rule of law in order to do so.

### 6. THE CONCEPT OF KNOWLEDGE

The basis for the foregoing reading of the knowledge requirement in the M'Naghten Rules is essentially epistemological. When we say that someone knows something, we standardly mean either (a) that he holds true beliefs about the object of his knowledge or (b) that his beliefs can be rationally justified. Thus my belief that it is raining outside my window counts as knowledge if it is based on the fact that it is raining outside my window, just as your belief that the current President of Ireland is a woman counts as knowledge if it is based on the fact that the current President of Ireland is Mrs Mary Robinson. Similarly, my belief that cigarette smoking causes lung cancer counts as knowledge since it is based on the overwhelming statistical evidence that these phenomena are causally related,[91] notwithstanding the fact that they may not in fact be causally related and may be shown not to be in the future. In other words, although knowledge typically implies true beliefs, it is sometimes consistent with false ones, its distinguishing mark being that the beliefs that constitute it, whether true or false, can be described as valid inferences from the relevant available evidence.[92]

On this view, insane beliefs are not knowledge and someone acting on them does not know what he is doing since he is unable to take account of the obvious fact that they are not warranted by the objective evidence. Thus there is no significant epistemological difference between a defendant who kills his victim in the pathological belief that he is fending off a fatal attack, on the one hand, and one who kills in the insane belief that he is carrying out divine instructions or delivering him to a better life, on the other—the types of cases traditionally

90 Supra, n. 33.

91 Cutler, 'A Review of the Statistical Evidence on the Association between Smoking and Lung Cancer' (1955) *50 J Am Stat A* 267; Doll and Hill, 'Smoking and Carcinoma of the Lung; a Preliminary Report', (1950) *2 BMJ* 739; 'A Study of the Aetiology of Carcinoma of the Lung (1952) *2 BMJ* 1271; 'The Mortality of Doctors in Relation to their Smoking Habits; Preliminary Report' (1954) *1 BMJ* 1451; *Sunday Press*, 21 February 1993.

92 Unjustified true beliefs do not therefore count as knowledge. See Raden, *Madness and Reason* (London, 1985) pp.58-9.

covered by the Rules and traditionally excluded by them, respectively. In both cases, the holder of the relevant beliefs does not know what he is doing because he has no means of checking their validity or the validity of the desires to which they give rise, in the way a sane person does, before deciding to act on them, the fact that he may or may not have a putative justification for his actions being irrelevant to this conclusion.

## 7. THE ARGUMENT FROM PSYCHIATRY

This view of the insanity defence is supported by the psychiatric account of serious mental disorder. In modern psychiatry, insanity is generally understood as a pervasive inability to engage reality: as a failure of 'reality testing', to use the term of art favoured by psychiatrists. Hence the standard distinction between the psychotic disorders and the less serious neurotic and personality disorders which do not involve loss of contact with reality. For example, schizophrenia is standardly defined as:

> a large group of disorders, usually of psychotic proportion, manifested by characteristic disturbances of language and communication, thought, perception affect and behaviour which last longer than six months. Thought disturbances are marked by alterations of concept formation that may lead to misinterpretation of reality, misperceptions, and sometimes to delusions and hallucinations. Mood changes include ambivalence, blunting, inappropriateness, and loss of empathy with others. Behaviour may be withdrawn, regressive and bizarre.[93]

Thus the schizophrenic's inability to 'test reality' is not confined to the fact that he has false perceptions: that he sees and hears things that are not there. If it were, the category of schizophrenia would be limited to cases of psychotic hallucination. On the contrary, it denotes a broadly based cognitive failure which includes the kind of thought disorder that leads to faulty reasoning and judgment as well as purely perceptual errors caused by hallucination. The schizophrenic is as likely to draw erroneous conclusions from accurately perceived

93 American Psychiatric Association, *Glossary of Diagnostic and Statistical Manual*, 3rd edn. (Boston, 1980), pp. 120-1.

objective evidence (the misinterpretation of reality) as he is to mistake the flux of his own consciousness for such evidence, or to rely on private sensations that have no objective correlative in the real world as a guide to action (hallucination). Unlike the sane person, 'he is not able to keep his responses to the external world separate from the fantasy processes that are going on at the same time.'[94] This aspect of schizophrenic thinking has frequently been described as over-inclusion: the inability to distinguish the shared, public meanings of words and concepts from their private, purely subjective associations.[95] As Radden has observed:

> The schizophrenic's beliefs and ideas are unrealistic not only in being false—which they undeniably are—but in being subjective, rather than public or intersubjective. When this is emphasised the separation of defects of perception (hallucination), from defects of thought and reasoning (over-inclusion), seems an artificial one. We can recognize that it is as much the reality of intersubjective meanings as of sensory items which the schizophrenic fails to 'test'. It is not reality in the sense of some objective standard of truth which fails to be acknowledged; it is rather reality in the sense of the features which are shared between other thinkers and perceivers—the aspects on the basis of which there is public agreement in judgment.[96]

This point is crucial to the understanding of severe paranoia and psychotic depression. Typically the paranoid schizophrenic does not hallucinate.[97] He is not beset by devils or prompted by supernatural powers.[98] Indeed it is doubtful if he can even be accused of faulty reasoning in the strict syllogistic sense. As the scientific literature indicates, severe paranoia is characterized by the ability to construct

94 Maher, *Principles of Psychopathology: An Experimental Approach* (New York, 1966), p. 412.

95 Schwartz (ed.), *Language and Cognition in Schizophrenia* (New York, 1978), p. 239 et seq. See generally Pavey, 'Verbal Behaviour in Schizophrenia: A Review of Recent Studies' (1968) *70 Psychological Bulletin* 121; Seeman, 'Analysis of Psychotic Language: A Review and Synthesis' (1970) *31 Diseases of the Nervous System* 92; Maher, 'The Language of Schizophrenia: A Review and Interpretation' (1972) *120 BJ Psychiat* 3.

96 Op. cit. p. 78-9.

97 Kraepelin, *Lectures in Clinical Psychiatry* (New York, 1968) p. 145.

98 Ibid.

an elaborate and highly logical system of reasoning on the basis of accurately perceived experience.[99] The paranoid schizophrenic does not imagine the slights and hostilities that he encounters in his dealings with others, he is merely more sensitive to them than the ordinary person. Thus his paranoid beliefs are often grounded in the real attitudes of others towards him. What distinguishes the paranoid individual from the sane person is rather his inability to form a balanced judgment about the traces of hostility encountered in the normal course of social intercourse. He typically fails to detect any of the positive feelings that others have for him, to the extent that his general outlook gradually hardens into a pervasive sense of victimization which eventually overwhelms his judgment and may lead to a decision to take drastic action against his fancied persecutors.[100] Viewed epistemologically, the paranoid person does not know what he is doing because the beliefs that guide his actions are necessarily partial or incomplete. His beliefs do not count as knowledge because he is unable to test them against the relevant available counter-evidence of affection and esteem to which a sane person would have ready access.

Severe depression is also typically free of hallucination and so, like paranoid schizophrenia, does not entail loss of contact with physical reality. Yet there is no doubt that severe depression can reach psychotic proportions or that the depressive psychotic is unable to 'test reality' in the standard psychiatric sense. Hence the reference to mood changes—'ambivalence, blunting, inappropriateness and loss of empathy with others'—in the standard definition of schizophrenia, quoted earlier.

Nor does the fact that severe depression is manifestly an affective disorder involving a derangement of non-cognitive states of feeling (as distinct from cognitive states of thought) affect this conclusion.[101] In the final analysis, moods and feelings, whether of depression or elation, involve cognitive states in that they entail very general beliefs about the world and how it is likely to affect one's vital interests. Just as the paranoid schizophrenic has a chronic expectation that others will treat him badly, so the severe depressive is pathologically convinced that others—including members of his immediate family—regard him as a worthless failure.[102] This belief constitutes his governing

99 See Cameron, *Personality Development and Psychopathology* (Boston, 1963) pp. 477-8.

100 Cameron, ibid.

101 American Psychiatric Association, *Diagnostic and Statistical Manual of Mental Disorders*, 3rd. edn. (Washington, 1980) p. 87.

102 Beck gives the example of a depressive who 'when a friend was too busy to chat

outlook or perspective on everyday life, to the extent that he is apt to interpret the routine indifference of others as solid confirmation of his own sense of failure and worthlessness, and to dismiss as insignificant (or even not to notice) any evidence that conflicts with his gloomy expectations in this regard.

Like the paranoid schizophrenic, the depressive is at once convinced of the veracity of his view of the world and blind to the biased or partial character of the evidence on which it is based. In extreme cases, his gloomy outlook may harden into one of outright despair and lead him to seek a drastic solution to his perceived predicament, such as killing those who depend on him.[103] Even in such cases, however, the essentially cognitive nature of the depressive's derangement is clear: typically he kills in the belief that death will deliver the deceased (or some significant other) from his earthly travail, the 'inappropriateness' of his response consisting in his inability to evaluate his motives in the light of the shared, intersubjective criteria by which they are ordinarily judged.[104]

In conclusion, it can be seen that the psychiatric conception of serious mental illness cuts across the distinctions associated with the traditional interpretation of the M'Naghten Rules. Whereas that interpretation turns on a narrow concept of psychosis that is arbitrarily confined to cases of hallucination, on the one hand, and cases of complete moral illiteracy of a kind that precludes any awareness of the difference between right and wrong, on the other,[105] the psychiatric conception is based on a criterion of 'reality testing' that includes the inability to make sound judgments, i.e., to draw reasoned conclusions from the relevant available evidence as a prelude to action.

Thus the psychiatric conception also embraces the categories of

with her on the 'phone, thought "She doesn't want to talk to me any more."' If her husband came home late from the office, she decided that he was staying away to avoid her. When her children were ill-natured at dinner time, she thought, 'I have failed them': 'The Development of Depression: A Cognitive Model' in Friedman and Katz (eds.) *The Psychology of Depression: Contemporary Theory and Research* (Washington, 1974), p. 10. See generally Beck, *Depression: Clinical, Experimental and Theoretical Aspects* (New York, 1967); *Cognitive Therapy and the Emotional Disorders* (New York, 1976); (with Rush, Shaw and Emery) *Cognitive Theories of Depression* (Pennsylvania, 1978).

103 *HM Advocate v. Sharp* 1927 JC 66. The accused, who was otherwise sane and intelligent, killed two of his children in the pathological belief that it was the only way of sparing his wife the financial burden of looking after them. See also *S v. Kavin* 1978 (2) SA 731 (W), infra, ch. 3.6.

104 Ibid.

105 Supra, 2.2.

paranoid schizophrenia and depressive psychosis even in cases where the paranoid's or depressive's actions lack the colour of putative justification. And while this may not in itself be a sufficient reason for adopting the psychiatric approach as a model for the legal criterion of insanity, it is submitted that the fact that that approach also accords with the standard epistemological account of knowledge[106] establishes the case for adopting it beyond reasonable doubt. A certain amount of disagreement between law and psychiatry as to the meaning of insanity is perhaps inevitable, given the very different aims of the respective disciplines.[107] But agreement between them should be possible, and is certainly desirable, to the extent that it is enjoined by a common-sense understanding of the familiar way in which knowledge and ignorance affect action.

## 8. CONCLUSION

Although the argument of this chapter has been that the existing wording of rule 3 of the M'Naghten Rules is consistent with both the common-sense and psychiatric conceptions of serious mental disorder, it is submitted that there is a compelling case for reformulating the rule in a way that does not depend on the contentious concepts of whether the accused 'knew' the 'nature and quality' of his act or that it was 'wrong.' The following formula seems appropriate:

> In order to establish a defence of insanity, it must be proved that, at the time of committing the act, the accused was suffering from a mental disorder or defect such that he was incapable of acting rationally in the sense that he was unable to assess the reasons or conclusions that prompted his actions against the relevant available evidence and the criteria by which they are ordinarily judged.

This form of words would free the insanity defence from the burden of the restrictive interpretation we have been criticising, while at the same time preserving the cognitive core of the Rules and enabling the courts to produce the right result in all of the cases in which there is a strong moral impulse to acquit on the grounds of insanity. It would

106 Infra, 2.6.
107 For a wide-ranging discussion of this point, see Hall, *General Principles of Criminal Law* (New York, 1960), p. 455 et seq; supra, ch 1.

also greatly simplify the insanity defence by removing the need for any additional provisions dealing specifically with insane delusions, such as those contained in rules 1 and 4, respectively.[108]

It should however be noticed that the revised formulation retains the notion of mental disorder or defect as a necessary condition of the insanity defence. This distinguishes it from the 'disability of mind' defence suggested by Fingarette and Hasse as a replacement for the insanity plea.[109] On their formulation 'disability of mind' embraces any impairment of an accused's mental powers such as 'to disable him at least to some material extent from rational control of his conduct in respect to the requirements of the criminal law'.[110] As we shall see in chapter 6, the insanity defence is *sui generis,* largely because of the regime of compulsory hospitalization (in a criminal lunatic asylum) associated with it. For this reason it seems inappropriate to treat it as a species of a larger genus (embracing mental impairments other than those caused by illness or defect) in the way suggested by Fingarette and Hasse. Moreover, as we shall see in chapter 3, there are good reasons for eschewing the language of control in dealing with the typical cases covered by the insanity defence.

108 Supra, 2.2.
109 *Mental Disabilities and Criminal Responsibility* (Berkeley, 1979), pp. 200, 265.
110 Ibid.

## [3]

# Volitional Insanity

### 1. THE RULE IN *DOYLE*

In *Doyle v. Wicklow County Council,*[1] the Supreme Court recognized the existence of the defence of volitional insanity in Irish law. The question of insanity formed part of a Case Stated which arose out of a claim for compensation for criminal injuries in the Circuit Court. It had been proved in the court below that a youth of seventeen had deliberately burned down the applicant's abattoir with the intention of destroying the premises and its contents. It had also been established that the boy was medically insane, in the sense that he was suffering from a mental disorder—unidentified in the report—which caused him to believe that his love of animals entitled him to burn down the abattoir and that he would not be liable to criminal prosecution or punishment for doing so. And there was uncontested psychiatric evidence that the boy was so determined to carry out his plan that he would have waited until there was no one around who might have tried to stop him.[2]

The net issue for the Circuit Court was whether the boy was legally sane: if he was, the injuries were criminal and the applicant was entitled to compensation; if he was not, the application would fail on the grounds that no crime had been committed. The problem for the Supreme Court was to decide the criterion of insanity to be applied when determining this issue. Delivering the judgment of the Court on this question, Griffin J repeated the familiar refrain that the M'Naghten Rules did not provide a comprehensive test of insanity. Since the Rules were framed in answer to a series of questions about the legal effect of insane delusions, he felt that they should be read in the light of that limitation, and without prejudice to the

1 [1974] IR 55.
2 [1974] IR at 57.

possible exculpatory effect of other forms of serious mental disorder. This had been the position in Irish law since Kennedy CJ first stated it in 1935, in *O'Brien,*[3] and he accepted that judge's view that it was consistent with the modern approach to psychiatric disorder.[4]

As to how the psychiatric understanding of serious mental disorder should be incorporated into the insanity defence, Griffin J held that the crucial question was whether mental disorder prevented a person from controlling his actions, quoting Henchy J's celebrated words in the *People (AG) v. Hayes* (Central Criminal Court, 30 November 1967), as follows:

> In the normal case, tried in accordance with the M'Naghten Rules, the test is solely one of knowledge: did [the accused] know the nature and quality of his act or did he know that the act was wrong? The rules do not take into account the capacity of a man on the basis of his knowledge to act or to refrain from acting, and I believe it to be correct psychiatric science to accept that certain serious mental diseases, such as paranoia or schizophrenia, in certain cases enable a man to understand the morality or immorality of his act or the legality or illegality of it, or the nature and quality of it, but nevertheless prevent him from exercising a free volition as to whether he should or should not do that act. In the present case the medical witnesses are unanimous in saying that the accused man was, in medical terms, insane at the time of the act. However, legal insanity does not necessarily coincide with . . . medical . . . insanity, but if it is open to the jury to say, as say they must, on the evidence, that this man understood the nature and quality of his act, and understood its wrongfulness, morally and legally, but that nevertheless he was debarred from refraining from assaulting his wife fatally because of a defect of reason, due to his mental illness, it seems to me that it would be unjust, in the circumstances of this case not to allow the jury to consider the case on these grounds.[5]

It is easy to sympathize with the Supreme Court's decision in *Doyle.* The question of the proper scope of the insanity defence urgently

3 [1936] IR 263.
4 [1974] IR at 70-1.
5 [1974] IR at 71; FitzGerald CJ, Budd, Henchy and Walsh JJ concurring.

needed to be resolved. The Court of Criminal Appeal had already accepted that the traditional test of insanity was too narrowly drawn, and had thrice signalled, in *O'Brien*,[6] *Boylan*[7] and *McGrath*,[8] respectively, that it might be prepared to countenance a plea of irresistible impulse[9] in an appropriate case. Moreover, it had become clear, as can be seen from the passage just quoted from Henchy J's judgment in *Hayes*, that trial judges, perhaps emboldened by the Court of Criminal Appeal's pronouncements on the matter, had actually moved beyond the confines of the M'Naghten Rules when directing juries on the question

6 [1936] IR 263.

7 [1937] IR 449.

8 An unreported decision of 1960 cited by O'Hanlon in 'Not Guilty Because of Insanity' (1968) *3 Ir. Jur.* (n. s.). 61 at 71.

9 An early—perhaps the earliest—attempt to raise the plea of irresistible impulse occurred in *Earl Ferrers* [1760] 19 St Tr 885: 'If they [the witnesses] have not directly proved me so insane as not to know the difference between a moral and an immoral action, they have at least proved that I was able to be driven and hurried into that unhappy condition upon very slight occasions... If I could have controlled my rage, I am answerable for the consequences of it. But if I could not, and if it was the mere effect of a distempered brain, I am not answerable for the consequences': ibid. at 894. The plea was unsuccessful as it was not then recognized as a ground of insanity; but it would almost certainly have failed in any event given that the report discloses clear evidence of planning and delay on the defendant's part: infra, 3.3. Writing in 1842, Prichard, the superintendent of the Bristol asylum, described the type of insanity traditionally associated with the plea in the following terms: 'In this disorder the will is occasionally under the influence of an impulse, which suddenly drives the person affected to the perpetration of acts of the most revolting kind, to the commission of which he has no motive. The impulse is accompanied by consciousness; but it is in some instances irresistible; some individuals who have felt the approach of this disorder have been known to take precautions against themselves; they have warned, for example, their neighbours and relatives to escape from their reach till the paroxysm should have subsided': *On the Different Forms of Insanity in Relation to Jurisprudence*, (London, 1842), p. 112. Prichard did not think that irresistible impulse should be regarded as a species of legal insanity: ibid. This conclusion was at first shared by Stephen, who was familiar with the work of contemporary psychiatrists, including Prichard: 'On the Policy of Maintaining the Limits at Present Imposed by Law on the Criminal Responsibility of Madmen' in *Juridical Society Papers 1855-58* (London, 1855), p.71; but was later completely repudiated by him. Hence his addition to the M'Naghten Rules to the effect that the defence of insanity should also be available where the accused was 'prevented by disease affecting the mind ... from controlling his own conduct': *Digest of Criminal Law*, (London, 1877), p. 173; a point which he developed with conviction in his *History of the Criminal Law of England*, (London, 1883), p. 246. Indeed, the M'Naghten Rules notwithstanding, Stephen J (as he had then become) left the issue of irresistible impulse to the jury in *R v. Davis* [1881] 14 Cox C C 563. This example was followed in *R v. Fryer* [1915] 24 Cox C C 405. The Court of Criminal Appeal finally re-

of insanity.[10] There was even some evidence—exemplified in Kenny Js direction in *Coughlan*[11]—that the issue of insanity was being left to juries in terms that were much wider than anything that had been contemplated by the Court of Criminal Appeal in the *O'Brien, Boylan* and *McGrath* cases. If consistency and uniformity were to be restored to the defence, there was an obvious need for a clear, authoritative statement on the meaning of legal insanity from the Superior Courts. And given that the legislature had virtually abolished the death penalty in 1964,[12] thereby greatly diminishing the practical significance of the insanity plea, the Supreme Court understandably felt that it should not pass up the opportunity presented by the instant case to make such a statement, notwithstanding its stated misgivings about the appropriateness of tackling a major issue in the theory of criminal liability in the context of a claim for compensation under the criminal injuries code.[13]

## 2. DETERMINATION AND CONTROL

Yet it is far from clear that the holding in *Doyle* represents an entirely satisfactory solution to the problems posed by a restrictive interpretation of the M'Naghten Rules. A defendant who is unable to control his actions by reason of mental illness certainly does not deserve to be punished for them—on the general principle that a person is not responsible for failing to do the impossible. But how is a jury to decide the issue of control? Is the formula adopted by the Supreme Court to the effect that the defendant must be 'debarred

asserted the authority of the Rules in *R v. True* [1922] 16 Cr App Rep 164. The defence of irresistible impulse was rejected as 'a fantastic theory' and declared not to be part of English criminal law in *Kopsch* [1925] Cr App Rep 50. For a fascinating account of the history of attempts to introduce the defence by legislation, see Walker, op. cit., 106-12. The notion of irresistible impulse has been recognized in theory, but not in practice, in Irish law: see infra, 3.3. The question of whether or not there is any psychiatric basis for the notion of irresistible impulse is one of the principal themes of the remainder of this chapter.

10 Thus in *AG v. McDonagh* [1973] 107 ILTR 169, Gannon J told the jury that: 'If it be established by evidence to your satisfaction that at the time of committing the act the will of the accused was so defective that he was unable to control his actions and that such defect of will was due to mental illness the proper verdict would be guilty but insane'.

11 *Irish Times,* 28 June 1968; see chapter 1.6.

12 The Criminal Justice Act of that year restricted the scope of the death penalty to cases of capital murder.

13 [1974] IR at 66.

from refraining'[14] from committing the act to be taken literally? If it is, then it may well be that a *Doyle*-type defendant is not entitled to the defence, since the fact that a defendant was determined to do something does not entail, and may exclude, the conclusion that he was unable to refrain from doing it. Indeed this point seems to have been accepted by Griffin J when he said, *obiter*, that '[h]aving regard to the findings of the learned Circuit Court judge and the [psychiatric] evidence . . . it seems to me that the respondents have not made out a case that legal insanity absolved the youth, who set fire to the abattoir, from criminal responsibility . . .'[15] Griffin J did not elaborate on this point, correctly deciding to leave what was essentially an issue of fact for determination by the Circuit Court, yet it seems fair to say that his misgivings stemmed from the fact that the claim that the boy was unable to control his behaviour did not sit easily with the uncontested evidence that he was determined to burn down the abattoir as a protest against the killing of animals and did burn it down for that reason.[16]

Typically we describe someone as determined to do something if we learn that he had difficulty trying to do it or had to overcome obstacles in order to do it. Thus we would say that a parent was determined to send her children to university if she had to take a second job in order to afford the fees, or that an athlete was determined to run the marathon if he had to train in freezing weather conditions.

Moreover, this conclusion holds notwithstanding the fact that what the agent wanted to do was bizarre or even profoundly irrational. The one-legged athlete who 'runs' the marathon may be eccentric, but if he manages to finish it seems quite natural to say that he was determined to do so. Similarly, the child who goes out of his way to hit his baby sister with a hammer may be too young to understand what he is doing, yet in certain circumstances it might be appropriate to say the he showed great determination in hitting her. Indeed the last example is instructive, since it is clear that our impulse to excuse the child would not turn on the fact that he showed such determination. The child is not responsible for hitting his sister because, being a child, he is incapable of appreciating the consequences of his actions; and it seems plainly wrong to treat his determination to hit her as proof (or even as evidence) that he was unable to control his behaviour, or to suggest that this is why we feel impelled to excuse him. A person who is determined to do something intends to do it and is prepared

14 [1974] IR at 71.
15 [1974] IR at 71-2.
16 [1974] IR at 56-7.

to do everything in his power to carry out his intention. Far from showing an inability to control one's behaviour, evidence of determined effort shows that the relationship between thought and behaviour is functioning normally—even in cases where the agent's intentions show a radical want of reason.

Naturally if we learned that the child in our example was assailed by an overwhelming impulse to strike his sister we would still want to excuse him for doing so. But notice that in these circumstances we would not say that the child was *determined* to hit his sister. And we would not say that he was determined to hit her because, *ex hypothesi,* he had no control over that outcome. Given that the impulse was overwhelming, he would have ended up hitting her even if didn't want to—even, indeed, if he had been determined not to! Thus our impulse to excuse the child on these facts would survive even if it turned out that he was *doli capax.*[17] For even if the child understood the consequences of his actions, it would still be true that he was unable to control them, and a person who is unable to control his actions is not morally responsible for them for that reason and quite independently of any other reason.

## 3. *DOYLE* AND SCHIZOPHRENIA

Nor is it clear that a strict interpretation of the Supreme Court's formula will always produce the right result in the paradigm case contemplated by Henchy J when laying down the formula, in *Hayes,*[18] i.e., in a case of paranoid schizophrenia in which the accused knew what he was doing in the physical sense and that it was legally wrong. An example will make this clear. Take the straightforward case of a defendant who kills his victim in the delusional belief that she was party to a conspiracy to destroy his business interests, and let us suppose that he planned the killing meticulously by luring his unsuspecting victim to an isolated location and by postponing the fatal attack until he was sure there was no one around to foil it. Plainly the defendant would not be entitled to the defence of insanity on the traditional view of the Rules, as Henchy J correctly implied,[19] since his claim that he killed his victim because he believed that she was persecuting him

17 In other words, if he was sufficiently mature to understand what he was doing.

18 Supra, 3.1.

19 Ibid.; the following conclusion is based on the assumption that the defendant knows that killing is a form of homicide.

entails the conclusion that he knew the physical character of his action and that it was contrary to law—in other words, because there is no description of the killing that remains faithful to the facts that precludes that conclusion.

Similarly, he would hardly be entitled to the defence on a criterion of irresistible impulse, since that notion is inconsistent with the evidence of meticulous planning and delay[20] and since the Court of Criminal Appeal has repeatedly held that the plea of irresistible impulse must be supported by the evidence. Indeed that was the reason why that Court, although prepared to accept the defence of irresistible impulse in principle, consistently refused to admit it in practice.[21]

But if the evidence on which the plea of insanity is based must be consistent with the terms of the plea, in what sense can we say that the defendant in the instant hypothetical case was unable to control his actions? Plainly not in the literal sense, since it is difficult to imagine a convincing description of the killing that remains faithful to the facts of the case that warrants that conclusion. If there was evidence that the defendant was somehow acting against his will, or that he tried but failed to control his behaviour, the situation might be different. But all the evidence—of planning and delay—points in the opposite direction.

Nor can we get round this difficulty by re-describing the facts in psychiatric terms, although this may be what Henchy J had in mind when he sought to justify the new control test by appealing to the scientific understanding of mental illness.[22] For evidence of the ability to engage in elaborate planning and scheming of the kind under discussion here is actually part of the psychiatric definition of extreme paranoia. This is clear from Kraepelin's classic definition of the condition as 'the insidious development of a permanent, unshakeable delusional system from inner causes in which clarity and order of thinking, willing and action are completely preserved'. Kraepelin goes on:

> In this disease . . . there occurs regularly a mental working up of

20 See *S v. Kavin* [1978] (2) SA 731 (W). Interestingly, the issue of irresistible impulse was not raised in Doyle, notwithstanding the fact that the Irish case law on volitional insanity—supra, 3.1; and note immediately following—had hitherto been expressly based on it.

21 *People (AG) v. O'Connor* [1933] L J Ir 130; *People (AG) v. O'Brien* [1936] IR 263; *People (AG) v. Boylan* [1937] IR 449; *People (AG) v. Manning* [1954] 89 ILTR 155; and see the additional authorities cited by O'Hanlon [1868] *3 Ir Jur (n.s.)* 61 at 71.

22 Supra, 3.1.

> the delusion to form a delusionary view of the world—in fact a 'system'. The disease leads to a 'derangement' of the standpoint which the patient takes up towards the events of life . . . First, suspicions begin to appear which gradually become certainties and steadfast convictions. The delusions become connected with real perceptions and occurrences which are construed only in morbid and prejudiced ways; hallucinations never come under observation or only quite occasionally . . . The paranoid patients are generally in a condition without gross disturbances and still able to engage in some profitable business.[23]

This view of the illness is confirmed by the American Psychiatric Association's definition of paranoia as:

> A rare condition characterized by the gradual development of an intricate, complex, and elaborate system of thinking based on (and often proceeding logically from) misinterpretation of an actual event. A person with paranoia often considers himself endowed with unique and superior ability. Despite its chronic course, this condition does not seem to interfere with thinking and personality.[24]

## 4. *DOYLE* AND MELANCHOLIA

Similar difficulties arise in relation to the depressive defendant who kills his victim after long brooding on imagined wrongs or the seeming hopelessness of his circumstances, such as the chronic depressive who finally decides to kill his family to save them from the results of his poverty.[25] He cannot be heard to say that he did not know what he was doing in either the *Codère*[26] or *Windle*[27] senses, since the substance of his plea is that he killed his family in order to save them from penury, i.e., because the facts that constitute his psychosis exclude the kind of ignorance traditionally recognized under the Rules.[28] But

23 *Lectures in Clinical Psychiatry* (New York, 1968), p. 145.
24 *Diagnostic and Statistical Manual of Mental Disorders,* 3rd edn. (Washington, 1980), p.100.
25 The facts of S v. Kavin [1978] (2) SA 731 (W).
26 [1916] 12 Cr App Rep 21.
27 [1952] 36 Cr App Rep 85.
28 See ch. 2.2.

is it not also true that these facts preclude him from relying on the sort of control test adopted by the Supreme Court in *Doyle?*[29] If a sane man killed his family in order to save them from the gas chambers, we should certainly want to excuse him for doing so—either on the grounds that his choice was heavily constrained by his desperate plight or because it represented the lesser of two evils in the circumstances (if that is not the same thing). But it would not occur to us to say that he (should be excused because he) was unable to control his actions, since the notion of making a choice—particularly a difficult choice—and subsequently acting on it presupposes the ability to exert such control. The claim that A did something that he decided to do for the reason that he decided to do it is simply incoherent without the assumption of volitional control on A's part.

Now if the idea of acting on prior decisions and choices is incoherent without the assumption of volitional control in the case of the sane defendant, it must also be incoherent in the case of the medically insane depressive. Since he too acted for a reason, albeit a profoundly irrational reason, and gave effect to his prior decisions and choices by acting for that reason, it seems equally inappropriate to try to complete a description of the killing in his case by adding: 'but he couldn't control his actions.' As in the case of the paranoid schizophrenic discussed previously, the element of volitional control seems actually to be entailed in any credible description of the facts that constitute his psychosis and its associated reaction. If we describe his case by saying that he killed his family because of a pathological belief that it was necessary to do so in order to save them from penury—and it is difficult to know how else to describe it—the claim that he was nevertheless unable to control his behaviour would destroy the force of the 'because' in that description, since it would follow that his pathological beliefs played no significant causal role in the killing. Alternatively, if we make no reference to the causal role of his beliefs when describing the killing, as a strict application of the *Doyle* test[30] requires us to do, we will not be describing a case of depressive psychosis at all, since part of what it means to suffer from that condition is that one's behaviour is causally affected by pathological beliefs and desires.[31]

29 Supra, 3.1.
30 Ibid.
31 See the studies carried out by Beck, supra, ch. 2, n. 102. See also Cameron, *Personality Development and Psychopathy* (Boston, 1963), p. 521 et seq.

But what about the drug addict who kills for money to feed his habit? Since we know that an addict cannot control his craving for drugs, surely he is insane even on a sharp application of the *Doyle* test?[32] Once again, this conclusion does not follow. The addict who kills for money to feed his habit may have no control over his craving for drugs, since the craving is a direct product of the addiction, or at least part of what it means to be addicted. There is therefore no question of his being responsible for his addiction or on account of his addiction. The killing is also a product of the addiction, but in an entirely different sense. It is a product of a desperate decision to satisfy the addiction and is, therefore, a volitional action in precisely the same sense as the depressive's decision to kill his family or the paranoid's decision to kill his fancied persecutor are volitional actions.

Nor should we baulk at this conclusion. It may well be that there are genuine cases of compulsive behaviour, such as compulsive handwashing and (possibly) kleptomania, in which the element of volitional control is missing in the sense that the agent cannot will not to do or repeat a particular action. And it goes without saying that a defendant whose action was deficient in this sense is entitled to the benefit of the kind of control test laid down in *Doyle*.[33] The argument here is that it is a fiction—and a dangerous fiction in the case of drug addicts—to suppose that the kinds of action we have been analysing are genuine cases of compulsive behaviour, or that this is why we should be prepared to excuse those who perpetrate them.

This is clear from the fact that psychiatrists limit the category of genuine compulsive behaviour to cases of severe akrasia, i.e. cases where a person's beliefs and desires all support one course of action and yet the person persistently does another, to the specific exclusion of cases in which the agent's desires coincide with his behaviour. Thus Cameron describes a case of compulsive handwashing as follows:

> Sally returned home . . . with a fully developed handwashing compulsion which did not go away. She soon had an ugly, painful dermatitis . . . ugly and painful or not, the hands and forearms had to be scrubbed every time Sally went to the toilet and every time she had a 'sensual sensation' or thought about contamination.[34]

32 Supra, 3.1.
33 [1974] IR 55.
34 Op. cit., p. 392.

In contrast with the bogus cases of compulsive mania we have been discussing, the compulsive handwasher acts against her better judgment. In the bogus cases, the paranoid schizophrenic, the depressive and the drug addict, respectively, did exactly what they wanted to do, notwithstanding the fact that what they wanted to do was strange and their reasons for wanting to do it (at least in the first two cases) delusional; whereas she repeatedly did something that she didn't want to do and, since compulsive personality disorder is not a psychosis, that she had a good reason for not doing given the ugly and painful condition of her hands. What distinguishes her case from theirs is that she was unable to translate her beliefs and desires into appropriate action in the way that they were manifestly capable of doing. She was therefore quite literally 'debarred from refraining' from acting as she did,[35] whereas they merely appear to be, or have been made to appear so by judicial fiat. In a word, the element of akrasia,[36] of acting against one's better judgment, which is the distinguishing mark of genuine cases of compulsive behaviour, is present in her case but absent in theirs.

Admittedly, the case of the homicidal drug addict poses special problems, since it seems obvious that narcotics addiction affects self-control in a way that paranoid schizophrenia and psychotic depression do not. Yet it is submitted that the fact that it does not obliterate self-control, in the way that the compulsive manias do, suggests that it is more properly dealt with by means of a defence of diminished responsibility[37] rather than a defence of insanity (at least in cases in which it is unaccompanied by psychosis).

*Mutatis mutandis,* the same considerations apply to the psychopathic defendant, i.e., the defendant who kills or injures his victims in order to satisfy his violent (usually sexual) desires and impulses. Given the limitations of upbringing and character normally associated with this

35 In the words of Culver and Gert, the compulsive hand washer 'lacks the volitional ability to will to wash his hands. This paradoxical situation, of willing what one does not have the volitional ability to will, arises because having the volitional ability to do X includes as a necessary feature willing not to do X in appropriate circumstances. The volitional ability to will to do X requires that one can will not to do X. A compulsive hand washer wills to wash his hands, but since he cannot will not to wash his hands, he lacks the volitional ability to will to wash his hands': *Philosophy and Medicine* (London, 1982), p. 116. See also Gert and Duggan, 'Free Will as the Ability to Will' in Fischer, ed., *Moral Responsibility* (London, 1986), p. 212.

36 For a detailed philosophical analysis of the concept of akrasia, see Davidson, *Essays on Actions and Events* (London, 1985), ch. 2.

37 See ch. 8.

personality type,[38] the psychopathic killer is almost certainly less able to keep his violent impulses in check than the ordinary individual, and thus seems naturally to attract the defence of diminished responsibility, even if he is arguably less entitled to it than someone in the grip of an all-consuming addiction. But it is submitted that he is not entitled to the defence of insanity on a strict application of the control test as the element of akrasia, or of not being able to do what one wants to do, also seems to be missing in his case: like the addict who kills his victim in order to feed his habit for drugs, he too does exactly what he wants to do by translating his beliefs and desires into appropriate action.

This conclusion is of especial importance in Ireland given that the Supreme Court has said that the psychopathic killer is covered by the control test.[39] Indeed, as the discussion of the concept of mental disorder in chapter 4 illustrates, the recognition of psychopathy as a species of volitional insanity is an example *par excellence* of the folly of allowing pragmatism to override principle in the operation of the insanity defence.

## 6. THE LIBERAL INTERPRETATION OF THE CONTROL TEST

A possible solution to the raft of problems we have been discussing would be to treat the *Doyle* formula[40] as a metaphor for the loss of autonomy occasioned by severe mental disorder rather than as a strict test of volition. The argument might be that the defendant was unable to control his behaviour in the sense that he was unable to control the flow of pathological beliefs and desires that gave rise to his homicidal actions and that cut him off from the common stock of fellow-feelings that enable the sane man to control his violent impulses.[41] On this version of the control test, the fact that the defendant was able to control his behaviour, in the strict sense that he was able to translate his beliefs and desires into appropriate action, would not

38 See the discussion of psychopathy, infra, ch. 4.6; see also ch. 8.
39 Ibid.
40 Supra, 3.1.
41 A version of this argument was used by Alexander Cockburn in his defence of Daniel M'Naghten: 'I trust that I have satisfied you . . . that the disease of partial insanity can exist—that it can lead to a partial or total aberration of the moral senses and affections, which may render the wretched patient incapable of resisting the delusion, and lead him to commit crimes for which morally he cannot be held responsible': 4 St. Tr. (n.s). at 859. See supra, n. 9.

be fatal to a plea of volitional insanity, since it might still be true that his mind was so deranged that he did not have access to the kind of moral information that provides the ordinary individual with perspective on his actions and a sense of empathy with those who might be affected by them.

The logic of the liberal interpretation was considered by the Royal Commission on Capital Punishment in its discussion of the *Ley* case:

> Ley, because of his insanity, lived in a twylight world of distorted values which resulted not so much in his being 'incapable of preventing himself' from committing his crime, in the strict sense of those words, as in his being incapable of appreciating, as a sane man would, why he should try to prevent himself from committing it. It seems to us reasonable to argue that the words 'incapable of preventing himself' should be construed so as to cover such states of mind; that they should be interpreted as meaning not merely that the accused was incapable of preventing himself if he had tried to do so, but that he was incapable of wishing or of trying to prevent himself, or incapable of realizing or attending to considerations which might have prevented him if he had been capable of realizing or attending to them. If each of Ley's acts are considered separately, it would be difficult to maintain that he could not have prevented himself from committing them. Yet if his course of conduct is looked at as a whole, it might well be argued that, as a result of his insanity, he was incapable of preventing himself from conceiving the murderous scheme, incapable of judging it by other than an insane scale of ethical values, and, in that sense, incapable of preventing himself from carrying it out. If the addition to the M'Naghten Rules were construed in this way, it would serve its purpose well, and the Rules thus amended should cover most of the cases where a defence of insanity ought to be admitted.[42]

The liberal approach has been adopted in several jurisdictions. In Scotland, in *H.M. Advocate v. Kidd,* Lord Strachen left the issue of insanity to the jury as follows:

> The question really is this, whether at the time of the offence charged the accused was of unsound mind. I do not think you

42 *Report of the Royal Commission on Capital Punishment (1949-53),* Cmnd. 8932 (London, 1953), p. 111.

> should resolve this matter by inquiring into all the technical terms and ideas that the medical witnesses have put before you. Treat it broadly, and treat the question as being whether the accused was of sound or unsound mind. That question is primarily one of fact to be decided by you, but I have to give you these directions. First, in order to excuse a person from responsibility for his acts on the grounds of insanity, there must have been an alienation of reason in relation to the act committed. There must have been some mental defect, to use a broad neutral word, a mental defect, by which his reason was overpowered, and he was thereby rendered incapable of exerting his reason to control his conduct and reactions. If his reason was alienated in relation to the act committed, he was not responsible for that act, even although otherwise he may have been apparently quite rational. What is required is some alienation of the reason in relation to the act committed . . .
>
> At one time, following English law, it was held in Scotland that if an accused did not know the nature and quality of the act committed, or if he did know it but did not know he was doing wrong, it was held that he was insane. That was the test, but that test has not been followed in Scotland in the most recent cases. Knowledge of the nature and quality of the act, and knowledge that he is doing wrong, may no doubt be an element, indeed are an element, in deciding whether a man is sane or insane, but they do not, in my view, afford a complete or perfect test of sanity. A man may know very well what he is doing, and may know that it is wrong, and he may none the less be insane. It may be that some lunatics do an act just because they know it is wrong. I direct you therefore that you should dispose of this question in accordance with the directions which I have given, which briefly are, that there must be alienation of reason in regard to the act committed . . .[43]

This approach was followed by the Second Division (which included Lord Strachen) in the civil case of *Breen v. Breen*, where Lord Patrick said that, notwithstanding the fact that the Court had expressly accepted that 'the case is not one of total alienation of reason, since the doctors are agreed that the defender knew the nature and quality of his acts and knew that they were wrong', the question was whether the accused's conduct 'was influenced by his insanity, so that he was disabled from

43 1960 JC 61 at 70-1.

forming a rational decision in regard to it'.[44] *Kidd* and *Breen* have since been followed in a number of unreported cases and, in Gordon's view, 'can be taken to represent the current position [in Scots law]'.[45]

The liberal approach has also been adopted in South Africa. The decision in *S v. Kavin*[46] is an interesting example of how it operates in practice. In that case the defendant killed his wife and two of his children and attempted to kill a third child. He was severely depressed about his financial circumstances and wanted to reunite his family, whom he dearly loved, in heaven. The court accepted that he knew what he was doing and that it was wrong, but held that he was not guilty of murder on the grounds that his mental illness had prevented him from acting in accordance with that appreciation, notwithstanding the fact that there was uncontested psychiatric evidence that his actions were planned and that the killings amounted to 'a slow and deliberate course of conduct' such that he could 'not be said to have suffered from an irresistible impulse' or even to have acted compulsively.[47] The decision was inspired by the Rumpff Report[48] which had expressly recommended that the legal test of insanity should reflect the fact that the human personality was an integrated whole rather than a set of watertight compartments, and that the conative function of self-control could be eroded, even to the point of disintegration, by the constant prodding of pathological beliefs and desires (of the kind experienced by paranoids and depressives), i.e., by a severe disturbance of the cognitive functions of perception and understanding.[49] This recommendation was incorporated in section 78 (1) of the Criminal Procedure Act 1977, and *Kavin*[50] was the first case to test the scope of the new formula. Section 78 (1) provides as follows:

> A person who commits an act which constitutes an offence and who at the time of such commission suffers from a mental illness or mental defect which makes him incapable

44 1961 SC 158 at 185.
45 Op. cit. at 375-6.
46 [1978] (2) SA 731 (W).
47 1978 (2) SA at 737-8; per Irving Steyn J.
48 *Report of the Commission of Inquiry into the Responsibility of Mentally Deranged Persons* (Cape Town, 1967). The Commission, named after its chairman, Mr Justice Rumpff (as he then was), was appointed after Demetrio Tsafendas was found unfit to stand trial for the murder of the then Prime Minister of South Africa, Dr Verwoerd.
49 Ibid., at 9: 7-33.
50 1978 (2) SA 731 (W).

(a) of appreciating the wrongfulness of his act; or

(b) of acting in accordance with an appreciation of the wrongfulness of his act, shall not be criminally responsible for such act.

The language of the South African formula is similar to the test proposed in the American Law Institute's Model Penal Code (which, by 1980, had been adopted by twenty eight states and ten of the eleven federal circuit courts), which allows the defence of volitional insanity to an accused who by reason of mental illness 'lacks substantial capacity to conform his conduct to the requirements of the law.'[51] It also echoes the relevant wording in article 20 of the German Criminal Code, which provides that the defendant must be 'incapable of acting according to his perception.'[52]

Unfortunately, it is not entirely clear from the wording of the *Doyle* formula[53] that this is how the Supreme Court intended the issue of control to be left to the jury. The formula speaks of the defendant being 'debarred from refraining from [acting] because of a defect of reason, due to his mental illness...', which does suggest an erosion of intellectual autonomy of the kind we have been discussing. Moreover, since Henchy J's stated reason for introducing the formula, in *Hayes*,[54] was to bring cases of paranoia and severe melancholia within the ambit of the insanity defence, it is submitted that his words should be interpreted in a way that guarantees that result. And it should be noted that Henchy J appeared to favour this interpretation when the *Doyle* case was sent back to the High Court. There he allowed the appeal against the decision to award compensation for the loss resulting from the burning of the abattoir,[55] notwithstanding Griffin J's *obiter dictum* in the Supreme Court,[56] to the effect that the evidence did not support the new plea. On the other hand, it cannot be gainsaid that Griffin J's *dictum*, uttered when that judge was delivering the judgment of the Supreme Court on the issue of insanity, is a clear indication that the formula was intended as a strict test of volitional control.

51 MPC, 4.01; see ch. 1 n. 39; *McGlynn* [1967] IR 232.
52 See the section on German law in ch. 9.3.
53 Supra, 3.1.
54 Ibid.
55 [1974] IR at 74.
56 [1974] IR at 71-2.

## 7. THE WEAKNESS OF THE LIBERAL APPROACH

On the assumption that paranoia and melancholia are, in the words of the Royal Commission on Capital Punishment, 'cases where a defence of insanity ought to be admitted',[57] the great strength of the liberal approach is that it enables the courts to achieve this result in a reasonably principled way. The weakness of the approach is the lingering sense of unreality occasioned by the assumption that the reason we excuse the insane is because they cannot control their behaviour. If anything this is heightened (rather than reduced) by the candid way in which advocates of the approach have attempted to re-define self-control as the erosion of intellectual autonomy. The core of this idea seems to be the claim that mental disorder sometimes prevents a person from rationally evaluating whether he ought to do what he wants to do, in the way that a sane person is quite properly assumed to be able to do. Hence Lord Strachen's *dictum* to the effect that 'there must have been an alienation of reason in relation to the act committed ... some mental defect, by which his reason was overpowered, and [the defendant] . . . thereby rendered incapable of exerting his reason to control his conduct and reactions.'[58] Hence too the Royal Commission's conclusion that the defendant in the *Ley* case was 'incapable of preventing himself from conceiving the murderous scheme, incapable of judging it by other than an insane scale of ethical values . . . incapable of realizing or attending to considerations which might have prevented him had he been capable of realizing or attending to them ... and, in that sense, incapable of preventing himself from carrying it out.'[59]

Now the striking thing about these formulations is that they go to the question of the defendant's appreciation of what he is doing. They deal with the way in which knowledge and understanding affect action: the central issue in the cognitive test of insanity as laid down by the M'Naghten Rules. Admittedly, they seek to expand the traditional interpretation of that test by asking whether the defendant was in a position to make an informed judgment about the significance of his proposed course of action. But even this move fits quite naturally with what is ordinarily understood by knowledge. On the common epistemological assumption that knowledge entails a valid inference from the relevant available evidence, a defendant who is too deranged

57 Op. cit.
58 Supra, 3.6.
59 Ibid.

to give proper weight to the ethical significance of his actions or to access the common considerations by which they are ordinarily judged, cannot be said to know what he is doing in any non-trivial sense.[60]

As we have seen, this was the kind of reasoning adopted by the Australian and Canadian courts when seeking to re-define the traditional knowledge requirement in *Stapleton*[61] and *Swain*,[62] respectively. The M'Naghten Rules had been interpreted as limiting the knowledge criterion to a perceptual grasp of the physical nature and quality of action and a bare awareness of the moral rules governing the defendant's behaviour, and the reasoning in those cases was that genuine knowledge also presupposes the kind of understanding that enables the mentally healthy individual to assess the impact of his behaviour on others and on society at large.[63] It is also the kind of reasoning traditionally employed by the courts when dealing with the rebuttable presumption of *doli incapax* in the context of a plea of infancy, where the question is whether the defendant was old enough or mature enough to draw on the common criteria by which his actions are usually assessed.[64]

In other words, the claim that a defendant who was unable to make an informed decision about the propriety of what he wanted to do is not responsible for his actions is a familiar notion in the criminal law and works very well without the additional hypothesis that someone who is ignorant in this sense somehow cannot control his actions. It does not occur to us to ask whether a defendant who killed in the insane belief that his victim was the devil incarnate was able to control his actions, and it would not occur to us to ask this question in relation to the depressive who killed in order to re-unite his family were it not for the fact that the knowledge criterion in the M'Naghten Rules has been so restrictively defined.

In both cases the moral impulse to excuse the defendant stems from the manifest want of reason in the respective 'homicidal' schemes, the question of the accused's ability to control his behaviour being superfluous to this conclusion. That question arises in the second type of case for the purely technical reason that the control test has traditionally been seen as the only way out of the impasse created by the limitation of the Rules to cases where the defendant does not

60 Ch. 2.6.
61 [1952] 86 CLR 358 (HCA).
62 [1986] 50 CR (3rd) 97 (Ont CA).
63 Ch. 2.2-4.
64 Supra, 3.2.

know what he is doing in a purely physical sense, and would not arise at all if the Rules were expanded to take account of the ordinary epistemological principle that a person who is incapable of making a rational evaluation of his actions does not know what he is doing since he is not in a position to test his decisions and judgments against the shared understandings that govern ordinary life.

Nor does the fact that psychiatrists are prepared to testify that defendants are unable to control their actions in the sense understood by advocates of the liberal approach affect this conclusion. The very existence of the control test places defence psychiatrists under considerable pressure to tailor their evidence to it, since that is the only way of securing a just result in the penumbra of hard cases that fall outside the ambit of the Rules.[65] If the knowledge criterion were redefined in the way suggested above, the desired result could be achieved in such cases without resorting to that expedient.

This move would certainly produce the right result in cases of paranoia and melancholia given the psychiatric consensus that these are essentially cognitive failings of judgment and perspective—notwithstanding the associated mood (or feeling) disorders to which they also give rise.[66] Moreover, it would clarify the relationship between psychopathy[67] and the insanity defence. For while psychiatrists may be prepared to testify that the psychopath is entitled to the defence on the liberal version of the control test, on the grounds that it is generally agreed that someone with a psychopathic personality disorder is unable to empathise with the plight of his victims and their families,[68] it is abundantly clear that he is not entitled to it on the revised version of the knowledge test, i.e., when the liberal version of the control test is reformulated in epistemological terms.

If supported by evidence of upbringing and character, a chronic inability to empathise with one's victims may quite properly be considered as a potential extenuating circumstance when punishment is being imposed, or (depending on the weight of the evidence) as

65 'The triers of the facts do not first listen to the expert's testimony, decide that it signifies that the defendant was psychotic and then later ask themselves, as an independent question, whether he was insane, knew what he was doing, and so on. On the contrary, not only are the experts asked to testify in direct relation to the terms of the tests, but every statement they make is also interpreted as telling the triers of fact something about the accused's competence to understand and control his conduct': Hall, op. cit. at 527; see also ch. 5.5.

66 Ch. 2.7.

67 Ch. 4.6.

68 Ibid.

grounds for a defence of diminished responsibility. But lack of empathy with or indifference to the suffering one inflicts on other people is a moral rather than a cognitive failing: in the case of the psychopath it means that he has become so accustomed to gratifying his violent desires at the expense of other people that he no longer considers them as other than a means to that end. In other words, since psychopathy goes only to the perversion of the defendant's desires and the extreme lengths to which he is prepared to go to satisfy them, but does not touch his ability to understand what he is doing or to evaluate his actions in the light of ordinary moral sentiments, it does not qualify as a cognitive failing of psychotic proportions; and consequently, the current attitude of the Irish courts with respect to uncontested medical evidence of the disorder notwithstanding,[69] is not properly the province of the insanity defence.

For good measure, the proposed reformulation would have the added advantage of removing defendants suffering from affective, but non-cognitive, disorders like kleptomania (popularly known as compulsive stealing) from the ambit of the insanity defence. Kleptomaniacs would seem to be entitled to the defence under the liberal version of the control test, and (on the assumption that kleptomania is a genuine compulsive mania like compulsive handwashing) may even be entitled to it on the literal or strict version. Not surprisingly, there is no evidence that kleptomaniacs actually plead insanity; and, given the drastic dispositional consequences normally associated with the insanity verdict,[70] not to mention the moral incongruity of treating petty thieves as criminally insane, it seems right that they should not have to run the risk of having the plea foisted on them by judicial direction.[71]

Finally, the revised knowledge test would enable us to dispense with the fiction that a person can be sane in the cognitive sense and yet insane in some residual sense of interest to the law. Contrary to a widespread judicial misconception,[72] this assumption has no basis in modern psychiatry. If it were true, we should be able to identify cases

69 Ibid.
70 See ch. 6.
71 Cf Radden, op. cit. pp. 133 et seq., 160.
72 'I believe it to be correct psychiatric science to accept that certain serious mental diseases, such as paranoia or schizophrenia, in certain cases enable a man to understand the morality or immorality of his act or the legality or the illegality of it, or the nature and quality of it, but nevertheless prevent him from exercising a free volition as to whether he should or should not do that act': *per* Henchy J in *Hayes*, as approved by Griffen J in *Doyle* [1974] IR at 71; supra, 3.1.

of insanity unaccompanied by any significant impairment of the intelligence function; and, if we discount kleptomania for the reasons just given, no such cases exist, since a defendant who fails the liberal version of the control test will also fail the revised version of the cognitive test.[73] As we have seen,[74] the hypothesis of non-cognitive insanity holds up if and only if knowledge is defined in purely perceptual terms, since it is true that some psychotics know what they are doing in a physical sense. But it is patently false once knowledge is defined in the standard epistemological sense understood by psychiatrists: as the ability to formulate justified beliefs and desires and to test them against what is commonly known about the world. On that definition of knowledge, there is no such thing as non-cognitive or purely volitional insanity: all forms of serious mental illness are cases of cognitive insanity given that they are marked by an inability to test or justify beliefs and desires against the publicly available evidence—the existence of control tests and the legal fiction of volitional insanity to which they refer, notwithstanding.

## 8. CONCLUSION

In conclusion, it is submitted that the concept of volitional insanity is unsatisfactory both from a theoretical and practical point of view—because it appeals to the demonstrably redundant notion of the defendant's ability to control his actions and because it embraces the psychopathic defendant, respectively; and that the revised version of the concept of cognitive insanity, as embodied in the knowledge test proposed in chapter 2, is preferable to it since it not only produces the right result in cases of schizophrenia and psychopathy alike, but does so in way that achieves a perfect theoretical fit between the scientific and moral or common-sense understandings of mental illness, on the one hand, and the legal conception of madness as embodied in the insanity defence, on the other.

73 American Psychiatric Association, *Statement on the Insanity Defence* (Washington, 1982) p. 12. See generally Zilboorg, 'Misconceptions of Legal Insanity' (1939) 9 *Am J Orthopsychiat* 552. This was also Stephen's view: '[T]he absence of the power of self-control would involve an incapacity of knowing right from wrong': HCL 171. And in the modern Australian case of *Sodeman* [1936] 55 CLR 192, Evatt J said that 'It is quite out of accord with modern research in psychology to assert an absolute gap between cognition and conation': ibid. at 227. The point is developed at length in the *Rumpff Report,* op. cit. See also Hall, op cit., pp. 486-500.

74 In ch. 2.

[4]

# Mental Disorder

The discussion so far has been principally concerned with the kind of irrationality involved in serious mental illness, and with the way in which an insane want of reason affects criminal responsibility. This emphasis reflects the fact that throughout the common-law world the jurisprudence on insanity has traditionally concentrated on elucidating the notion of a 'defect of reason' as defined in the M'Naghten Rules, i.e., on specifying the meaning of the requirement that the accused did not 'know the nature and quality of his act or that it was wrong'; and on finding a way round the limitations of the received definitions of the key terms of this requirement.[1] In the result, only incidental mention has been made of the relatively neglected notion of 'disease of the mind' as used in the Rules, and it is to the elucidation of that notion that we now turn.

Although the question of what constitutes a valid 'defect of reason' has dominated insanity jurisprudence, the question of whether the defendant may be said to have been suffering from a 'disease of the mind' is logically prior to it. The fact that a defendant's reasoning powers have been impaired in the appropriate way is not enough to secure the insanity defence. It must first be established that the alleged 'defect of reason' was caused by a 'disease of the mind' (rule 3).[2] Unless the party raising the issue of insanity can do this, the fact that the impairment of the defendant's mental faculties qualifies as a 'defect of reason' is irrelevant.[3] This limitation also applies to the notion of volitional insanity. In Stephen's original formulation, the

1 Hall, op. cit., p. 472 et seq.

2 Supra, ch.2.2.

3 *Kemp* [1957] 1 QB 399 at 406; *Rabey* [1977] 37 CCC (2d) 461; 15 CR (3d) 225 (SCC); *Simpson* [1977] 35 CCC (2d) 337 (Ont CA).

test of volitional insanity was grafted on to the M'Naghten Rules, as the third limb of rule 3,[4] and this arrangement was preserved by the Supreme Court when establishing the defence of volitional insanity in *Doyle*. In the words of the Supreme Court in that case, where the defence of volitional insanity is raised the jury should be asked to decide 'whether the accused was debarred from refraining from [committing the act] because of a defect of reason due to mental illness . . . '[5]

## 1. THE PROBLEM OF DEFINITION

The meaning of the term 'disease of the mind' is a legal rather than a psychiatric question.[6] The issue is whether the accused's mental faculties were impaired by illness not whether he was suffering from a recognized mental illness.[7] Any pathological condition which interferes with the accused's reasoning powers in the appropriate way is therefore a 'disease of the mind' in the relevant sense, including purely physical diseases or states that are of only incidental concern to psychiatrists, such as arteriosclerosis,[8] epilepsy,[9] diabetes[10] and somnambulism.[11] In the words of Sir Owen Dixon (formerly Chief Justice of Australia):

> The reason why it is required that the defect of reason should be 'from disease of the mind', in the classic phrase used by Sir Nicholas Tindal [in the M'Naghten Rules], seems to me to be no more than to exclude drunkenness, conditions of intense passion and other transient states attributable either to the fault

4 *A History of the Criminal Law of England,* (London, 1883) vol. 2, p. 186.
5 [1974] IR 55 at 71.
6 *Kemp* [1957] 1 QB 399 at 406. See generally Fingarette, *The Meaning of Criminal Insanity* (New York, 1972).
7 *R v. Sullivan* [1983] 2 All ER 673 at 677 (HL); *Kemp* [1957] 1 QB 399 at 406; *Quick* [1973] QB 910.
8 *Kemp* [1957] 1 QB 399; infra.
9 *Bratty* [1963] AC 386; infra, 4.5 Cf Williams, *Textbook of Criminal Law* (London, 1978), pp. 610-11.
10 *Quick* [1973] QB 910 (CA); infra. But not, it seems, mental defects existing from birth or even from infancy: *R v. Straffen* [1952] Cr App Rep 132. *Aliter* in legal systems where the M'Naghten Rules have been codified: Cheang, *Criminal Law of Malaysia and Singapore* (Kuala Lumpur, 1990), p. 91.
11 *Burgess* [1991] 2 WLR 1206 (CA); infra, ch. 6.2.

> or to the nature of man. In the advice delivered by Sir Nicholas Tindal ... the words 'disease of the mind' were chosen because it was considered that they had the widest possible meaning. He would hardly have supposed it possible that the expression would be treated as one containing words of law to be weighed like diamonds. I have taken it to include, as well as all forms of physical or material change or deterioration, every recognizable disorder or derangement of the understanding whether or not its nature, in our present state of knowledge, is capable of explanation or determination.[12]

On this formulation 'disease of the mind' is not synonymous with disease of the brain. Indeed in *R v. Porter*,[13] its author (Dixon J, as he then was) told the jury that a 'disease of the mind' was a 'state of disease or disorder or mental disturbance arising from some infirmity, temporary or of long standing,' but did not mean 'that there must be some physical deterioration of the cells of the brain, some actual change in the material, physical constitution of the mind, as disease ordinarily means when you are dealing with other organs of the body where you can see or feel and appreciate structural changes in fibre, tissue and the like.' On the contrary, he went on, it meant 'that the functions of the understanding are through some cause, whether understandable or not, thrown into derangement or disorder.'[14]

This point was taken in *R v. Kemp*.[15] Having attacked her with a hammer, the defendant was charged with causing grievous bodily harm to his wife with intent to murder her. His defence was that he didn't know what he was doing as he had lost consciousness as a result of an arteriosclerotic episode that had cut off the blood supply to his brain. As arteriosclerosis is a physical disease, and as there was no evidence that it led to brain damage in his case, it was argued on behalf of the defendant that the malfunctioning of his brain was not a 'disease of the mind' in the relevant sense. Rejecting this argument, Devlin J (as he then was) said:

> The law is not concerned with the brain but with the mind, in the sense that 'mind' is ordinarily used, the mental faculties of reason, memory and understanding. If one reads for 'disease of

12 'A Legacy of Hadfield, M'Naghten and Maclean' (1957-58) *31 ALJ* 255 at 260.
13 [1936] 55 CLR 182.
14 [1936] 55 CLR at 188-9.
15 [1957] 1 QB 399.

> the mind' 'disease of the brain,' it would follow that in many cases pleas of insanity would not be established because it could not be proved that the brain had been affected in any way, either by degeneration of the cells or in any other way. In my judgment the condition of the brain is irrelevant and so is the question of whether the condition of the mind is curable or incurable, transitory or permanent.[16]

In other words, the limits of the notion of 'disease of the mind' are determined by the concept of pathology: 'defects of reason' stemming from an underlying pathological condition fall within the ambit of the notion; conversely, those springing from non-pathological causes are excluded by it.[17] Non-pathological causes may be internal to the defendant. Hence Sir Owen Dixon's reference to drunkenness and provocation.[18] Or they may be external, such as a blow to the head resulting in concussion, the consumption of alcohol or drugs and failure to take a prescribed medication.

In *R v. Quick*[19] the defendant was charged with a statutory assault on a patient under his care. The defendant was a diabetic and had been drinking on the day of the incident. There was evidence that he had acted contrary to his doctor's advice in having only a small breakfast and no lunch. His defence was that he did not know what he was doing as he was suffering from hypoglycaemia at the time of the incident. The evidence of hypoglycaemia was intended to support a plea of automatism but the trial judge ruled that it was tantamount to a defence of insanity and the defendant pleaded guilty. His conviction was set aside on appeal on the grounds that the issue of automatism should have been left to the jury. Since the hypoglycaemic episode was induced by the defendant's failure to follow his doctor's advice after taking insulin, it should not have been attributed to his diabetes, and therefore could not be said to have been caused by a 'disease of the mind'.

## 2. SZASZ AND THE REVOLUTION IN NEUROPHYSIOLOGY

The use of the terms 'disease' and 'illness' in connection with mental phenomena has been repeatedly criticised as illogical by Szasz. In his

16 [1957] 1 QB at 407; cf 4.2 infra.
17 *Burgess* [1991] 2 All ER 769 (CA); *Bingham* [1991] *Crim LR* 443 (CA).
18 (1957-58) *31 ALJ* at 260; supra.
19 [1973] QB 910 (CA).

view, the notion of disease implies the existence of a set of observable symptoms that can be correlated with an identifiable organic state which is their underlying cause, and is inapt when this condition cannot be met.[20] In a recent article he put the matter thus:

> Many scientists, doctors, and laypeople believe that if a genetic defect caused a mental illness or a lesion was found in the brains of mentally ill patients, it would prove that mental illnesses exist and are like any other disease; [but] this is not so. If mental illnesses are diseases of the central nervous system, they are diseases of the brain, not the mind. If mental illnesses are the names of (mis)behaviours, they are behaviours, not diseases. A screwdriver may be a drink or an implement. No amount of research on orange-juice-and-vodka can establish that it is a hitherto unrecognised form of carpenter's tool.[21]

One difficulty with this view is that it is not clear that Szasz is right in claiming that diseases are always identified by a set of symptoms and an observable organic state with which the symptoms can be correlated. As Radden has argued:

> Some of the difficulty here concerns the technical question of access to the underlying malfunction presupposed in an organic notion of disease. Because many diseases are still known and identified by their symptoms rather than by any underlying organic condition, the position at which Szasz seems to hint—that the organic malfunction must be *observable*—is overstated. The organic malfunction must be *presupposed;* it does not have to be observed for the accurate ascription of the term 'disease'.[22]

In any event, the difficulty identified by Szasz disappears if the concept of disease is taken to refer to a process rather than a fact; in other words, if it is broadened to include (as well as physical lesions and their symptoms) a constitutional proneness or predisposition which, given certain conditions, will eventually result, to a greater or lesser degree, in a breakdown of normal functions. Claridge has recently developed this point as follows:

20 For example, see his *Law, Liberty and Psychiatry*, 2nd. edn., (New York, 1989), p. 12.

21 (1991) *338 The Lancet* 1574.

22 Op. cit., p. 22.

> Physical diseases can be broadly divided into two types. There are, on the one hand, some diseases characterised by a clearly discontinuous change in bodily functioning and traceable to some discreet cause, often external in origin; the infectious diseases are an example. But other diseases have a different quality. These are the *systemic* diseases, which have their origins in the internal state of the organism and arise as a transformation and ultimate breakdown of otherwise normal functions. A good example is essential hypertension, in which sustained high blood pressure eventually brings about irreversible signs of disease, not only in the cardiovascular system, but in other organs as well, including the eyes, the brain and the kidney... [T]he equivalent in the psychological domain, to blood pressure in essential hypertension—or similar processes in other systemic physical diseases—is the genetically influenced variations in brain organisation which underly temperamental and personality differences . . . the latter can, simultaneously, be construed as dispositions to varying forms of mental disorder; and . . . the emergence of such disorder is, in essence, a transformation of these biological dispositions into signs of illness. As in the physical systemic illnesses, the transformation may be mild or incomplete. This may be for a variety of reasons: a relative weakness of the temperamental qualities in question, the degree to which modifying influences during the person's life have afforded protection against severe disorder, and an absence of triggering factors in the individual's immediate environment. Because it is sometimes incomplete, translation of normal function into disorder gives rise to a genuine spectrum of abnormality which corresponds to the distinction between mild and serious mental disorder. It is only at the extremes that the disease 'entities' of psychiatry become clearly definable.[23]

On this reasoning it does not matter that the so-called functional schizophrenias are invariably identified in terms of their so-called 'symptoms' (of thought and language disorder) and cannot be shown conclusively to be rooted in an underlying brain dysfunction. They can be described as diseases—rather than merely as 'the names of (mis)behaviours'—as long as they can be correlated with a pre-existing tendency to disorder, and there is a reasonable chance that their

23 *Origins of Mental Illness* (Oxford, 1985), pp. 9-10.

organic substructure will eventually be discovered. As we shall see presently, the reasonableness of this assumption is not in doubt.

Admittedly, this suggests, following Szasz, that these disorders are diseases of the brain rather than the mind, and therefore the province of the neurological sciences rather than psychiatry; but that is a point that need not concern lawyers. The legal problem posed by the defendant who does not understand what he is doing by reason of a more or less stable pattern of thought disorder is the same whether his condition is neurological in nature or has some other as yet unknown cause. If it is known or suspected that the defendant's condition is neurologically based, then it is obviously desirable—although not essential—that evidence to this effect be put before the jury. But as long as its causes remain unknown, it would be imprudent of the law to disallow medical evidence of communication and thought disorder simply because it happens to be given by psychiatrists. In either case, if the medical evidence discloses that his beliefs fit a recognized pattern of thought disorder and that there are reasonable grounds for supposing that the disorder is real rather than feigned, the accused should have a good defence to a criminal charge *provided the degree of thought disorder satisfies the relevant legal standard of responsibility.*

In other words, the question of whether the manifestations of the disorder can be linked to an underlying brain dysfunction or biochemical state, though fundamentally important from a scientific point of view, is ultimately irrelevant to the question of criminal responsibility. As we saw in the preceding chapters, responsibility does not turn on whether the accused was suffering from a disease, but on whether his condition prevented him from relating to the world in the standard epistemological sense. The belief that people who cannot do this are mentally ill or mad is part of the common stock of understandings that govern everyday life, and is unlikely to be shaken by the news that the so-called functional schizophrenias may not (or at least have not as yet been shown to) be biologically rooted. For this reason alone, the law is constrained to act on the assumption that the terms 'mental illness' or 'mental disease' describe real psycho-pathological conditions or states.

As regards the *scientific* issue involved here, it is submitted that, Szasz's well-known argument to the contrary notwithstanding,[24] the

24 Szasz's argument is essentially that the so-called symptoms of schizophrenia are not real symptoms because, unlike the symptoms of physical diseases, they involve a judgment on the part of the clinician—for example, in the case of a patient who thinks he is Napoleon or that he is being persecuted by the Communists, a

evidence in favour of the hypothesis that the so-called functional schizophrenias will eventually turn out to be organic in nature is impressive.[25] There are three schools of thought. The first points to the conclusion that at least some types of schizophrenia involve a substantial genetically inherited contribution, in the sense that some people can be shown to have a higher propensity to develop schizophrenia than others.[26] The evidence for this conclusion comes from pedigree and twin studies, respectively:

> First, there is the fact that the risk for any given individual varies in an orderly manner according to his or her degree of relatedness to a known schizophrenic. Bearing in mind that the lifetime risk in the general population is about 1 per cent, this figure increases to roughly 3 per cent for second degree relatives (grandparents, nephews and so on), to 10 per cent for siblings, and to as high as 45 per cent for the child of two parents who are themselves diagnosed as schizophrenic. Secondly, more recent twin studies have continued to confirm that MZ twins are more often concordant for schizophrenia than DZ twins . . . averaged out over a number of studies, it is still the case that where one twin is schizophrenic there is a 45 per cent chance of the other member becoming so, if the pair is monozygotic: the corresponding figure

judgement to the effect that the patient is *not* Napoleon or is *not* being persecuted by the Communists, respectively. '[T]he statement 'X is a mental symptom' involves rendering a judgment. The judgement entails, moreover, a covert comparison or matching of the patient's ideas, concepts or beliefs with those of the observer and the society in which they live. The notion of mental symptom is therefore inextricably tied to the *social*, and particularly the *ethical*, context in which it is made, just as the notion of bodily symptom is tied to an *anatomical* and *genetic* context': Szasz, n. 20, p. 13. One obvious difficulty with this view is that the clinical assessment of physical symptoms also presupposes the kind of shared socio-cultural context between doctor and patient which Szasz claims is unique to psychiatric diagnosis. For example, the clinical evaluation of pain—which he instances as a classical example of a physical symptom: ibid.—would be impossible without 'a covert comparison or matching of the patient's ideas, concepts or beliefs with those of the observer and the society in which they live.' Without a shared network of taken-for-granted assumptions about its meaning (of the kind which psychopaths—infra, 4.6—are thought not to have access to), a patient's descriptions of pain and a doctor's understanding of those descriptions could never achieve the status of a genuine communication.

25 For an excellent summary of the last thirty years' work in the area, see Blakemore, *The Mind Machine* (London, 1990), pp. 124-31.

26 For a comprehensive review of the evidence, see Gottesman and Shields, *Schizophrenia: The Epigenetic Puzzle* (Cambridge, 1982).

> for dizygotic pairs is about 15 per cent... the relative concordance rates consistently observed for the two types of twin—about three times greater for MZ than for DZ pairs—add weight to the importance of heredity in the aetiology of the disorder.[27]

Powerful additional evidence for the heredity hypothesis is available from studies of adopted and fostered schizophrenics. The original study in this genre—which followed up two groups of fostered children, one with schizophrenic biological mothers, the other without—found that 17 per cent of the first group (those who were reared apart from a schizophrenic mother) eventually developed the illness themselves, whereas none of the second group (those reared apart from 'normal' mothers) did.[28] More recently Kety and his colleagues have found that the biological parents of children who later became schizophrenic are significantly more likely to suffer from the condition themselves that the adoptive parents of such children.[29]

The argument from genetics has been criticised on the grounds, *inter alia,* that since adoption often involves families from the same socio-economic group, it does not make adequate allowance for the influence of environmental factors; and because it does not allow for the possible influence of pre-adoption (and even pre-natal) experiences. For example, it is known that schizophrenics tend to be born in winter and to suffer from asthma and immunological deficiency, which raises the possibility—and this is the second school of thought—that their condition may be a product of infection or some effect linked to temperature.

Thus one leading researcher has recently suggested that schizophrenia may be the result of a retrovirus affecting the DNA of the patient's chromosomes.[30] This hypothesis was triggered by the fact that it has been repeatedly found that pairs of *non-identical* twins are

27 Claridge, op. cit., p. 128-9.

28 Heston, 'Psychiatric disorders in foster home reared children of schizophrenic mothers', (1966) *112 BJ Psychiat* 819-25.

29 Kety et al, 'The types and prevalence of mental illness in the biologic and adoptive families of adopted schizophrenics' in Rosenthal and Kety (eds.) *The Transmission of Schizophrenia* (Oxford, 1968); 'The biologic and adoptive families of adopted individuals who became schizophrenic: prevalence of mental illness and other characteristics' in Wynne et al, (eds.) *The Nature of Schizophrenia: New Approaches to Research and Treatment* (New York, 1978).

30 Crow, 'Molecular pathology of schizophrenia: more than one disease process?' (1980) *280 BMJ* 66-8; et al, 'Monoamine mechanisms in chronic schizophrenia: post-mortem neurochemical findings' (1979) *134 BJ Psychiat* 249-56.

more likely to be schizophrenic that ordinary pairs of brothers and sisters.[31] On the assumption that non-identical twins (on account of their physical closeness in the womb and as babies) are more likely to have shared infections, both before and after birth, than are ordinary siblings, the idea is that the proposed virus interferes with the normal asymmetric development of the cerebral hemispheres and, in particular, with the left temporal lobe which in humans is associated with language and thought and which is known to be abnormal in many schizophrenics. Indeed:

> [S]pecific degenerative changes have been described [in relation to schizophrenics] in the parts of the temporal lobe that feed information into the hippocampus (concerned with memory formation) and other parts of the limbic system (which is concerned with emotional responses), as well as in the hippocampus itself. It may all add up to a failure of the normal proliferation and migration of nerve cells early in life, in regions on the left side of the brain that are concerned with language, visual perception, emotion and memory for words.[32]

The weakness in this hypothesis is that much of the evidence for it comes from the study of the autopsied brains of chronic schizophrenics who have had long courses of drug treatment. In other words, it is not clear that it allows for the possible causal influence of such treatment (and chronic illness itself) on the noticed degenerative changes in the brain.

The third school of thought attempts to link schizophrenia to a hidden defect in the chemistry of the brain. This hypothesis developed from the discovery, in the 1950s, of chlorpromazine and other antipsychotic drugs; and from the clinical finding that chlorpromazine in particular greatly reduced the positive symptoms (i.e., delusions and hallucinations) of schizophrenia. There are five steps in the argument.[33] First, it was quickly discovered that drugs of this type

31 Claridge, op. cit.

32 Blackmore, op. cit., p. 127; see also Gray et al, 'The neuropsychology of schizophrenia' (1991) *14 Behav Brain Sci* 1.

33 See Meltzer and Stahl, 'The dopamine hypothesis of schizophrenia: a review' (1976) *2 Schizophrenia Bull* 19-76; Haracz, 'The dopamine hypothesis: an overview of studies with schizophrenic patients' (1982) *8 Schizophrenia Bull* 438-69; Iversen et al, 'Pathophysiology of schizophrenia—causal role for dopamine or noradrenaline' (1983) *305 Nature* 577-8; Lozovsky et al, 'Modulation of dopamine receptor supersensitivity by chronic insulin: implications for schizophrenia' (1985)

affect the so-called dopamine neurotransmitter in the brain. Second, dopamine cells, which are found in groups in the mid-brain area, transmit their fibres to the basal ganglia, the limbic system, and the frontal lobe—the regions of the brain which control movement, emotion and reasoning, respectively. Third, under normal conditions dopamine travels—across the synapse—from the terminal of a nerve fibre to the receptors on its neighbouring neuron. Fourth, chlorpromazine and other anti-psychotic drugs reduce the movement of dopamine by blocking these receptors. Fifth, thus it follows that schizophrenia may be caused by too much dopamine in the limbic system and frontal lobe (although it has recently been suggested that the true cause is more likely to be too many receptors on the receiving nerve cells rather than the presence of too much dopamine).[34] This conclusion was bolstered by the discovery that amphetamine, which increases the amount of dopamine released by nerve fibre terminals, and L-dopa, a drug used to increase the flow of dopamine in order to control the symptoms of Parkinson's disease, both tend to produce the symptoms of schizophrenia.

The weakness of the 'dopamine hypothesis' is that there is no evidence for it apart from the known effects of dopamine-blocking drugs on schizophrenic patients. Moreover, it is accepted that these drugs actually work on only about one third of the schizophrenic population. But these flaws are far from being fatal. In Blakemore's words, they may mean 'either that the dopamine system is not the only pathway involved in the disease, or that schizophrenia is in fact a varied group of diseases—or both':

> The negative symptoms (poverty of speech, emotional flattening), which are characteristic of chronic schizophrenia and are relatively unaffected by anti-psychotic drugs, may be caused by the structural changes in the temporal lobe [the second school of thought discussed above]. The error in the dopamine system may account for the positive symptoms (delusions and hallu-

*343 Brain Research* 190-3; Tamminga et al, 'Schizophrenia symptoms improve with apomorphine' (1978) *200 Science* 567-8; Grace, 'Phasic versus tonic dopamine release and the modulation of dopamine system responsivity: a hypothesis for the etiology of schizophrenia' (1991) *41 Neuroscience* 1-24. For a recent review of the literature, see Goldberg and Huxley, *Common Mental Disorders* (London, 1992), pp. 75-81.

34 Davis et al, 'Dopamine in schizophrenia: a review and reconceptualization' (1991) *148 Am J Psychiat* 1474-86.

cinations), which are particularly severe during acute attacks of madness and which do respond well to drugs.[35]

In addition, recent work in the field of neuro-pharmacology suggests that the development of a drug capable of treating the negative as well as the positive symptoms of schizophrenia may be imminent. Many thought that this moment had arrived with the development of clozapine in the late 1980s; until it was found found that that drug causes a potentially fatal condition known as agranulocytosis (in which the body's white blood cells are broken down), albeit in only between 1 and 2 per cent of patients. The success of clozapine in treating the negative as well as the positive symptoms of schizophrenia was thought to be due to the fact that it blocked the serotonin—which is also a neuro-transmitter—receptor $5HT_2$ (in addition to the dopamine receptors blocked by chlorpromazine). Now it has been suggested that a new drug, HP 236, could achieve even better results with patients suffering from all forms of schizophrenia, without producing the unwanted side-effects associated with clozapine and chlorpromazine.[36] Apparently the new drug is being considered for clinical evaluation, pending the results of standard tests for toxicity.[37]

## 3. PATHOLOGICAL AND NON-PATHOLOGICAL FACTORS

The distinction between pathological and non-pathological factors is sometimes difficult to draw. If a blow to the head causes brain damage which in turn leads to a malfunctioning of the mind, it is submitted that the defendant is entitled to the defence of insanity. But a malfunctioning of the mind caused by concussion is not enough to support the defence.[38] Nor is a malfunction of the mind caused by drunkenness,[39] whereas one caused by *delirium tremens* is.[40] This does

35 Op. cit., p. 129; see also Crow, 'Molecular pathology of schizophrenia: more than one disease process?' (1980) *280 BMJ* 66-8; Claridge, op. cit. p. 186, who concludes that it is 'much more likely [that] extreme functioning of the limbic system—and hence dopamine pathways—forms part of a widespread abnormality involving the whole brain, and hence all neurotransmitters'; and (generally) Oades, *Attention and Schizophrenia* (Boston, 1982).

36 Hrib, 'HP 236 and Schizophrenia' 1992 *35 J Medicine and Chem* 2712.

37 Bradley, 'Healing without hurting the troubled mind' *New Scientist* 12 September 1992, p. 18.

38 *R v. Carter* [1959] VR 105; *Rabey* [1980] 54 CCC (2d) 1 (SCC); infra.

39 *Quick* [1973] QB at 929.

40 '[D]runkenness is one thing and the diseases to which drunkenness leads are

not mean that the distinction is a matter of expediency, as was suggested in *Quick*.[41] The question is whether the accused's reasoning powers were deranged by illness, and concussion and drunkenness are not illnesses, whereas brain damage and *delirium tremens* are. Nor does the fact that the relevant pathological condition, say epilepsy, may have been induced by some non-pathological factor, like a concussive blow, affect this conclusion. If it is clear that the blow produced the epileptic attack then, on the general principles of causation, the latter will quite properly be regarded as a *novus actus interveniens* with respect to the derangement of the accused's mental faculties, i.e., as having broken the chain of causation leading from the blow to the derangement.

This point was recently taken in *DPP v. Ellis*.[42] The defendant killed his victim in the course of a row during which he claimed the latter had been trying to blackmail him into participating in an armed robbery. There was medical evidence that the fatal blows may have been struck during an epileptic fit brought on by an earlier blow from the victim. Counsel for the accused contended that this entitled his client to an unconditional acquittal on the grounds of automatism: as the fit was induced by a blow to the head and was non-recurring, he argued that it did not constitute a mental illness nor require treatment and should not therefore attract the insanity defence. The trial judge ruled[43] that evidence of an automatist or epileptic fit disclosed the operation of a supervening illness and accordingly left the issue of insanity to the jury.[44]

But if the blow, or some other non-pathological factor, is the only thing that stands in a causal relationship with the derangement, it

different things; and if a man by drunkenness brings on a state of disease which causes such a degree of madness, even for a time, which would have relieved him from responsibility if it had been caused in any other way, then he would not be criminally responsible': *Davis* [1881] 14 Cox CC 563 at 564, per Stephen J; approved by the House of Lords in *DPP v. Beard* [1920] AC 479 at 501.

41 [1973] QB at 928; per Lawton LJ.

42 [1990] IR 291 (SC).

43 In light of the decision of the Court of Criminal Appeal in *People v. Messitt* [1972] IR 204, to the effect that 'If the accused or his advisors are not prepared to make the case that he is insane, the duty of putting such evidence as is available on the topic before the jury rests on the People, if the Attorney General is of opinion that the evidence is such that the jury might reasonably conclude that the accused was insane . . . It is not an answer to this to say that the accused does not wish this evidence to be given. One of the questions in issue is his sanity: his fitness to plead does not involve the conclusion that he is the only person to make a decision as to whether the issue of his insanity is to be considered by the jury': at pp. 213-4; per Kenny J, delivering the judgment of the court.

44 Infra, ch. 6.2.

seems quite natural to say that the latter was not caused by a 'disease of the mind.' In other words, in cases where there is no evidence of supervening illness, the jury should be given the opportunity to consider whether the defendant is entitled to a complete acquittal based on automatism. Unlike the pathologically deranged defendant whose condition may recur, the non-pathologically deranged defendant presents no danger to the public. In contrast, the special verdict of insanity, with its associated regime of hospitalization and treatment, seems more appropriate in cases in which the defendant's condition is likely to endanger the public by re-asserting itself, notwithstanding the fact that the condition may itself have been induced by a non-pathological factor.[45]

*Rabey v. The Queen*[46] affords a nice illustration of this problem. The appellant attacked his victim, a fellow geology student, with a rock sample and tried to choke her. He was charged with causing bodily harm with intent to wound. His defence was that he was unaware of what he was doing as he was in a dissociative state—i.e., a state in which the mind-behaviour link is not working—at the time of the incident. There was evidence that the dissociative state was caused by the powerful emotional shock which resulted from his discovery, shortly before the attack, that the girl, with whom he had been on friendly terms, did not reciprocate his feelings for her. It was argued on the appellant's behalf that a dissociative state caused in this way was not a 'disease of the mind' (within the meaning of the Canadian version of the M'Naghten formula). It was rather the effect of the psychological blow of the bad news and was therefore on a par with mental confusion caused by a physical blow, i.e., with simple concussion. There was supporting psychiatric testimony that mental confusion caused by psychological shock is not a neurosis and that someone suffering from it is liable to act as an automaton.

Part of the prosecution case was that the appellant's response to the girl's rejection of him was consistent with the symptoms of hysterical

45 This does not mean that a pathological condition must be prone to recur in order to qualify as a 'disease of the mind'. There are also considerations of retributive justice to be considered. 'It would be quite unreasonable to hold that a serious mental disorder did not constitute a disease of the mind because it was unlikely to recur. To so hold would be to exclude from the exemption from responsibility afforded by insanity, persons, who by reason of a severe mental disorder were incapable of appreciating the nature and quality of the act or of knowing that it was wrong, if such mental disorder was unlikely to recur': *Rabey* [1977] 37 CCC (2) 461 at 476 (Ont CA); per Martin J; affirmed [1980] 15 CR (3d) 225 (SCC)

46 [1980] 54 CCC (2d) 1 (SCC).

neurosis, and that the issue for the court was therefore whether he should be acquitted on the grounds of insanity. The trial judge took the view that the conflict of evidence raised a reasonable doubt that the defendant was in a dissociative state brought about by an external, non-pathological factor, and accordingly accepted the defence of automatism. The prosecution successfully appealed to the Ontario Court of Appeal and a new trial was ordered. The Supreme Court of Canada later affirmed the decision of the Court of Appeal by a majority of four to three, Ritchie J, on behalf of the majority, expressly adopting the following passage from Martin J's judgment in the court below:

> In my view, the ordinary stresses and disappointments of life which are the common lot of mankind do not constitute an external cause constituting an explanation for a malfunctioning of the mind which takes it out of the category of a 'disease of the mind.' To hold otherwise would be to deprive the concept of an external factor of any real meaning. In my view, the emotional stress suffered by the respondent as a result of his disappointment with respect to Miss X cannot be said to be an external factor producing the automatism within the authorities, and the dissociative state must be considered as having its source primarily in the respondent's psychological or emotional make-up. I conclude, therefore, that, in the circumstances of this case, the dissociative state in which the respondent was said to be, constituted a 'disease of the mind.' I leave aside until it becomes necessary to decide them, cases where a dissociative state has resulted from emotional shock without physical injury, resulting from such causes, for example, as being involved in a serious accident although no injury has resulted; being the victim of a murderous attack with an uplifted knife, notwithstanding the victim has managed to escape serious injury; seeing a loved one murdered or seriously assaulted, and the like situations. Such extraordinary external events might reasonably be presumed to affect the average normal person without reference to the subjective make-up of the person exposed to such experience.[47]

This seems right as far as dissociative reactions that are rooted in the defendant's subjective make-up are concerned, Dickson J's strong dissenting judgment notwithstanding.[48] But the remarks about

47 [1980] 54 CCC (2d) at 7.

48 [1980] 54 CCC (2d) at 28. And cf MacKay's view that 'if [a *Rabey*-type defendant]

dissociative states produced by external factors need careful scrutiny. Insofar as they entail the conclusion that such states do not come within the ambit of the concept of 'disease of the mind,' they are unexceptionable. But if they mean that non-pathologically induced dissociative states should invariably be treated as cases of automatism, they are open to serious objection. The authorities show that the plea of automatism is confined to cases of involuntary conduct,[49] and it is far from clear that dissociative reactions of the kind contemplated by Martin J necessarily fall into that category. Convulsive bodily movements and spasms induced by any of the listed factors certainly would,[50] but similarly induced complex bodily movements such as choking and driving almost certainly would not

is robust and not normally affected then he may have a good defence where the shock is severe; if on the other hand his dissociative state is triggered off by an everyday and 'ordinary' form of stress then he is to be regarded as suffering from a disease of the mind. But what in reality is the difference between these two types of case? In both the accused is in a dissociative state. But the former's condition is not 'pathological' since it is to be regarded as a 'transient state induced by some specific external factor' namely, the severe shock. How the latter's condition can become 'pathological' simply because he is more susceptible to shock or stress must remain a mystery. It is submitted then that the refinement of the 'external factor doctrine' offered in *Rabey* is most unsatisfactory..:'Non-Organic Automatism—Some Recent Developments' (1980) *Crim L Rev* 350 at 360. But this criticism seems misguided. The fact is that defendants who are abnormally susceptible to shock or stress are dangerous in a way that the normally susceptible defendant is not, and seem naturally to attract the insanity defence for that reason. This is true even in cases where it might be thought inappropriate to commit a *Rabey*-type defendant to a maximum security psychiatric institution, since the insanity defence can be adapted to provide for less drastic forms of psychiatric treatment, not excluding outpatient psychiatric care—as was recommended in England both by the Criminal Law Revision and Butler Committees: Cmnd 2149 of 1963 para 34 and cmnd 6244 of 1975 para 18.42, respectively. In contrast, the defence of automatism precludes this possibility as it amounts to a complete acquittal without conditions. For a review of the relevant Australian cases see Harding, 'Sane and Insane Automatism in Australia: Some Dilemmas, Developments, and Suggested Reforms' (1981) *4 Int J Law and Pychiat* 73.

49 'No act is punishable if it is done involuntarily; and an involuntary act in this context—some people nowadays prefer to speak of it as automatism—means an act done by the muscles without any control by the mind such as a spasm, a reflex action or a convulsion or an act done by a person who is not conscious of what he is doing, such as an act done while suffering from concussion, or while sleepwalking': *Bratty v. A-G* for NI [1963] AC 386 at 409; per Lord Denning. Automatism is confined to 'involuntary movement of the body or limbs of a person': *Watmore v. Jenkins* [1962] 2 QB 572 at 586; per Winn J. See generally, Mc Auley, 'The Action Component of *Actus Reus*' (1988) *23 Ir Jur* 218.

50. *Bratty* [1963] AC 386 at 395; per Lord Denning.

since they usually, though not invariably, entail the kind of voluntary control characteristic of standard action.[51]

This is not to say that a defendant who carries out a complex bodily movement in an externally produced dissociative state is automatically responsible for his actions. If the dissociative reaction involves a degree of mental confusion such that the defendant does not know what he is doing, he will generally be entitled to an acquittal on the grounds that he lacked *mens rea*. The point is rather that he is not entitled to be acquitted on the grounds of automatism, a distinction which could be vital in cases in which the prosecution does not have to prove *mens rea* (in the sense of intention or subjective recklessness). In *Watmore v. Jenkins*[52] the defendant was charged, *inter alia*, with dangerous driving. The case against him was that he had caused his car to career from one side of the road to the other for a distance of five miles, hitting a number of vehicles along the way and forcing others to take drastic evasive action, and finally coming to a halt by colliding with a parked car on the opposite side of the road. His defence was that he didn't know what he was doing as a result of a dissociative state brought on by the after-effects of hepatitis. It was accepted that the defendant was a diabetic and that the hypoglycaemic episode was caused by a sudden and unpredictable change in the condition of his liver which had upset the hydrocortezone level in his body. The court of first instance stated a case on the issue of automatism to the Divisional Court, but that court sent back a direction to convict the defendant as charged, Winn J delivering its judgment:

> The finding of a condition which 'may be likened to sleep-walking or to a fit of epilepsy' is not a finding that there was a state identical with those states in respect of absence of control of the will; the finding that 'the body may continue to do things it is used to doing' is not a finding that everything the respondent's arms, legs and eyes did throughout those five miles was a thing his body was used to doing; the finding that 'he continued to perform the functions of driving, after a fashion' tends to negative rather than support a conclusion that the whole of such performance was involuntary or unconscious . . .
>
> The charge of dangerous driving was fully established by the facts unless the evidence failed to exclude beyond reasonable doubt the existence of a state of automatism extending through-

51 See the discussion of *Watmore v. Jenkins* [1962] 2 QB 572, infra.
52 [1962] 2 All ER 868.

> out the whole of the distance or stretches of road to which it related. For reasons already stated, the findings of the justices do not support a conclusion that already, before the material time, there had occurred in this case such a complete destruction of voluntary control as could constitute in law automatism. The court will send back this charge of dangerous driving with a direction to convict.[53]

## 4. DISSOCIATIVE STATES AND STANDARD ACTIONS

The proper limits of the defence of automatism have recently been considered by the Western Australian Court of Criminal Appeal. In *R v. Falconer*[54] the defendant was charged with the murder by shooting of her estranged husband. It was accepted that the killing took place against a background of violence and sexual assault by the deceased against the defendant and two of their daughters; and that, on the day of the incident, the deceased had unexpectedly returned to the family home and, notwithstanding the existence of a non-molestation order against him, sexually assaulted the defendant, taunted her with the suggestion that neither her nor their daughters' allegations of sexual abuse would be believed in court, and attempted to grab her by the hair. From that point the defendant said she remembered nothing until she found herself on the floor with her shotgun by her and her dead husband on the floor nearby. The medical evidence was that on her account of the circumstances her conduct and behaviour before and after the shooting were consistent with a dissociative state in which she was unaware of her actions. The trial judge refused to leave the issue of automatism to the jury on the grounds that there was insufficient evidence to support it.

Delivering the judgment of the Western Australian Court of Criminal Appeal, Malcolm CJ held that this was a misdirection and allowed the appeal. In his view the medical evidence to the effect that the events that occurred on the day of the killing could have caused the defendant to panic and enter a full-blown dissociative state was enough to raise a reasonable doubt as to whether the accused was acting as an

53 [1962] 2 All ER at 874. See also *Broome v. Perkins* [1987] 85 Cr App Rep 321, where similar reasoning was applied to deny the defence of automatism to a defendant who apparently took evasive action whilst driving in what he claimed was a state of unconsciousness due to sudden illness. Cf *King* [1962] SCR 746 (SCC).

54 [1989] 46 A Crim R 83.

automaton when she shot her husband:

> The issue in the present case was whether the jury, if satisfied, that the appellant shot her husband, could infer that she did so with the intention to kill him. The question whether the shooting was a conscious or voluntary act of will on the part of the appellant was highly relevant to the issue of intent. The evidence of the assault on the day of the shooting and Mr Falconer's taunting of the appellant, given her general emotional and mental state, was on the medical evidence capable of giving rise to involuntary conduct. Consequently, the evidence derived in that way, coupled with the appellant's own evidence gave rise to an issue of voluntariness which should have been left to the jury.[55]

The difficulty with this reasoning is that, even if we insist that the appellant was in a dissociative state, it is not clear that her actions were involuntary. On the contrary, since there is no evidence that she was armed with her shotgun when her husband came on the scene, we must assume that she fetched it from wherever it was stored, aimed it at least in the general direction of her husband and pulled the trigger—in other words, that she performed the kind of complex action that, as the decision in *Watmore v. Jenkins*[56] illustrates, is not easy to reconcile with the hypothesis of automatic involuntary conduct, i.e., with a set of bodily movements over which the agent has no control. Given the verbal and physical taunts to which she had been subjected, it is submitted that the better view is that the claim that she was in a dissociative state when she killed her husband means no more than that she flew into a state of 'blind' panic, fear or rage when her husband tried to grab her by the hair, and killed him whilst in that state. This was simply the point at which she 'snapped' under the cumulative strain of his on-going attacks on her and her family.

In short, this analysis suggests that a *Falconer*-type defendant is typically only entitled to the defence of provocation (rather than automatism) and, consequently, should be convicted of manslaughter (rather than acquitted *tout court*). Admittedly, this solution poses its own problems since there will undoubtedly be some cases in which the provocation is so extreme that the defendant is arguably entitled to a complete acquittal on moral or culpability grounds (to the extent that not even a nominal or suspended sentence for manslaughter would be retributively appropriate). However, it is submitted that this

55 [1989] 46 A Crim R at 91.
56 Supra, 4.3.

is an argument for expanding the defence of provocation to a full-blown acquittal—on the grounds that this would enable to courts to provide for such cases without doing violence to the classic principle that the defence of automatism is confined to cases where the link between the accused's mental processes and his behaviour has been completely severed as opposed to merely impaired.[57]

The fundamental importance of this principle is dramatically illustrated by the recent case of *DPP v. Courtney*,[58] where the defendant admitted killing the deceased by repeatedly smashing a brick into her face. His defence to a charge of murder was that he was suffering from a condition diagnosed as post-traumatic stress disorder, such that a remark he alleged the woman made to him before the attack, and her screams when she regained consciousness as he drove her to the scene of the killing some time after initially assaulting her, threw him into a state of acute panic and triggered the flurry of involuntary blows which caused her death. In the ringing phrase of counsel for the defence, the disorder and the panic combined to produce a pattern of behaviour that amounted to a 'non-mentally processed reaction' on the defendant's part and, consequently, to a defence of volitional insanity. Although the defence was rejected by the jury—in all probability because of the abundant evidence of deliberation and control entailed in driving the victim to the mountains after he had knocked her unconscious, it is worth examining the logic of defence counsel's argument in some detail.[59]

At the outset, it should be said that the concept of 'non-mentally processed reaction' is entirely apt when referring to the kind of behaviour that should be treated as involuntary for legal purposes; it serves as a graphic reminder that a behavioural event is an action if and only if it is a causal product of the agent's mental state, i.e., if it realizes or gives effect to one or more of his beliefs, intentions or desires. A bit of behaviour that does not meet this condition is not an action because it cannot be connected to the person whose behaviour it is in a way that enables us to say: 'he did it'.[60] We cannot say 'he did it' in this sort of case because the attribution of agency only makes sense if it is clear that the agent satisfied one or more of his beliefs, intentions or desires by doing whatever the 'it' in that phrase happens to stand for.

57 See ch. 1.5; supra, n. 49.

58 *Irish Times* and *Irish Independent*, 22 January 1993.

59 'Why we found him guilty' *Irish Independent*, 23 January 1993; the claim of post-traumatic stress disorder was based on evidence of the defendant's experience as a soldier in the Lebanon.

60 See ch. 1.5; for a detailed analysis of the problems involved in the attribution of agency, see McAuley, op. cit.

Thus it is simply incoherent to say 'Patrick drove his car from Dublin to Monaghan, but none of the bodily movements involved in that exercise were connected with any of his prior or contemporary mental states'. If Patrick did indeed *drive* his car from Dublin to Monaghan, then the second part of this proposition must be false. Contrariwise, if the second part of the proposition is true, then the first part must be false. Patrick does not have to *intend* to go to Monaghan, much less *desire* to go there, before we can say he *drove* there. He might, for example, take a wrong turn and end up in Monaghan in the mistaken belief that he was on the road to Clones. But he must intend to drive *somewhere,* i.e, there must be a causal connection between that mental state and the bodily movements involved in driving to Monaghan, before we can say that he *drove* there. If no such connection exists—if, for example, Patrick has a stroke at the wheel but by some miracle his limbs continue for a time to perform the bodily movements involved in steering the vehicle and pressing the accelerator, we naturally want to say that he was not then *driving* to Monaghan, because from that point onwards these movements are not his mental 'products'.[61]

To summarise the discussion so far, the burden of the theory of action on which the *Courtney* defence was based is that actions are mental products in the sense that they are caused by cognitive mental states such as intentions, desires and beliefs; and that behavioural events that do not answer this description are properly regarded as automatic and therefore beyond the reach of the criminal law. It seems to follow from this theory that behaviour produced or caused by extreme *emotional* states—whether of fear, panic, rage or some combination of these—should be treated as automatic involuntary conduct for legal purposes, on the grounds that these states effectively break the causal chain between mind and behaviour that is an essential feature of standard action. As we have seen, this assumption was a key ingredient in defence counsel's argument in *Courtney,* in the sense that it was contended that the accused could not control his actions because he killed in a frenzy of violence facilitated by post-traumatic stress disorder and triggered by his victim's screams when she regained consciousness and realised she was being abducted.

Leaving aside the fact that the defendant was convicted of murder in that case, and allowing for the fact that defence counsel is obliged

61 See the discussion of *Watmore v. Jenkins* in the previous section.

to do the best he can for his client in the circumstances, it is submitted that this reasoning is fatally flawed.[62] Although superficially appealing, its intellectual cogency rests on an imagined antinomy between the cognitive and affective functions of the mind and, in particular, on the mistaken belief that extreme emotional states are non-cognitive in character. As we saw in chapter 2,[63] depressive states, even when extreme, though primarily emotional or affective in nature, have a crucial cognitive element in that they entail specific beliefs about the patient's worth as a human being and value to others; and may entail more general beliefs about the hopelessness or pointlessness of life. To the extent that the patient relies on these beliefs as a basis for behaviour, the results are clearly actions notwithstanding the fact that the results may be entirely mistaken (because the beliefs that gave rise to them are themselves mistaken).

Similarly, a person who does something out of fear, panic or rage is also acting cognitively in the sense that his behaviour is a direct expression of his assessment of the state of the world as it affects him at that moment, whether or not that assessment is rooted in an underlying mental disorder. If his assessment is skewed by mental disorder—say by a psychotic fear that he was being eaten from the inside by worms or, to take Courtney's claims at face value, in the sense that post-traumatic stress disorder caused him to feel threatened by the remark he attributed to the deceased or to panic and become enraged or frightened by her screams when she regained consciousness as he drove her from the city to the mountains—anything he does on the basis of that assessment, including lashing out at his screaming victim, and grabbing a rock and repeatedly striking her with it, is an action in the straightforward sense that it is plainly mediated and guided by one or more of his mental states. In short, it *is* a causal product of his mind and therefore cannot be a 'non-mentally processed reaction'.

In conclusion, it is submitted that the concept of a frenzied outburst of violence, such as occurred in the *Courtney* case, does not preclude the performance of standard actions. Standard action requires cognitive interaction with the environment such that the agent's behaviour—e.g., the fact that he repeatedly struck his victim with a brick—can be shown to stand in a causal relationship with one or more of his mental states—e.g., with a belief that he had to stop his victim screaming or that she might report him to the police. In the

62 See ch. 1.5.
63 See 2.7.

final analysis, all emotional states entail a belief or beliefs, however general, about the environment. Notwithstanding the intensity of the emotional state a defendant happens to be in, it follows that the things he does on account or as a result of it are genuine actions.

## 5. INSANE AUTOMATISM

The defendant who kills or injures his victim in an involuntary movement while unconscious due to illness—e.g., the epileptic who strikes his victim in a convulsive spasm—presents even more difficult problems. The nearest analogues are *Bratty v. A-G* for Northern Ireland[64] and *Sullivan v. DPP.*[65] In *Bratty* the defendant strangled a girl with one of her stockings. His defence was that he was unaware of what he was doing as the attack occurred during the psychomotor stage of an epileptic seizure, and this was held to be evidence of insanity. The result was the same in *Sullivan* where the defendant also attacked his victim during an epileptic seizure. But these cases can be distinguished from the instant hypothetical case. Acquitting the defendant in that case on the grounds of insanity seems inappropriate as it is not clear that he has committed an *actus reus,* i.e., that the outcome can be attributed to him as agent; whereas the element of agency or voluntary action was clearly present in the *Bratty* and *Sullivan* cases. In other words, the hypothetical case looks more like a case of automatism than insanity. Yet allowing the defendant to rely on automatism seems equally inappropriate given that his condition may recur and that he is likely to be a danger to others if and when it does.

There is no easy solution to this problem. But it is submitted it would help if the courts were to limit the category of insane automatism to cases of involuntary action due to illness involving a risk of recurrence. This arrangement would reflect the fact that the element of agency is missing in these cases while at the same time signalling that the defendant is suffering from a potentially dangerous condition. Cases of the *Bratty* and *Sullivan* type, which are sometimes misleadingly included in the category of insane automatism,[66] could then be more accurately classified as cases of insanity *simpliciter;* and

64 [1963] AC 386.
65 [1984] AC 156.
66 For example, by Burchell et al, *South African Criminal Law and Procedure,* vol 1 (Cape Town, 1983), pp. 286-7. The idea that the defence of insanity presupposes a voluntary act on the defendant's part is clear from the form of the insanity verdict: see ch. 6.1.

cases of involuntary action resulting from non-recurring illnesses (like strokes and heart failure) and external factors, as cases of automatism *simpliciter.*

## 6. THE PROBLEM OF PSYCHOPATHY

Decisions such as *Porter*[67] and *Kemp*[68] depend on an integrated reading of the key terms in rule 3 of the M'Naghten Rules:[69] 'disease of the mind' is defined as any pathological condition that leads to a recognized 'defect of reason.'[70] This approach poses no problems as regards physical illnesses, since the concept of physical pathology is relatively stable. Doctors may disagree about the aetiology of arteriosclerosis or diabetes, for example, but no one disputes that these conditions are diseases. And no one disputes that they are diseases because they conform to the normal pattern of physical pathology: the symptoms associated with them are known and understood, and treated on the basis that they reflect an underlying disease state in the person suffering from them.[71]

But the approach could lead to serious difficulties in the area of mental illness. For example, how should the courts treat a defendant whose 'defect of reason' was allegedly caused by psychopathy, given that there are genuine grounds for doubting whether psychopathy is a mental illness in the normal psychiatric sense? Some psychiatrists use the term to refer to a pattern of repeated anti-social behaviour in the face of criminal punishment[72]—recidivism, as criminologists call

67 [1933] 55 CLR 182.
68 [1964] 2 QB 341.
69 Supra, ch. 2.2.
70 Supra, 4.1.
71 Supra, 4.2.
72 The World Health Organization has defined psychopathy as a 'personality disorder with a predominantly sociopathic or asocial manifestation . . . characterized by disregard for social obligations, lack of feeling for others, and impetuous violence or callous unconcern. There is a gross disparity between behaviour and the prevailing social norms. Behaviour is not readily modifiable by experience, including punishment. People with this personality disorder are often affectively cold and may be abnormally aggressive or irresponsible. Their tolerance to frustration is low: they blame others or offer plausible rationalizations for the behaviour which brings them into conflict with society': *Mental Disorders: Glossary and Guide to their Classification in Accordance with the Ninth Revision of the International Classification of Diseases* (WHO,1978), point 301.7.

it—apparently on the assumption that the incorrigibly persistent offender must be mentally ill.[73] But this definition is hopelessly circular,[74] since there is abundant criminological evidence that most persistent offenders are not mentally ill in either the psychotic or neurotic sense, i.e., in any sense other than the fact that they have been labelled as psychopaths.[75]

Others classify psychopathy as a mental illness on the grounds that it seems to be linked to the personality traits—lack of fellow feeling, aggressiveness, impulsiveness, egocentricity, callousness, unreliability, lack of remorse—associated with the persistent offender. Hence the McCords' classic definition:

> The psychopath is asocial. His conduct often brings him into conflict with society. The psychopath is driven by primitive desires and an exaggerated craving for excitement. In his self-centred search for pleasure, he ignores the restrictions of his culture. The psychopath is highly impulsive. He is a man for whom the moment is a segment of time detached from all others. His actions are unplanned and guided by his whims. The psychopath is aggressive. He has learned few socialized ways of coping with frustration. The psychopath feels little, if any, guilt. He can commit the most appalling acts, yet view them without remorse. The psychopath has a warped capacity for love. His emotional relationships, when they exist, are meagre, fleeting, and designed to satisfy his own desires. These last two traits, guiltlessness and lovelessness, conspicuously mark the psychopath as different from other men.[76]

This account seems equally unsatisfactory. Apart from the fact that the mentioned characteristics are notoriously vague and difficult to

73 This was the approach taken in *Blocker v. United States* [1961] 288 F 2d 853 (USCADC). *Blocker* is discussed in Becker, 'Durham Revisited: Psychiatry and the Problem of Crime: Part II' (1973) *Psychiatric Annals* 1 at 12.

74 '[T]he psychopath's mental disorder is inferred from his antisocial behaviour while the antisocial behaviour is explained by mental disorder . . . [t]he offender suffers from diminished responsibility if anything has impaired his responsibility': Wootton, *Crime and the Criminal Law,* 2nd. edn. (London, 1981), p. 117.

75 For example, see Penrose, 'Mental Disease and Crime: Outline of a Comparative Study of European Statistics' (1939) *BJ Med Psychol* 18; Gibbens, 'Psychiatry and the Abnormal Offender' (1956) *Medico-Legal J* 24; Lopez-Rey, *Crime: An Analytical Appraisal* (London, 1970), pp. 119-23.

76 W and J McCord, *The Psychopath: An Essay on the Criminal Mind* (New York, 1964) pp. 16-7.

measure, and seem to be shared, to a greater or lesser degree, by people generally, the concentration of more than a few of them in a single individual is quite consistent with the hypothesis of moral wickedness or depravity unaccompanied by mental disorder. Unlike his psychotic counterpart, it seems that the psychopathic killer understands what he is doing: there is no suggestion that his homicidal motives are epistemologically biased. On the contrary, they seem to proceed from the markedly deviant character of his desires rather than any defect of understanding, and this is why our impulse to excuse him on the grounds of insanity seems to falter. Naturally the law should be prepared to make some allowance for someone 'suffering' from what psychiatrists call 'psychopathic personality disorder'—on the general principle that we are not responsible for the formation of our characters or personalities. In cases where there is evidence that a defendant's deviant sexual desires or violent impulses probably interfered with his capacity for self-control, it is submitted that this could be done by means of a plea of diminished responsibility. By definition, the concept of diminished responsibility acknowledges that there are factors which interfere with self-control without obliterating it, and seems therefore ideally suited to the apparently dual character of psychopathy.

In contrast, the assumption that psychopathy is a mental disorder that necessarily involves persistent anti-social behaviour arbitrarily excludes consideration of the moral dimension of the condition. On this assumption, the defendant's violent actions, and the deviant impulses and desires which give rise to them, are regarded as 'symptoms' of an underlying illness state, and we do not normally hold people responsible for having the symptoms of an illness. In other words, the classification of psychopathy as a mental illness settles the underlying moral issue by fiat, and that is unacceptable from a legal point of view.[77] To the extent that there is a widespread, common-sense belief that the incorrigibly persistent offender who gives vent to his deviant desires and impulses is at least partially responsible for his actions, the law should be prepared to accommodate it—notwithstanding anything that psychiatrists may say to the contrary.

On the assumption that the psychopathic defendant is not entitled to the insanity defense, perhaps the solution to this problem is to define 'disease of the mind' in a way that excludes psychopathy (or any other condition, such as homosexuality, whose pathological status seems genuinely in doubt). This could be done on the grounds that

77 See the discussion of *Blocker*, supra, ch. 1, n. 39.

mental illness is typically defined in terms of a specific cognitive defect that may or may not lead to deviation from the fundamental norms of social life; whereas the concept of psychopathy has no meaning apart from the behavioural or moral deviations it is used to denote, and the cluster of deviant desires and attitudes—the so-called personality disorder—associated with them.[78]

The alternative is to allow psychopathy as a 'disease of the mind' but to insist that it does not entail a recognized 'defect of reason'. This approach has recently been adopted by the Supreme Court of Canada, in *Kjeldsen v. The Queen*,[79] but it does not commend itself on logical grounds. For if psychopathy really is a mental illness, and violent anti-social conduct one of its symptoms, the conclusion that someone suffering from it does *not* have a 'defect of reason' seems patently false. Moreover, given the psychopath's assumed inability to restrain his violent impulses, this conclusion is virtually impossible to sustain in jurisdictions, like Ireland, that recognize the liberal version of the control test.[80] Indeed, once psychopathy is classified as a 'disease of the mind', the only way of guaranteeing the conclusion that someone said to be suffering from it does not have a 'defect of reason' is by ensuring that the concept of 'defect of reason' is itself defined in a way that excludes the inability to restrain one's violent impulses, i.e., in a way that cancels what psychiatrists generally regard as one of the classic symptoms of psychopathy! Apart from the rampant illogicality of this move, it would have disastrous consequences for the plea of volitional insanity, since it would also deny the defence of insanity to defendants thought to be incapable of controlling their behaviour as a result of mental illnesses other than psychopathy. Given that the control test solves most of the problems associated with the traditional reading of the M'Naghten Rules,[81] that seems too high a price for ensuring that the psychopathic defendant does not slip through the filter of the insanity defence.

The argument that psychopathy is not an illness and should not be treated as such for legal purposes does not entail the conclusion that psychopaths are psychologically normal. On the contrary, there is a large body of experimental evidence which suggests that many psychopaths have extremely low physiological arousability and a significantly higher pain threshold than the average

78 Supra.
79 [1982] 64 CCC (2d) 161 (SCC).
80 See ch. 3.6.
81 Ibid.

individual.[82] Insofar as these findings can be correlated with the classic psychopathic personality traits of impulsiveness, callousness and lack of remorse or shame with respect to the infliction of suffering on others, they suggest that psychopathy is more a personality disorder than a form of moral depravity; in other words, they appear to contradict the view of psychopathy being presented here.

To some extent the personality traits associated with psychopathy can be explained sociologically: as the result of poor parental guidance or early exposure to a criminal subculture—in other words, as a product of faulty socialisation. But environmental causes do not tell the whole story, since many psychopaths do not appear either to have been neglected (or overindulged) by their parents or corrupted by their environments.[83] Thus it seems plausible to assume that (in these cases at least) there may be a constitutionally in-built resistance to physical conditioning at the root of the psychopathic personality. Indeed, on this view, psychopathy might be regarded as an illness in the broad sense of that term defended above: as a biologically determined predispositional inability to empathise with human suffering.[84]

However, it is important to stress that the nature of the relationship between the organic basis of psychopathy (assuming there is one) and the personality and behavioural traits associated with it remains a mystery. Indeed, such evidence as there is suggests that the psychopath's basic insensitivity to physical punishment is not reflected in an inability to learn to avoid other kinds of punishment; on the contrary, he seems perfectly capable of taking the necessary avoiding action when faced with the threat of non-physical punishment—for example, the threat of financial loss.[85] Moreover, it is well established that psychopaths are perfectly capable of deferring gratification when it suits them to do so.[86] As Claridge has observed:

> [N]otwithstanding the fact that the psychopath has a basic insensitivity to punishment, the way this disposition comes to be elaborated so as to guide his real-life behaviour clearly depends on psychological processes . . . that are quite

82 This evidence is reviewed at length in Hare, *Psychopathy: Theory and Research* (New York, 1970).

83 Claridge, op. cit., p. 97.

84 Supra, 4.2.

85 Schmauk, 'Punishment, arousal and avoidance learning in sociopaths' (1970) *76 J Abnormal Psychol* 325-35.

86 Widom, 'A methodology for studying non-institutionalised psychopaths' in Hare and Schalling (eds.) *Psychopathic Behaviour* (New York, 1978).

distant from those mechanisms which in a purely biological sense may account for his temperament.[87]

In other words, whether or not psychopathy has an organic basis, and whether or not we classify it as a psychological abnormality, there seems little doubt that it is not an illness, even in the attenuated sense of that term being relied on here; and that the psychopath is and should continue to be regarded as a relatively autonomous moral agent. In contrast to the position regarding the functional psychoses,[88] there are no grounds for assuming that the mechanisms linking the physiology of the condition to personality and behaviour—to the kinds of things that psychopaths do as well as their reasons for doing them—will eventually be laid bare or shown to stand in a causal relationship with one another. Indeed, it is obvious that there is no direct causal nexus between the alleged physiological basis and behavioural symptoms of psychopathy; as we have seen, the former is routinely overridden by the psychological processes of human decision and choice.[89] Moreover, this conclusion is strengthened by the fact that the decisions and choices involved in psychopathic behaviour are epistemologically normal, in the sense that the are not distorted by a cognitive inability to 'test reality' of the kind associated with psychosis.

Yet it seems equally obvious that we need to allow for the experimental evidence that psychopathy is a psychologically abnormal condition that may well have a discrete physiological basis. Hence the earlier description of the psychopath as a '*relatively* autonomous moral agent'. The qualification implied by the term 'relatively' in this description is intended to bring out the element of personality disorder or abnormality that seems to mark the condition and that, by analogy with other extremes of temperament, may in certain circumstances—for example, if it was very severe—justify a finding of diminished responsibility. It also serves as a useful reminder that, given the biological context of all human action, there is no such thing as *absolute* moral autonomy; and, consequently, that criminal responsibility is not necessarily incompatible with biologically determined variations of temperament and personality of the sort which may well underpin psychopathy.

The appellate courts in Ireland have not as yet had to decide whether psychopathy comes within the purview of the insanity defence, although it is submitted that, in this regard, the dye has already been

87 Op. cit., p. 99.

88 Supra, 4.2.

89 For further discussion of this point, see JJ and JAB Ray, 'Some apparent advantages of subclinical psychopathy' (1982) *117 J Soc Psychol* 135-42.

cast by the Supreme Court. In *DPP v. O'Mahony*[90] the appellant was convicted of murder and appealed to the Supreme Court on the grounds that the trial judge had erred in law in refusing to leave the issue of diminished responsibility to the jury. His contention was that since the defence of diminished responsibility formed part of the common law, the jury should have been given the opportunity to return a verdict of manslaughter. This contention was rejected by the Supreme Court on the grounds that the defence of diminished responsibility could not be said to be part of the common law as it was created by section 2 of the English Homicide Act 1957, and that the operation of the M'Naghten Rules by the English courts prior to that date proved conclusively that section 2 was not declaratory of a pre-existing common law rule.[91] Moreover, referring to the issue of psychopathy, Finlay CJ, who delivered the judgment of the court, stated that:

> Having regard to the definition of insanity laid down by this Court in *Doyle v. Wicklow County Council* [(1974) IR 55] . . . it is quite clear that the appellant in *R v. Byrne* [(1960) 2 QB 396 (CA)] . . . a sexual psychopath who suffered from violent perverted sexual desires which he found it difficult or impossible to control [but who was not otherwise mentally ill] . . . if tried in accordance with the law of this country on the same facts, would have been properly found to be not guilty by reason of insanity [*sic*].[92]

Although this statement was *obiter*, and in part a recitation of the facts in *Byrne*, it is significant for at least two reasons. First, both the language and the logic of the statement indicate a clear acceptance of the disease or illness model of psychopathy: the defendant in *Byrne* is described as being entitled to the insanity defence because (there was uncontested medical evidence that) he '*suffered* from violent perverted sexual desires which he found it difficult or impossible to control',[93] i.e., he is presented as someone whose *violent desires and behaviour per se* are deemed to be symptoms of a pathological condition that automatically brings him within the ambit of the test of

90 [1986] ILRM 244.

91 Interestingly, it does not appear from the report whether the court was asked to consider the position in Scots law where the defence of diminished responsibility has been recognized as part of the common law since 1867; ch. 8.2.

92 [1986] ILRM at 248-9.

93 Italics added.

volitional insanity laid down in *Doyle*.[94] In other words, the statement is a classic example of the dogmatic view of psychopathy criticised above, as it precludes the possibility that a *Byrne*-type defendant might be partially responsible for giving vent to his violent impulses. Indeed, it is submitted that it would be difficult for a jury directed in terms of the statement to return a conviction even where it felt that the defendant was *entirely* responsible for his actions—since it borders on the perverse to say that someone is responsible for exhibiting the symptoms of an illness.

Second, not surprisingly given its source, the statement is apt to be taken as declaratory of the existing practice of the courts where the plea of insanity is supported by uncontested medical evidence of psychopathy. Put bluntly, this means that the defence of volitional insanity could be used to fill the vacuum created by the absence of a defence of diminished responsibility. As we shall see in chapter 6, this state of affairs is highly unsatisfactory as it involves the risk of the compulsory indefinite hospitalization of defendants acquitted of murder on the grounds of insanity who are not mentally ill, in the sense that they are not suffering from a psychosis, as well as the possibility of a steady stream of applications for release by these 'patients' on the grounds that they have been 'rehabilitated' and are therefore no longer a danger to themselves or others.

It is now accepted that the solution to this problem is to create a defence of diminished responsibility, thereby enabling the courts to tackle the dual nature of the psychopathic killer by means of a wide discretion to recommend treatment and/or impose punishment according to the requirements of the individual case; and, in this regard, it is to be hoped that the rumours that the government is shortly to introduce the new defence prove to be true.[95] As already indicated, this solution accords with a common-sense analysis of the problem of psychopathy and is required by the network of moral assumptions that guarantee the legitimacy of the criminal justice system in a civilized society.

94 Ch. 3.1.

95 See, for example, *Irish Independent*, 13 February 1991; 23 January 1993. The gap between these dates suggests that those awaiting the new legislation should not hold their breaths.

[5]

# Proving Insanity

## 1. GENERALLY

It is clear from rule 2[1] that the judges in *M'Naghten* intended to put the onus of proving insanity on the accused, and there is a long line of authority supporting this conclusion.[2] Insanity is therefore an exception to the general rule that the onus of proof in a criminal case rests on the prosecution. This was explicitly acknowledged by the House of Lords when formally adopting the general rule in *Woolmington v. DPP*.[3] If the accused raises the defence of insanity, he must prove it on the balance of probabilities: the standard of proof required of the plaintiff in a civil action.[4] He is not required to prove the matter beyond all reasonable doubt: the standard of proof normally required of the prosecution. This means the accused must be acquitted if the jury think it more likely than not that he was insane in the appropriate sense. But it is not enough for the accused to discharge the ordinary evidentiary burden that arises in relation to pleas other than insanity, i.e., to raise a reasonable doubt that he might have been insane at the relevant time.

In the South African case of *S v. Kennedy*[5] there was common cause that the appellant was suffering from a disease of the mind which might have prevented him from knowing what he was doing, and it was argued on his behalf that the trial judge should therefore have told the jury that it was for the prosecution to prove that it did not have that effect. The Appellate Division rejected this argument on the grounds that the trial judge was right to insist that the appellant

1 Supra, ch. 2.2.
2 *Stokes* [1848] 3 Car & Kir 185; *Layton* [1849] 4 Cox CC 149; *Smith* [1910] 6 Cr App Rep 19; *Coelho* [1914] 30 TLR 535; *Bratty* [1963] AC 386.
3 [1935] AC 462.
4 *Sodeman v. R* [1936] 2 All E R 1138 (PC).
5 1951 (4) SA 431 (A).

must prove the alleged defect of reason on the balance of probabilities notwithstanding that sufficient evidence had been led to show that there was a reasonable chance that it may have existed.

It is arguable that the burden of proof resting on the defendant in insanity cases is heavier in Irish law than in other common-law legal systems. In *AG v. Fennell*[6] the Court of Criminal Appeal held that it was not a misdirection to tell the jury that the accused had to prove the matter 'beyond all reasonable doubt'. In the words of Sullivan CJ, delivering the judgment of the Court:

> If the onus, according to the authorities, is to be established 'clearly' or 'specifically' or 'to the reasonable satisfaction of the jury', it is, in the opinion of this Court, only 'chopping logic' to say that in this case the use of the words 'beyond reasonable doubt' adds any greater burden to the onus on the accused.[7]

There is some support for this view in *AG v. Boylan*[8] where it was held that it was acceptable to tell the jury that the accused must prove the issue of insanity to their 'reasonable satisfaction', although it is submitted that it is straining language to say, with Sullivan CJ in *Fennell*,[9] that this phrase, standing alone, imposes a requirement that the accused must put the matter beyond all reasonable doubt. It could equally be argued that these words do no more than require the defendant to show that his claim might plausibly be true. Moreover, Sullivan CJ's reasoning has been heavily criticised in *Carr-Briant*, on the grounds that it was based on the mistaken assumption that the trial judge in *Sodeman v. R*[10] had relied on the proposition 'that the burden of proof of insanity that lay upon the prisoner was as strict and onerous as the burden of proof that lay upon the Crown with regard to the facts which the prosecution had to establish.'[11] In the opinion of Humphreys J, delivering the judgment of the Court of Appeal, 'what Sullivan CJ is purporting to quote as the direction of the trial judge was merely the argument of counsel for the appellant as to the effect of that direction, an argument not accepted by the Privy Council'.[12]

6 [1940] IR 445.
7 [1940] IR at 450-1.
8 [1937] IR 449.
9 [1940] IR at 450-51.
10 [1936] 2 All ER 1138.
11 [1943] 2 All ER 156 at 158.
12 Ibid.

Naturally the prosecution is required to prove insanity beyond all reasonable doubt if it is part of its own case and to disprove it beyond all reasonable doubt where it has been introduced by the defence and proved on the balance of probabilities.[13] If the accused puts his state of mind in issue, it is a question of law for the court as to whether or not he has raised a defence of insanity. If the trial judge rules that the defence of insanity has been raised on the evidence, it is his duty to instruct the jury accordingly, irrespective of the views of the prosecution or the defence.[14]

## 2. THE EXTENT OF THE REVERSE ONUS

The degree of conflict between the reverse onus in insanity cases and the general rule that the prosecution must prove its case should not be exaggerated. The conflict is real enough where the defendant is claiming that he did not know what he was doing in the physical sense—for example, where he stabs his wife in the mistaken belief that she is a poisonous snake—as this amounts to a denial of *mens rea.* In cases of this kind the effect of the reverse onus is to require the defence to disprove part of the prosecution case, albeit on the balance of probabilities.[15] But this is not true where the defendant alleges that he did not know what he was doing in the non-physical sense or that it was wrong, since the prosecution is not required to prove either that an accused understood his actions or knew that they were legally or morally right.[16] *Mutatis mutandis,* the same consideration applies where the defendant is claiming that he was unable to control his actions. In these cases the special rule certainly increases the burden of proof normally resting on the defendant: what would normally be an evidentiary burden of merely introducing evidence to support a claim becomes a probative burden of establishing that the claim is probably true.[17] But it does not require the defendant to disprove part of the prosecution case—unless the latter is defined in a way that

13 This follows from *Woolmington,* supra, and from the analogous rule that, if the prosecution introduces the issue of unfitness to plead, it must prove it beyond all reasonable doubt: *Robertson v. R* [1968] 3 All ER 557. But cf Lord Denning's judgment in *Bratty* [1963] AC at 411.

14 *Ellis* [1990] 2 IR 291; *Bratty* [1963] AC 386.

15 Cf Williams, *Criminal Law: The General Part* (London, 1961), p. 165. See also *Cottle* [1958] NZLR 999 at 1019.

16 Because these things are entailed in the presumption of sanity; supra, ch. 2.2.

17 *Sodeman v. R* [1936] 2 All ER 1138; Carr-Briant [1943] KB 607.

requires the prosecution, and only the prosecution, to establish every fact relating to the case against the accused; and on this criterion even the evidentiary burden normally resting on the accused would be inconsistent with the general rule!

However, the reverse onus in insanity cases is difficult to justify.[18] It is not necessary as a safeguard against frivolous and vexatious insanity pleas. If vigorously applied, a rule requiring the prosecution to challenge medical evidence of mental disorder,[19] coupled with the ordinary evidentiary burden normally resting on the accused to introduce sufficient evidence to enable the trial judge to leave a contentious issue to the jury, seems perfectly adequate in that regard. This arrangement works perfectly well where the defendant is trying to secure a complete acquittal on the grounds of automatism, where the risk of frivolous and vexatious pleas is arguably greater, so it seems anomalous not to apply it in situations where he is merely hoping to secure a special verdict which automatically involves indefinite detention in a criminal lunatic asylum.[20]

### 3. RECENT CANADIAN DEVELOPMENTS

The constitutionality of reverse onuses has been considered by the Canadian courts. In *R v. Appleby*[21] the Supreme Court of Canada held that the words 'presumed innocent until proven guilty according to law ' in section 2(f) of the Canadian Bill of Rights:

> must be taken to envisage a law which recognizes the existence of statutory exceptions reversing the onus of proof with respect to one or more ingredients of an offence in cases where certain specific facts have been proved by the Crown in relation to such ingredients.

In the opinion of the Court, this was because Lord Sankey, in *Woolmington,*[22] in addition to excluding the insanity defence from the ambit of the presumption of innocence, had expressly provided for statutory exceptions to it. *Appleby* was widely criticized, not least for

18 See generally Cross, *The Golden Thread of the English Criminal Law: The Burden of Proof* (Rede Lecture, 1976); Williams, 'Offences and Defences' (1982) 2 *LS* 233.
19 Infra, 5.4.
20 Infra, ch. 6.2.
21 [1972] SCR 303 at 316.
22 [1935] AC 368.

equating 'according to law' in section 2(f) with whatever the legislature decides, thereby reducing the presumption of innocence to a 'quite harmless and useless platitude.'[23] It has recently been overruled in *R v. Oakes,* where the Supreme Court of Canada held that:

> a provision which requires an accused to disprove on a balance of probabilities the existence of a presumed fact which is an important element of the offence in question violates the presumption of innocence in s. 11(d) [of the Canadian Charter of Human Rights]. If an accused bears the burden of disproving on a balance of probabilities an essential element of an offence, it would be possible for a conviction to occur despite the existence of a reasonable doubt. This would arise if the accused adduced sufficient evidence to raise a reasonable doubt as to his or her innocence but did not convince the jury on a balance of probabilities that the presumed fact was untrue.[24]

The decision in *Oakes* has been welcomed as having 'restored the cornerstone precept of the presumption of innocence to a new and firm footing [in Canadian law].'[25] Yet it is unlikely that the decision affects the plea of insanity. The Supreme Court of Canada only had to deal with a reversal of the onus of proof of an essential element of an offence in that case, whereas the issue of insanity is normally not even an ingredient of the prosecution case (let alone part of the definition of an offence); and when it is it is clear that the prosecution must prove it beyond all reasonable doubt. Moreover, the decision was confined to the constitutionality of reverse onuses created by statute and not at common law.

### 4. MEDICAL EVIDENCE: THE RULE IN *DIN*

The party alleging insanity is not required to introduce medical evidence,[26] although there appear to be no recent reported cases of a successful insanity defence unsupported by such evidence.[27]

23 Mandell, 'The Presumption of Innocence and the Canadian Bill of Rights: *Regina v. Appleby* (1972) *10 Osgoode Hall LJ* 450 at 464-5.
24 [1986] 50 CR (3d) 1 at 25 (SCC).
25 Stuart, *Canadian Criminal Law* (Toronto, 1987), p. 44.
26 *R v. Dart* [1878] 14 Cox CC 143; *A-G for South Australia v. Brown* [1960] 44 Cr App Rep 100 (PC); *Manning* [1955] 89 ILTR 155.
27 With the notable exceptions of *Hadfield* and *Earl Ferrers*—discussed in ch. 2.1—such cases were the norm in the eighteenth century. Medical evidence of insanity

Normally medical evidence of insanity is given by doctors who have clinically examined the accused (although the M'Naghten Rules provided for evidence from doctors who had merely observed the accused in the course of his trial, albeit only in cases where the facts were not in dispute and the question became 'one of science only').[28] This principle was established in *R v. Frances*,[29] where the court took the view that the practice of allowing medical evidence that was not clinically based should be discontinued on the grounds that it usurped the function of the jury. The principle of the paramountcy of the jury's view of the medical evidence was re-affirmed in the modern case of *R v. Matheson*,[30] although the Court of Appeal conceded that if the medical evidence was 'all one way' a jury verdict which disregarded it should be set aside.

It is the duty of the prosecution to probe the soundness of medical evidence relating to an accused's state of mind.[31] In *R v. Din*[32] the

continued to be a relative rarity even after asylum doctors became acknowledged as experts in the nineteenth century: Walker, op. cit., p. 119. In English law the position is now governed by the Criminal Procedure (Insanity and Fitness to Plead) Act 1991, s. 1 (2) and the Criminal Procedure (Insanity) Act 1964, s. 4 (6) as amended. Section 1 (2) provided that neither a special verdict (of insanity) nor a finding of unfitness to plead will be returnable except on the evidence of two doctors, at least one of whom must have expertise in the diagnosis or treatment of mental disorder. The effect of the section is to align the method of proving insanity with that of proving insanity under the Mental Health Act: infra, 5.5.

28 'We think the medical man, conversant with the disease of insanity . . . who never saw the prisoner previously to the trial, but who was present during the whole trial, and the examination of all the witnesses, cannot be asked his opinion [as to the accused's state of mind at the time of the act] because this question involves the determination of the truth of the facts deposed to, which it is for the jury to decide . . . But where the facts are admitted or not disputed, and the question becomes substantially one of science only, it way be convenient to allow the question to be put in that general form, though the same cannot be insisted on as a matter of right': 4 St Tr, n s, 847 at 932.

29 [1849] 4 Cox CC 57.

30 [1958] 42 Cr App Rep 145. The defence in *Matheson* was diminished responsibility: infra, ch. 8.

31 The practice in common-law legal systems of treating psychiatric witnesses as if they were testifying to ordinary matters of fact—by examining, cross-examining and re-examining them and then leaving it to the jury to decide who was telling the truth—has been criticised: Walker, op. cit., 120-1. It has been suggested that it would be more appropriate—and of greater assistance to juries—if the courts could proceed in the manner of their civilian counterparts and appoint their own experts with a view to gaining an independent assessment of an allegedly insane accused's mental state, but this proposal was rejected by the Royal Commission on Capital Punishment: *Report*, p. 71. Proposals along these lines are likely to fall foul of the growing international scepticism about the reliability of psychiatric diagnoses and witnesses generally: supra, ch. 1.3; infra, ch. 8.3. See also infra, 5.5.

32 [1962] 42 Cr App Rep 116.

defendant pleaded diminished responsibility to a charge of murder. His plea was supported by the evidence of two doctors who had diagnosed him as suffering from paranoia. It was established in cross-examination that the doctors did not believe that the defendant's beliefs, assuming they were paranoid, brought him within the M'Naghten Rules, but the prosecution had not probed them on the more fundamental point of whether the beliefs that led to the killing might not have been rationally based. This emerged in the trial judge's questioning of the medical witnesses when both admitted that there were rational grounds for the defendant's suspicions that his wife was having an affair with a mutual friend and that there was no evidence of paranoia other than the defendant's suspicions in that regard. The trial judge advised the jury accordingly, and the defendant was convicted.[33]

In *DPP v. Buckley*[34] the defendant pleaded insanity to a charge of murdering a woman he had met in a public house and taken back to his flat. His plea was supported by his own oral testimony that he killed the woman so that he could have sex with the corpse, and by the evidence of two consultant psychiatrists who said that they were convinced Buckley was psychotic but suffered from a species of that malady not yet recognised by psychiatric nosology! The psychiatrists called by the prosecution testified that Buckley suffered from a serious personality disorder but was not insane. When the evidence concluded counsel for the prosecution drew attention to the fact that the defence psychiatrists had interviewed the defendant on only one and two occasions, respectively, whereas one of the psychiatrists testifying for the prosecution had been in charge of the investigation into Buckley's mental state over a period of several months, while the other was the Director of the Central Mental Hospital where that investigation had been carried out. He also pointed out that the defendant had not mentioned his claim that he killed in order to have sex with the corpse in the course of several incriminating admissions he had made to the gardai, whom he had told he killed his victim because '[I] was sick of women leading me on.' The trial judge directed the jury to apply the *Doyle*[35] test, and they duly rejected the insanity plea and found the defendant guilty of murder.

It is however doubtful if either the rule in *Din*[36] or an equivalent

33 The conviction was upheld on appeal.
34 *Irish Times,* 24 November 1989.
35 Supra, ch. 3.1.
**36 [1962] 42 Cr App Rep 116.**

rule is strictly applied by the Irish courts. Indeed if it were, few, if any, schizophrenic defendants (apart from those covered by the M'Naghten Rules), and certainly no psychopathic defendant, would get the benefit of the control test laid down in *Doyle*:[37] as the analysis in chapter 3 illustrates, neither schizophrenia nor psychopathy go to a defendant's capacity to control his actions. As it happens, the control test has regularly, if infrequently, been applied in favour of schizophrenic defendants since it was introduced in 1974,[38] and, if the Supreme Court's statement, in *O'Mahony*,[39] is to be believed, is also available in cases of psychopathy. This suggests that medical evidence of either of these conditions would generally be enough to secure the insanity defence, and is unlikely to be challenged by either the prosecution or the trial judge—most probably on the *bona fide* assumption that the point of the new test was to broaden the scope of the insanity defence to include the mentioned conditions. Indeed, this was precisely why the Chief Justice concluded, in *O'Mahony*,[40] that psychopaths were entitled to the insanity defence in Irish law.

The alternative explanation—that juries simply ignore trial judges' warnings about the soundness and/or relevance of medical evidence of schizophrenia or psychopathy to the legal criteria of insanity—seems less likely to be true, if only because it begs the question as to why juries should pay less attention to judicial summings-up in this regard after 1974 than before; and because, apart from Griffen J's *dictum* in *Doyle*,[41] there is no record of judicial scepticism in this regard since that case was decided. Indeed, the relevant *dicta* point in the opposite direction.[42]

Nor does the *Buckley*[43] case cast doubt on this conclusion. The prosecution's challenge in that case coincided with the fact that the psychiatrists who had clinically examined the accused while he was in the Central Mental Hospital awaiting trial did not believe that he was insane; whereas the argument here is that the prosecution tends not to challenge medical evidence of insanity when the psychiatric team conducting the clinical examination is testifying for the *defence*.

This state of affairs is of little or no consequence in the case of

37 [1974] IR 55 (SC).
38 I am grateful to the Director of Public Prosecutions for this information.
39 [1986] ILRM 244; supra, ch. 4.6.
40 [1986] ILRM at 248-9.
41 Supra, ch. 3.1.
42 This point is developed in relation to the discussion the Supreme Court's decision in *O'Mahony* in ch. 4.6.
43 *Irish Times*, 24 November 1989.

schizophrenic defendants, as the vast majority of those who get the benefit of the control test on foot of medical evidence of schizophrenia would almost certainly be entitled to an acquittal on the grounds of insanity on the revised version of the knowledge test worked out in chapter 2. Our concern is rather with successful insanity defendants who would have failed that test, i.e., with those defendants who knew what they were doing in the conventional epistemological sense but who were nevertheless acquitted on foot of uncontested medical evidence of psychopathic personality disorder—in other words, with the rump of successful insanity defences that are really cases of diminished responsibility which, in the absence of an appropriate defence, neither the prosecuting authorities nor the courts wish to see punished with a mandatory life sentence.

The solution to this dilemma is plainly to introduce a defence of diminished responsibility to cater for hard cases of mental disorder that do not meet the legal definition of insanity, thereby enabling the trial judge to use his discretion when deciding whether and how much punishment and/or treatment is appropriate in the light of the medical evidence relating to the accused's mental state. Indeed it is submitted that the availability of that defence acts as an incentive both to the prosecuting authorities and the courts to take a strict view of the medical evidence in cases where the defence alleges insanity. This course of action would also help to solve the problem, implicit in the *Gallagher*[44] saga, of defendants found guilty but insane on a murder charge who subsequently apply (to the government)[45] for release on the grounds that they are no longer mentally ill. It goes without saying that genuinely rehabilitated defendants should be released in these circumstances, given that the verdict of guilty but insane is an acquittal in law and that the confinement of accused persons consequent on it is not a legal punishment.[46] But it is patently inappropriate that this procedure should be abused by defendants who may have feigned mental illness or who—like the majority of psychopathic defendants—were sufficiently responsible for their actions to merit a substantial term of imprisonment.

## 5. PSYCHIATRIC EVIDENCE AND THE BINARY VERDICT

The words 'not guilty' constitute one of the most mysterious phrases

44 [1991] ILRM 339.
45 Infra, ch. 6.3.
46 Ibid.

in the criminal law. As Walker has observed, '[t]hey may mean that what was done was not criminal, or that it was not done by the accused, or that it was done by him in circumstances that excuse him morally. Yet the law tries to preserve the fiction that there are only two verdicts, guilty or not guilty. Even a finding that is obviously of a third kind, such as the special verdict of insanity, must be disguised as one or other'.[47] The binary verdict is largely a relic of early modern penology: in the days when all serious crimes were capital offences, it was an accurate reflection of the fact that the main task for the courts was to decide whether or not the defendant should be sentenced to death. Now that judges have more choice in the matter of sentencing, the either/or logic of the binary verdict looks increasingly anachronistic; although it still makes sense in legal systems that retain the fixed penalty for murder.

The binary verdict poses special difficulties for psychiatrists testifying on the issue of insanity. The principal difficulty derives from the fact that mental illness is a matter of degree or deviation from the norm of mental health,[48] whereas the concepts of guilt and innocence imply radical differences of kind rather than degree. For example, psychiatrists testifying for the defence may feel that the accused exhibits some of the symptoms associated with a particular form of psychosis, but have genuine doubts as to whether he exhibits enough of the appropriate symptoms to warrant an unequivocal diagnosis. Doubts of this kind are normal in a discipline that purports to be scientific and should on that account be aired in court, but if they are aired the resulting testimony is apt to seem hesitant and imprecise and to be criticised as such by the prosecution. Since this is likely to undermine the value of the evidence in the eyes of the jury, and could lead to the conviction for murder of someone who is mentally ill and does not deserve to be punished, psychiatrists are apt to tailor their evidence in a way that disguises its weaknesses from a strictly legal point of view, and to be encouraged in this course of action by counsel for the defence.[49]

This difficulty is compounded by the fact that the labels used in psychiatric nosology are intended to function as 'ideal types' or

47 Op. cit., p. 244.

48 See generally, Gross, *The Psychological Society* (New York, 1978). The spectrum ranges from cases of 'the most pervasive and severe derangement—sheer lunacy or psychosis—at the one extreme to minor, specific neurotic reactions like a faintly unusual or dysfunctional attitude towards love, or neatness or enclosed spaces, at the other': Radden, op. cit., p. 3; see also ch. 4.2.

49 See Arens, *Insanity Defence* (New York, 1974), p. 29 et seq; p. 103 et seq.

approximations of real illness states, and do not necessarily refer to mutually exclusive clusters of symptoms. In other words, they include some symptoms that are rarely seen in individual cases, and others that may be associated with several different psychiatric labels and illness states.

Thus psychiatrists who adhere to Kraepelin's classification[50] distinguish four different types of schizophrenia: catatonia, which is distinguished by the statue-like postures assumed by those who suffer from it; hebephrenia, which is marked by a radical deterioration of reasoning including a tendency to hallucinate; paranoia, which is usually identified by the presence of delusions of persecution unaccompanied by a tendency to hallucinate or any deterioration of reasoning; and 'simple' schizophrenia, where the patient loses touch with ordinary life to the extent that his responses seem disconnected and inappropriate but do not normally include delusions, hallucinations or catatonic posturing. However, adherents to this classificatory scheme readily admit that it is not cast in stone, and that the symptoms it predicts for each type of schizophrenia do not always appear in individual cases of that type; whereas the symptoms it excludes sometimes do appear. For example, hebephrenics, who normally hallucinate, sometimes do not, while paranoids, who rarely hallucinate, sometimes do.[51]

From a purely scientific perspective, taxonomic approximations of this kind are perfectly acceptable, since they can always be adjusted in the light of new empirical evidence, and can be discarded altogether if and when the psychiatric community comes up with a better or more economical way of organising the data. In the context of the criminal process, however, they are apt to seem vague and over-inclusive precisely because they do not appear to support an unequivocal diagnosis, and may even lead to disagreement between psychiatrists testifying on the same side. Like the problem of 'hesitant' or 'tentative' diagnoses already mentioned, disagreements of this sort can easily be misrepresented—often unintentionally—to juries as evidence of the inherent unreliability of psychiatric testimony and rejected by them on those grounds.[52]

The availability of a plea of diminished responsibility would go some way towards resolving these difficulties. Since a finding of diminished responsibility enables trial judges to give effect to evidence of mental

50 See Kraepelin, op. cit., p. 140 et seq.
51 See Mayer-Gross et al., *Clinical Psychiatry* (London, 1960), p. 127.
52 Walker, op. cit., p. 245 et seq.

illness in a way that does not completely exclude the defendant's responsibility for his actions, it effectively relieves the pressure on psychiatrists to 'beef up' or disguise their testimony in the way required by the 'all or nothing' logic of the binary verdict, thereby virtually eliminating the risk of evidence of psychopathy being passed off as evidence of insanity. This in turn reduces the pressure on juries when deciding whether or not to give effect to medical evidence of mental disorder, as well as providing the courts with a more accurate picture of the accused's mental state for sentencing purposes. The weakness of the plea of diminished responsibility is that it is typically confined to the crime of murder,[53] whereas evidence of mental disorder may be relevant to the issue of responsibility irrespective of the crime charged. Like the binary verdict, this limitation is an anachronistic throwback to the days when the point of introducing psychiatric evidence was to help the defendant escape the gallows by means of the insanity defence.

Some legal systems get round this difficulty by means of a mechanism enabling trial judges to make hospital or guardianship orders in respect of defendants who have been shown to have committed an offence the penalty for which has not been fixed by law—in effect, all crimes other than murder—but is one of imprisonment. In England, for example, section 37 of the Mental Health Act 1983 provides that in cases of this kind a person who is proved to have committed an offence may be committed to a mental hospital or to the guardianship of a local social services authority, on condition that two medical practitioners, one of whom must be approved by the Secretary of State as having special competence in the diagnosis and treatment of mental disorder, agree that this course of action is warranted in the circumstances. In such cases the verdict is in effect one of 'guilty of the act charged but not responsible for it on the grounds of mental disorder', although this is not made explicit as it is still not politically correct openly to prescind from the assumption that the binary verdict is universal. Incidentally, 'the relative importance of hospital orders in practice is seen by the fact that [in England and Wales] in 1986 no person charged with murder was found unfit to plead, only one was acquitted on the ground of insanity, 55 charges of murder were reduced to manslaughter on the ground of diminished responsibility, but hundreds of hospital and guardianship orders are made every year'.[54]

53 See ch. 8.
54 Smith and Hogan, *op. cit.* p. 215.

## 6. THE LIMITS OF PSYCHIATRIC EVIDENCE

The rules governing the admission of psychiatric testimony (and expert testimony generally) are based on the assumption that the jury is unable to determine the facts on the issue addressed by the expert. Hence Lawton LJ's celebrated *dictum* that:

> Jurors do not need psychiatrists to tell them how ordinary folk who are not suffering from any mental illness are likely to react to the stresses and strains of life.[55]

This arrangement poses no problems where the defendant is seeking to rely on a recognised mental illness since it is generally conceded that psychiatrists are uniquely qualified to comment on the nature and effects of such illness. But it can lead to difficulties where the defence is seeking to introduce medical evidence falling short of mental illness in support of the defence of diminished responsibility. Reviewing the Scottish authorities on diminished responsibility, Lord Cooper observed:

> You will see, ladies and gentlemen, the stress that has been laid in all these formulations upon weakness of intellect, aberration of mind, mental unsoundness, partial insanity, great peculiarity of mind, and the like . . . it will not suffice in law for the purpose of this defence of diminished responsibility merely to show that an accused person has a very short temper, or is unusually excitable and lacking in self-control. The world would be a very convenient place for criminals and a very dangerous place for other people, if that were the law. It must be much more than that.[56]

The practical effect of this limitation can be seen in the way in which the courts have sought to restrict the sorts of conditions that can be relied on as underlying causes of diminished responsibility. As we shall see in chapter 8, the currently dominant model of diminished responsibility is based on section 2 of the English Homicide Act 1957. One of the requirements of section 2 is that, in order to get the benefit

55 *R v. Turner* [1975] QB 834 at 841 (CA). Commenting on Lawton LJ's words, O'Flaherty J recently stated that 'It seems to the court that the law in Ireland is the same: *DPP v. Kehoe* [1992] ILRM 481 at 486 (CCA).

56 *H.M. Advocate v. Braithwaite* [1945] JC 55 at 56; infra, ch. 8.2.

of a plea of diminished responsibility, an accused must have been suffering from an 'abnormality of mind (whether arising from a condition of arrested or retarded development of mind or any inherent causes or induced by disease or injury)'. Moreover, it is well established that the normal range of human emotions and weaknesses—such as anger, hate, jealousy and hot-temperedness—do not qualify as potential causes of 'abnormality of mind' within the parenthesis to section 2.[57]

Recently, however, there have been signs that this consensus may be breaking up.[58] In *Whitworth v. R*[59] the defendant sought to base the defence of diminished responsibility on an alleged psychological 'scar' caused by a sexual assault when he was seven years old. Delivering the judgment of the Queensland Court of Criminal Appeal, Derrington J said that a psychological 'scar' could be an injury in the required statutory sense, and that:

> One . . . condition of the mind which may be an inherent cause of an abnormal state of mind is the inherent limitation of the mind to withstand stress. It is not unreasonable to say that most if not all ordinary minds are vulnerable to abnormality if the stress applied is sufficiently severe and protracted, and in an appropriate case it is this limitation of such tolerance to stress which may constitute, in the context of such stress, an inherent cause for the abnormality of mind . . . it is immaterial that the condition of abnormality of mind, as distinct from the underlying cause, may be ephemeral . . .[60]

Derrington J did not have to decide whether expert evidence of psychological trauma or stress tolerance levels was admissible. But since these are complex psychological matters, it is submitted that it is little short of fiction to suppose that juries will always be capable of dealing satisfactorily with them without the assistance of such evidence, or that they need to be protected from the kind of expert qualified to shed light on them.

This point was taken by the High Court of Australia in *Murphy v.*

57 *R v. Gittens* [1984] 1 QB 698; *R v. Purdy* [1982] 2 NSWLR 964; *R v. McGarvie* [1986] 5 NSWLR 270. The New South Wales legislation on diminished responsibility copies section 2 of the Homicide Act 1957: infra, ch. 8.3.

58 See Hunter and Bargen, 'Diminished Responsibility: 'Abnormal' Minds, Abnormal Murders and What the Doctor Said' in Yeo (ed.), *Partial Excuses to Murder* (Sydney, 1991).

59 [1987] 31 A Cr R 453.

60 [1987] 31 A Cr R 453 at 472-3.

*The Queen*[61] There the issue was the admissibility of a psychologist's report which cast doubt on the accused intellectual abilities and, consequently, on the statements attributed to him by the police (which involved him in a particularly brutal murder). The psychologist's report stated that the accused was neither mentally retarded nor brain damaged but, as a result of poor education and a deprived childhood, had the mental age of a ten year old. The trial judge disallowed the evidence on the classic ground that as the accused had no organically-based abnormality, expert evidence was quite literally irrelevant. The guiding assumption was that the jury was perfectly capable of assessing the defendant's abilities since they fell within the normal physiologically determined range.

By a majority of five-to-two, the High Court of Australia rejected this contention, taking issue specifically with Lawton LJ's statement in *Turner*:[62]

> There are difficulties with such a statement. To begin with, it assumes that 'ordinary' or 'normal' has some clearly understood meaning and, as a corollary, that the distinction between normal and abnormal is well recognised. Further, it assumes that the common sense of jurors is an adequate guide to the conduct of people who are 'normal' even though they may suffer from some relevant disability. And it assumes that the expertise of psychiatrists (or, in the present case, psychologists) extends only to those who are 'abnormal'. None of these assumptions will stand close scrutiny.[63]

On the principle that one swallow does not a make a summer, it would be unwise to see *Murphy* as marking the end, or even the beginning of the end, of the rule that expert psychological testimony must be confined to establishing whether or not the accused has a recognised mental illness. Yet it seems clear that the position articulated by the majority in that case is more suited to the complexities affecting the analysis of human behaviour than the established rule. As we saw in chapter 4,[64] it is probably a mistake to see mental illness and mental health as radically discontinuous states. Given the sub-clinical prehistory of the so-called systemic physical diseases, and allowing for

61 [1989] 86 ALR 35; [1988-89] 167 CLR 94 (HCA).

62 Supra.

63 [1989] 86 ALR 35 at 47-8. The majority judgment, from which this passage is taken, was delivered by Mason CJ and Toohey J, Brennan and Dawson JJ dissenting.

64 4.2.

the biological basis of all human behaviour, it seems safer to conceptualise mental illness as a point on a continuum: as the point at which an innate—probably genetic—predisposition to illness finally manifests itself as a full-blown clinical disorder.

On this view, the distinctions between normal and abnormal psychology, and between psychology and psychiatry, seem artificial. Since these disciplines all contribute to our understanding of how the normal shades off into the pathological, and since psychology in particular is concerned with the mechanisms that link our innate predispositions to our behaviour, it seems entirely right that juries should have access to the insights thrown up by them in an appropriate case. This does not mean that criminal courts should abandon common-sense assessment of ordinary human action, or that juries should no longer be trusted to evaluate human motive and intention. The point is rather that neither should be compelled to disregard the *additional* evidence regarding the springs of human action provided by the behavioural sciences.

The burden of that evidence is that temperament and personality, as mediated by environmental factors, influence action to a greater or lesser degree; and that variations of temperament and personality are in turn correlated with deeper variations in the organisation of the central nervous system.[65] As we saw in chapter 4,[66] some personality variations—psychopathy, for example—are quite consistent with rational action and, therefore, with moral and criminal responsibility. In these cases expert evidence is unlikely to enhance, and may impede, the jury's deliberations on the question of responsibility. In contrast, other personality variations do seem to be conditioned by intrinsic neurobiological factors. For example, it is known that highly anxious subjects are likely to react more strongly to punishment-signalling stimuli than the psychologically normal individual, and that this dimension of personality is associated with an overactive ascending reticular formation: the region of the brain that controls emotional arousal.[67] The argument here is simply that scientific evidence of this kind, i.e., evidence tending to confirm the existence of factors that reduce the margin of freedom or rationality that we associate with

65 The literature on this topic is vast; for an excellent summary, see Claridge, op. cit., ch. 2.

66 Op. cit.

67 Grey, 'The Psychophysiological basis of introversion-extraversion' (1970) *8 Behav Res and Therapy* 249-66; (generally) *The Neuropsychology of Anxiety,* (Oxford, 1982). For a recent review of the relevant literature, see Goldberg and Huxley, *Common Mental Disorders* (London, 1992), pp. 75-81.

standard action, should be admissible irrespective of whether or not it discloses a recognised mental illness.

Admittedly, the absence of a general defence of diminished responsibility would make it virtually impossible for juries (though not, of course, for sentencers) to give effect to such evidence. But that is not a good reason for maintaining the *status quo*. Indeed, the argument for admitting expert evidence wherever it is relevant to a proper understanding of the true nature of an accused's actions is also an argument for the kind of graduated scale of culpability entailed in the notion of diminished responsibility and, consequently, for making that defence available across the board.

[6]

# Verdict and Disposition

## 1. THE FORM OF THE VERDICT

Prior to 1800 the verdict in insanity cases was 'not guilty' and a successful defendant was entitled to an unconditional acquittal. The verdict was modified by the Criminal Lunatics Act of that year to not guilty 'on the ground of insanity' and the court was required to make an order detaining anyone who got the benefit of the new verdict until the government's pleasure was made known.[1] The verdict was changed again by section 2 of the Trial of Lunatics Act 1883,[2] which provided that where a person was:

> insane, so as not to be responsible, according to law, for his actions at the time when the act was done or the omission made . . . the jury shall return a special verdict to the effect that the accused was guilty of the act or omission charged against him, but was insane as aforesaid at the time when he did the act or made the omission.

This change, which was introduced at Queen Victoria's behest,[3] has been repeatedly criticized as illogical[4]—on the grounds that the proposition that a defendant is not responsible in law for his actions entails the conclusion that he is *not* guilty. Strictly speaking, this criticism is misguided since a section 2 verdict merely presupposes that the defendant has committed an *actus reus,* not that

1 See Appendix 1 for the full text of the Act.
2 See Appendix 2 for the full text of the Act.
3 Walker, op. cit., p. 189.
4 *Report of the Committee on Insanity and Crime* (1924), Cmd. 2005; per Sir Herbert Stephen (son of Fitzjames Stephen); Cross and Jones, op. cit., p. 60; McDowell, 'Time for Change' *Irish Independent,* 13 February 1991.

he has been found guilty in any fuller sense.[5] As excuses generally illustrate, there is nothing improper in the contention that a defendant acted unlawfully but was not responsible for his actions. This is the logical form of defences—such as duress or mistake—which rely on the claim that the defendant is not to blame for his bad actions.

Moreover, as Walker has argued,[6] since a successful defence of insanity entails keeping the accused in custody, the Victorian formula can be defended on the grounds that it is more consistent with a legal system in which the practical effect of a verdict of 'not guilty' is normally the unconditional liberation of the accused. On this view, the 'guilty . . . but insane' verdict should be retained because, like 'guilty' verdicts generally, it signals that the accused is liable to restraint. On the other hand, there is some force in the argument that the *shorthand* version of a section 2 verdict—'guilty but insane'—is anomalous and confusing as it looks suspiciously like a contradiction in terms, and that this difficulty would be cleared up by a verdict of 'not guilty by reason of insanity (or mental disorder)', such as was introduced in England by section 1 of the Criminal Procedure (Insanity) Act 1964 and recommended by the Henchy Report in 1978.[7] Although neither alternative is entirely satisfactory, it is submitted that the seeming illogicality of the *status quo* is preferable to the factually misleading implications of the current English formula and the Henchy proposal based on it.

The Victorian formula should not be confused with the verdict of 'guilty but mentally ill' currently available in twelve of the United States of America.[8] The former is a fully-fledged insanity verdict

5 This point was also overlooked by contemporary critics of section 2, but not by Queen Victoria herself: Walker, op. cit., 189-92. She envisaged the change in the form of the verdict introduced by section 2 as a deterrent to would-be assassins, arguing that it was fallacious to assume that the legally insane were necessarily beyond the reach of the law's formal disapproval, and in this she may also have been correct as she suffered seven assassination attempts prior to the change but none in the ensuing eighteen years: Walker, ibid.

6 Op. cit., p. 192.

7 Third Interim Report of the Interdepartmental Committee (chaired by Mr Justice Henchy, then of the Supreme Court) on Mentally Ill and Maladjusted Persons. *Treatment and Care of Persons Suffering from Mental Disorder Who Appear Before the Courts on Criminal Charges* (1978) p. 21 (hereinafter the *Report*).

8 See generally Mackay, 'Post-Hinkley Insanity in the USA' (1988) *Crim LR* 88. The relevant states are Alaska, Delaware, Georgia, Indiana, Kentucky, Illinois, Michigan, New Mexico, Pennsylvania, South Carolina, South Dakota, and Utah. The verdict was first introduced in Michigan in 1976: Mackay, op. cit., p. 91.

whereas the latter functions by way of an alternative to the insanity verdict and is intended to cater for cases where the type or degree of mental disorder from which the defendant is suffering is thought to be insufficiently grave to justify a finding of 'not guilty by reason of insanity.' In practice this means that the American formula is reserved for cases of psychopathy (as well as cases of psychosis which fall outside the ambit of the insanity criterion) where, without prejudice to the defendant's responsibility for his actions, some form of psychiatric treatment or therapy is thought to be appropriate. In other words, it represents a compromise solution to the problem posed by psychopathic defendants in those states where public opinion is thought to regard such defendants as responsible for their bad actions and to require that fact to be formally reflected in the verdict of the courts.[9]

Like its Victorian counterpart, the American verdict has also been criticized as illogical.[10] This charge would be well-founded if 'mentally ill' meant 'legally insane', since a guilty verdict normally presupposes that the defendant has the requisite criminal capacity. But since the verdict is routinely interpreted as referring to mental illnesses that do not go to criminal capacity, i.e., that function as extenuating circumstances only, and since the recognition of extenuating circumstances is perfectly consistent with a finding of guilt or responsibility, the charge of illogicality seems misplaced. Moreover, as it implies both responsibility and the need for treatment, the verdict of 'guilty but mentally ill' can be defended on the grounds that it sends out exactly the right signal in cases where a mixture of penal and therapeutic measures seems appropriate—such as that of a defendant who kills his victim during a bout of depression but who does not qualify for the insanity defence on the grounds that his condition has not interfered with his ability to 'test reality.'

Finally, in cases where it is felt that a defendant deserves to be convicted of murder notwithstanding evidence of mental illness—for example, where there appears to be no causal connection between the illness and the wrongful act or the evidence discloses no more than a mild neurosis—the verdict is preferable to one of 'diminished responsibility' since the latter necessarily results in a conviction for a lower degree of homicide.

9 See Plaut, 'Punishment versus Treatment of the Guilty but Mentally Ill' (1983) *J Crim L Criminol* 48.

10 See generally, Hoffman, *Rationalization of Insanity: An Analysis of the Guilty But Mentally Ill Provision in Illinois* (Ann Arbor, 1987).

Ironically, the American practice notwithstanding, therapeutic measures seem entirely inappropriate in cases of psychopathy given the firm evidence that that 'condition' is not amenable to treatment.[11] Indeed, it is submitted that, where there is no evidence of mental illness other than psychopathy, this evidence suggests that it would be better if the 'guilty but mentally ill' verdict were taken to signal no more than that the courts are entitled to adjust the quantum of punishment normally imposed for the offence charged. However, this would further complicate a defence that is already regarded as unduly difficult to operate in practice.[12]

The American verdict has also been criticized on the grounds that it assumes that psychopathy is a mental illness in the face of powerful arguments to the contrary,[13] and is probably unconstitutional.[14]

## 2. THE EFFECT OF THE VERDICT

Although a successful plea of insanity has long been treated as an acquittal for procedural purposes,[15] most legal systems provide a right of appeal against it.[16] This was also recommended by the Henchy Report[17] and, it is submitted, would be a desirable reform given that a verdict of insanity can be returned on foot of evidence led by the prosecution or as a result of a ruling by the court.[18] The fact that the verdict is an acquittal has the important consequence that the courts have no role in the detention of persons who get the benefit of it. Section 2(2) of the Trial of Lunatics Act 1883 requires the court to order the detention of persons acquitted on the grounds of insanity 'in such a place and in such a manner as the court shall direct till [the government's] pleasure shall be known.'[19] In other words, once the detention order is made the question of whether it

11 Supra, ch. 4.6.

12 See Mackay, op. cit., p. 91.

13 See Klofas and Weisheit, 'Pleading Guilty but Mentally Ill: Adversarial Justice and Mental Health' (1986) *Int J Law Psychiat* p. 491.

14 See Plaut, op. cit., p. 442.

15 *Felstead v. R* [1914] AC 534; *Duke* [1963] 1 QB 210.

16 For example, in English law the matter is governed by section 2 of the Criminal Procedure (Insanity) Act 1964.

17 *Report*, p. 39.

18 *People v. Messitt* [1972] IR 204 (CCA)—supra, ch. 4, n. 43; *DPP v. Ellis* [1990] 2 IR 291; *Kemp* [1957] 1 QB 399.

19 See appendix 2.

should continue and for how long is a matter for the government and the government alone.

This was accepted in Ireland until 1971 when the practice was introduced, following *State (O) v. O'Brien*,[20] of ordering the detention of persons found guilty but insane 'until further order of the court', apparently on the assumption that the decision as to how long a person should be detained under section 2 was a matter for the courts and not the legislature. This practice, which enabled detainees to apply to the *court* for release on the grounds that they were no longer a danger to themselves or others, has recently been declared invalid by the Supreme Court, in *DPP v. Gallagher*.[21] In the opinion of the Supreme Court, it would have been acceptable if a section 2 verdict was a conviction, since a detention order made in consequence of it would then be a sentence; and sentencing is a matter for the courts under the Constitution. But as a section 2 verdict is an acquittal and not a conviction, it followed that the courts had no further seisin of a case after it has been delivered; and, consequently, that there was nothing constitutionally untoward about the government's role in determining the length of detention orders made pursuant to it.

On the narrow issue of the logical implications of an acquittal on the grounds of insanity, the decision in *Gallagher* is unexceptionable. Moreover, it is to be welcomed insofar as it scotches the contention, also canvassed in *Ellis*,[22] that the relatives of an insane person's victim somehow have *locus standi* in any decision as to whether or not the insane person should be released from custody.[23] The danger in

20 [1973] IR 50 (SC). In 1956 the appellant was convicted of murder and *sentenced* according to section 103 (as adapted by section 133) of the Children Act 1908 to be 'detained in such a place and on such conditions as the [government] shall direct'. In 1957 he was certified to be insane and was moved to the Central Mental Hospital. In 1969 he applied to the High Court for an order of *habeus corpus*. That court directed his release on the grounds that as the power to select punishment was an integral part of the administration of justice, section 103 of the Act of 1908 was unconstitutional insofar as it purported to vest that power in the government. The decision of the High Court was upheld on appeal to the Supreme Court. As is clear from the text immediately following, the flaw in the argument from *O'Brien* was that it overlooked the fact that a guilty verdict under section 2, unlike a guilty verdict under section 103 of the 1908 Act, does *not* entail a conviction and sentence.

21 [1991] ILRM 339.

22 [1990] 2 IR 291.

23 Thus in *Ellis* counsel for the victim's family made a submission to the High Court to the effect that that court should retain seisin of the case: [1990] 2 IR at 301; whereas in *Gallagher* counsel for the victim's family was instructed to appear before the High Court to express its views in relation to any possible release: *Irish Times*, 15 January 1990.

that argument is that it is a recipe for the punitive or—what is worse—even vengeful detention of persons acquitted on the grounds of insanity.

Yet the decision should not be allowed to obscure the fundamental weaknesses in the dispositional arrangements affecting persons found guilty but insane. The most glaring flaw is that section 2 (2) provides that 'the court *shall* order the accused to be kept in custody as a criminal lunatic . . .'[24] A detention order is therefore mandatory once a section 2 (2) verdict has been delivered, and the court has no discretion to release the defendant either absolutely or conditionally. This arrangement is usually justified on the grounds of social defence: the insane defendant is subject to automatic detention on the presumption that he is dangerous, i.e., because it is taken for granted that a defendant whose pathological beliefs and attitudes led him to kill on one occasion may be driven to do so again.

This reasoning can be faulted on several grounds. First, there is no evidence that persons who have been diagnosed as mentally ill are more prone to violence than the mentally healthy. On the contrary, the empirical evidence shows that there is no significant difference between the two groups on this score. Second, there is no evidence that persons who have been acquitted on the grounds of insanity are more prone to violence than other violent killers or other offenders convicted of crimes of violence other than homicide.[25] Nor does the fact that psychopathy seems to be associated with serious crimes of violence affect these conclusions. As we saw in chapter 4,[26] since psychopathy is largely defined in terms of antisocial behaviour and as its status as a mental disorder depends on

24 Italics added. Incidentally, the Lunacy (Ireland) Act 1821 which replaced the provisions relating to the insanity defence in the Criminal Lunatics Act 1800—see appendix 1—and which was in turn replaced by s. 2 of the Trial of Lunatics Act 1883, left the question of the detention of insanity acquittees to the discretion of the court, by providing that 'the Court before whom the trial shall be had, shall, *if it shall be thought necessary or proper*, order such person[s] to be kept in strict custody . . . until the pleasure of the Lord Lieutenant, or other Chief Governor or Governors of Ireland for the time being, shall be known.' Italics added. See also ch. 7.6.

25 See Rabkin, 'Criminal Behaviour of Discharged Mental Patients: A Critical Appraisal of the Research', (1979) *86 Psychological Bulletin*, 1-27; and generally, Thornberry and Jacoby, *The Criminally Insane: A Community Follow-up of Mentally Ill Offenders* (Chicago, 1979); Steadman and Cocozza, *Careers of the Criminally Insane: Excessive Social Control of Deviance*, (Boston, 1974).

26 4.6.

its being so defined, it is hardly surprising that psychopaths tend to be over-represented among populations of convicted offenders and prisoners.

Third, a finding that an accused's insane beliefs or attitudes led him to kill on one occasion does not entail the conclusion that he is likely to kill for the same or similar reasons in the future. The presumption of dangerousness trades on the notion of insanity as a condition, i.e., as an abiding illness state which persists through time and may persist indefinitely. In other words, it implies a medical or psychiatric model of insanity. By contrast, the notion of insanity embodied in the insanity defence goes to the accused's state of mind at the moment he committed the wrongful act, and therefore implies nothing about the balance of his mind before or after the event that forms the basis of the charge against him. In short, the legal concept is a test of responsibility, not a diagnosis or description of an existing or potentially recurrent illness state.

French law recognizes the logic of this fundamental distinction by insisting on the automatic unconditional release of defendants acquitted on the grounds of insanity, and by subsuming the issue of whether or not defendants of this type should be hospitalized on the grounds of dangerousness under the ordinary law of civil commitment.[27] This arrangement can be criticized on the grounds, *inter alia,* that it means that the hospitalization of defendants acquitted on the grounds of insanity under French law generally depends on the initiative of their families. But it has the great merit that the issue of dangerousness must be decided on the basis of the acquittee's state of mind when civil commitment is being sought, thereby virtually eliminating the risk of the involuntary confinement of persons who are no longer, or were never, mentally ill.

Given the inquisitorial character of French criminal procedure, this arrangement stands in ironic contrast with the system of automatic indeterminate detention *in situ* in most common law countries. Under the common law system, the onus is on detainees to show why they should be released rather than on the government to show why they should be detained—an odd state of affairs in a legal culture not unknown for its superciliousness about the fact that it rightly regards the deprivation of liberty as a matter of fundamental constitutional significance.

Fourth, the presumption of dangerousness is inconsistent with the syntax of the criminal process. Indeed it can be argued that the

27 See the treatment of French law in chapter 9.2.

fact that a defendant was fit to plead raises a presumption that he is no longer insane and, consequently, that he is no longer dangerous.[28] At the very least, the fact that he was fit to plead suggests that the existing rule whereby insanity acquittees are automatically detained should be modified so as to require the trial judge to decide the issue of dangerousness in the light of the accused's state of mind at the time of trial.[29] Ideally the decision would be made by trial judges in the light of medical evidence from experts appointed by the court.

This is now the position in Italian law[30] and in the law of several of the United States of America.[31] In England section 5 of the Criminal Procedure (Insanity) Bill 1964, published under the auspices of the Criminal Law Revision Committee,[32] recommended that the court should be empowered to order an immediate release in cases in which it is satisfied on medical evidence that it is safe to do so having regard to the interests of society and the defendant. However, although this recommendation was subsequently repeated by the Butler Committee,[33] it has not become law.[34] A similar reform was recommended by the Henchy Committee[35] and, it is submitted, should be introduced in Ireland. Given the Supreme Court's clear statement, in *Gallagher*,[36] that an order made pursuant to a section 2 (2) verdict is not a sentence, there can be

28 Morris, 'Acquittal by Reason of Insanity', in Monaghan and Steadman (eds.), *Mentally Disordered Offenders: Perspectives from Law and Social Science* (New York, 1983), p. 68.

29 German and Singer, 'Punishing the Not Guilty: Hospitalization of Persons Acquitted by Reason of Insanity', (1976) *29 Rutgers L Rev* 1011 at 1076.

30 See the treatment of Italian law in chapter 9.3.

31 For a list of the relevant states, see Note, 'Commitment Following Acquittal by Reason of Insanity' (1968) *U Pa L Rev* 924.

32 Cmnd. 2149 of 1963 para 34.

33 *Report of the Committee on Mentally Abnormal Offenders,* Cmnd. 6244 of 1975 para 18.42.

34 The Criminal Procedure (Insanity and Fitness to Plead) Act 1991 does however increase the powers of disposal available to trial judges in insanity cases; these are now the same in insanity and unfitness to plead cases alike: viz., where the sentence for the offence is fixed by law, i.e., in murder cases, the court must make a hospital order restricting discharge without limitation of time; otherwise it may make 1) a hospital order restricting discharge either for a limited or unlimited time, 2) a guardianship order under the Mental Health Act 1983, 3) a supervision and treatment order under Sch. 2 of the 1991 Act, or 4) an order for absolute discharge.

35 *Report,* p. 29-31.

36 [1991] ILRM 339.

no justification for allowing it to function, albeit unintentionally, as a punishment.

Finally, the presumption of dangerousness is plainly false in relation to defendants acquitted on the grounds of insanity on foot of the psychological effects of an isolated bout of *physical* illness or of a chronic physical illness that has been brought under control by medication. As defendants of this type are not mentally ill, and as mental illness is generally regarded as a necessary condition of dangerousness,[37] it is difficult to justify the conclusion that they need to be automatically detained in the public interest.

This is not to suggest that the executive cannot be trusted with the decision as to whether a defendant is sufficiently dangerous to justify preventive detention. The point is rather that since preventive detention is such a drastic measure, the review process should begin *before* a defendant loses his liberty; and, in the nature of things, this means giving trial judges a discretionary power to order the immediate release of insanity acquittees with or without conditions. This move would be without prejudice to cases where an order of preventive detention was appropriate since there is no reason to suppose that trial judges would not act prudently in the exercise of their discretion in such cases.

*Ellis v. DPP*[38] nicely illustrates this thesis. The defendant was charged with the murder of a member of a gang which, he claimed, was blackmailing him into helping in an armed robbery. His defence was that he did not know what he was doing as he was in a dazed and confused state as a result of an epileptic episode, and that this entitled him to an acquittal on the grounds of automatism. The only medical evidence adduced at the trial was in support of the epilepsy claim, and neither the defence nor the prosecution introduced evidence of mental illness. The trial judge refused to leave the issue of automatism to the jury but directed them to consider the question of insanity—on the premise that evidence of any medical condition, not excluding purely physical conditions like epilepsy, that impairs an accused's reasoning or volitional powers in the appropriate way is tantamount to a plea of insanity.[39]

The defendant was duly acquitted on the grounds of insanity and detained in the Central Mental Hospital in compliance with section 2 (2) of the Trial of Lunatics Act 1883. He applied to the Central

37 See infra, 6.3; Morse, op. cit., p. 1048.
38 [1990] 2 IR 291.
39 This aspect of the insanity defence is discussed supra, ch. 4.1 and 4.3.

Criminal Court for release on the grounds that there was no evidence at his trial that he was mentally ill at the time of the killing, and that the hospital authorities had found no evidence that he was mentally ill when he was admitted and were satisfied that he was not now mentally ill. O'Hanlon J initially made an order of temporary release for a period of six months on foot of this application, on the assumption that the detention and release of persons who get the benefit of the insanity defence was a matter for the courts; but subsequently refused to make the order final at the end of the period of temporary release, on the grounds that, irrespective of the cogency of the medical evidence introduced by the defendant, the true legal position was that these were matters exclusively within the competence of the Minister for Justice.

On appeal the Supreme Court directed the trial judge to decide the issues of detention and release on the basis of the medical evidence before him, on the grounds that it would be unfair to the defendant to discount the Central Criminal Court's original assumption of jurisdiction in this regard notwithstanding that it may have been wrong in law. The defendant was accordingly returned to the Central Mental Hospital for further medical examination, and then released by order of the Central Criminal Court for a further period of one year on foot of the medical report from the hospital, only to be returned once more to the Central Mental Hospital when the period of release expired. Meanwhile, the Minister for Justice appointed a special committee to consider whether Mr Ellis's detention should be continued, which committee finally recommended that he should be unconditionally released.[40]

This incredible saga dragged on for over three years—largely, it must be said, because of the long delay in activating the review process once the period of detention had begun and because of the jurisdictional problem referred to in the preceding paragraphs. Yet it could have been avoided altogether had the trial judge been in a position to order the immediate release upon acquittal of a defendant who was plainly not mentally ill and whose acquittal on the grounds of insanity was equally plainly based on evidence of the effects of a well understood *physical* illness.

Alternatively, it is arguable that there should be a statutory rule prohibiting trial judges from making an order of compulsory psychiatric hospitalization unless and until there is clear medical

40 *Irish Times*, 22 November 1991.

evidence that such an order is necessary in the public interest.[41] A rule to this effect would protect defendants who, like Ellis and Sullivan,[42] acted during an epileptic episode or, like Quick,[43] when in a state of hyperglycaemia resulting from diabetes; and, it is submitted, would be preferable to leaving the question of hospitalization to the discretion of the court given that some judges may feel disinclined to run the risk of provoking public outrage by exercising their discretion in favour of defendants convicted of crimes of violence who are not mentally ill.

It would also solve the problem raised by *Burgess.*[44] There the defendant attacked and seriously injured his neighbour. In reply to a charge under section 18 of the Offences Against the Person Act 1861, he claimed that he had been sleep-walking throughout the incident and that this entitled him to a defence of non-insane automatism. The trial judge ruled that, in the absence of evidence that the condition had an external cause, his claim amounted to a defence of insanity and the defendant was acquitted on that basis. Although mindful of the 'apparent incongruity of labelling this sort of disability as insanity', and despite the fact that the three medical experts who gave evidence at the trial were agreed that recurrent violence during sleep-walking was highly unlikely, the Court of Appeal affirmed the verdict, with the result that the defendant was automatically committed to a psychiatric hospital. In the opinion of the Court, 'the absence of the danger of recurrence is not a reason for saying that [a condition] cannot be a disease of the mind' within the meaning of the M'Naghten Rules.[45]

Given that the insanity defence is a test of criminal responsibility,[46] it is submitted that this reasoning is sound. To the extent that his reasoning powers were disengaged as a result of somnambulism, and allowing for the fact that the latter is plainly not an external factor giving rise to automatism, Burgess comes clearly within the purview of the insanity defence. Admittedly, it is

41 This is the position in Italian law: infra, ch. 9.3.
42 [1984] AC 157.
43 [1973] QB 910; see also *Bingham* [1991] *Crim LR* 433.
44 [1991] 2 WLR 1206.
45 [1991] 2 WLR 1206 at 1212.
46 This point is discussed at length in ch. 1. Its importance is sometimes missed by commentators. For example, see White, infra ch. 7, n. 62 at p. 7, who appears to criticise the Criminal Procedure (Insanity and Fitness to Plead) Act 1991 for failing to align the legal and medical definitions of insanity; see also Sutherland and Gearty, infra n. 47.

arguable that defendants of this type should not be branded with the stigma associated with an insanity acquittal; although it is submitted that this difficulty could easily be cleared up by re-labelling the defence as an acquittal on the grounds of mental disorder or *mental impairment,* as the latter term transparently embraces those forms of impairment which do no arise from mental illness. Be that as it may, it is equally clear that a person who, in the opinion of all the expert witnesses at his trial, is neither mentally ill nor dangerous, should not be compulsorily hospitalized. Indeed, it may be that the automatic hospitalization of defendants of this type puts the government in breach of Article 5 of the European Convention on Human Rights.[47] It also helps to explain why so few defendants seek to rely on insanity either as a defence or as a plea in bar of trial.[48]

## 3. THE REVIEW PROCESS

Another major flaw in the arrangements affecting persons found guilty but insane is that there is no provision in the Trial of Lunatics Act for an automatic periodic review of detention orders made under section 2 (2). A detainee can apply to the government for a review and the government must use fair procedures when hearing his case.[49] But it is not obliged to carry out a review in cases where the detainee has not sought one. Thus in *Ellis* it was two years before a review was carried out at the defendant's request notwithstanding the highly unusual circumstance that his acquittal on the grounds of insanity did not entail a finding of mental illness and that there was no evidence to suggest that he had ever been mentally ill before the incident that formed the basis of the charge against him.

The Henchy Report recommended the establishment of a Review Body that would annually review all cases of detention as a result of an insanity verdict. Part of the contemplated Review Body's function was to ensure that detainees who were no longer a

47 Since it precludes the element of medical judgment which the European Court of Human Rights has insisted is an essential component of compulsory hospitalization: *Winterwerp v. The Netherlands* (1979) 2 EHRR 387, para. 39. See also, Sutherland and Gearty, 'Insanity and the European Court of Human Rights' (1992) *Crim. LR* 418.

48 This and related statistical matters are discussed in the epilogue.

49 *Gallagher* [1991] ILRM at 345

danger to themselves or others would be promptly released, i.e., that they would not be subjected to a regime of punishment. This recommendation was included in the Draft Criminal Justice (Mental Health) Bill 1978 published as part of the Report,[50] but it has never been enacted. The *Ellis* experience is a timely reminder that it should be.

The criteria employed when considering applications for release also deserve careful scrutiny. In both *Gallagher* and *Ellis,* the terms of reference given to the special committees established for this purpose were 'to advise the Minister for Justice as to whether the applicant is suffering from any mental disorder warranting his continued detention in the public and private interests (including the question of whether he would be a potential danger to any member of the public if released) . . .'[51] This suggests that mental disorder is a necessary condition of dangerousness and, consequently, that the detainee should be released if the committee finds no evidence of mental disorder. As we have seen, this view of the terms of reference is borne out by the decision in *Ellis*.[52] But it is not obvious from *Gallagher.*[53]

Gallagher shot and killed his girlfriend and her mother in front of witnesses in the grounds of Sligo General Hospital where the women had gone to visit a relative.[54] His girlfriend had wanted to end their relationship for some months prior to the incident but Gallagher refused to accept her decision and continued to call on her. At a wedding a week before the killing he attacked with a knife a young man who had danced with her. Three days before the incident his girlfriend complained to the police that he had raped her. When questioned by the police about the alleged rape Gallagher signed himself into the local mental hospital, but discharged himself the following day when his girlfriend decided she did not want to face the publicity associated with a rape trial and withdrew the charges. He then went to his home and procured the gun with which he shot the two women. After the killing he drove wildly around Donegal, eventually driving his car off a pier into the sea. He had handcuffed himself to the steering wheel but was rescued by the police who were pursuing him.

50 *Report,* ss. 20-3 infra, ch. 7.6.
51 *Evening Press,* 7 November 1991; *Irish Times,* 13 February 1991, respectively.
52 [1990] 2 IR 291.
53 [1991] ILRM 339.
54 For a detailed account of the facts and a history of the proceedings in *Gallagher,* see *Irish Times,* 20 July 1991.

At his trial for murder Gallagher admitted firing the fatal shots. There was conflicting psychiatric evidence of his condition at the time of the killings and subsequently. One psychiatrist testified that the handcuffing episode showed that his judgment and emotional control had been gravely impaired at the material time. Another gave evidence that he was taking slimming tablets which could have produced a paranoid schizophrenic reaction. Yet another testified that he did not believe the defendant was mentally ill when he shot the women as his actions were consistent with the ordinary human motives of jealousy and revenge. Gallagher was acquitted of murder on the grounds of insanity by a 10-2 majority verdict, and detained in the Central Mental Hospital. Six months later he applied to the High Court for release on the grounds that he was no longer insane in the opinion of the medical authorities at the Central Mental Hospital, but his application was rejected on the grounds that the detention of acquittees pursuant to section 2 (2) of the Trial of Lunatics Act 1883 was a matter for the executive; and this decision was subsequently upheld by the Supreme Court. The Minister for Justice then appointed a special committee to review Gallagher's application within the terms of reference specified above; and—just under a year later—this committee recommended that his detention should be continued.[55]

This decision would be unexceptionable were it not for the fact that the detainee had been protesting his sanity since shortly after his detention began and that the authorities at the Central Mental Hospital found no evidence that he was insane when admitted or subsequently. There is also the fact that, on the very day he announced his decision to keep Gallagher in the Central Mental Hospital, the Minister for Justice let it be known that he was soon to circulate details of a bill to reform the law of insanity which would include provision for a new defence of diminished responsibility.[56]

In other words, there is the suspicion that Gallagher is perceived by the government as the type of defendant who should be convicted of manslaughter and have his sentence reduced on the basis of a plea of diminished responsibility, and that the decision to continue his detention for the time being was motivated more by a concern to ensure that defendants of this type are seen not to be able to escape their just desserts by means of the insanity plea than by a dispassionate assessment of his state of mental health. These

55 *Evening Press,* 7 November 1991.
56 *Irish Times,* 8 November 1991.

remarks are not intended to impugn the integrity of the Minister's committee, but rather to point up the need for the speedy introduction of the promised new defence of diminished responsibility to cater for defendants who deserve neither to be acquitted nor punished in full, and who may require psychiatric treatment either in lieu of or in addition to an ordinary custodial sentence.

Finally, there is the question of what precisely is meant by the term 'mental disorder' in the context of the terms of reference? Is it confined to psychosis and schizophrenia or does it also embrace neurosis, psychopathy and the so-called personality disorders? This question is important given that the Supreme Court has declared, in *DPP v. O'Mahony*,[57] that psychopaths—specifically the *Byrne*-type defendant who acts out of violent perverted sexual desires he [says he] finds it difficult or impossible to control—are entitled to the insanity defence in Irish law; and that psychiatrists are apt to disagree as to the status of psychopathy as a mental disorder—some taking the view that it is not a mental disorder as it does not go to the cognitive functions, much less to the ability to 'test reality', others arguing that it is as it has been so classified by the authoritative Diagnostic and Statistical Manual of the American Psychiatric Association.[58]

Admittedly, psychiatrists may also disagree as to whether a particular patient is psychotic, as the recitation of the facts of *Gallagher* shows. But disagreements of that kind are quite different from the sort at issue here. They are disputes about whether a patient is actually suffering from a recognized mental illness, whereas we are talking about the deeper question of whether psychopathy should be recognized as a mental illness in the first place. The former can usually be resolved by further clinical examination, whereas the fact that the 'patient' may or may not exhibit the 'symptoms' normally associated with psychopathy is irrelevant to those who do not consider psychopathy to be a genuine mental illness. Irrespective of the merits of the competing arguments involved, it is highly undesirable that the decision to release or continue the detention of a detainee might depend on which view of the psychopathy issue the psychiatrist on one of the Minister's review committees happens to take—especially since the 'lay' members of these committees are unlikely to gainsay an expert colleague's views on a matter that seems to fall exclusively within the domain of psychiatry.

57 [1986] ILRM at 248-9.
58 See the discussion of psychopathy in chapter 4.6.

The solution to this problem is plainly to exclude psychopathy from the ambit of the insanity defence altogether, thereby absolving special committees from having to decide the thorny question of whether or not it is a mental disorder. The introduction of a defence of diminished responsibility would help to facilitate this outcome by giving trial judges and juries a realistic alternative to the insanity defence in cases where it seems appropriate to give effect to medical evidence of psychopathy. Nor is it an answer to this argument that no psychiatrist is likely to recommend the release of the kind of psychopath specifically contemplated by the Supreme Court in *O'Mahony*,[59] on the grounds that he or she does not believe that psychopathy is a mental illness. Indeed the fact that this is unlikely to happen strengthens rather than weakens the argument that preventive detention is likely to be abused—in direct contravention to the Supreme Court's ruling in *Gallagher*[60]—as a punitive measure as long as psychopaths are eligible for the insanity defence.

This may seem like a trivial matter when set against society's right to protection against the sadistic killer who happens not to be insane but who gets the benefit of the insanity defence on the grounds of psychopathy. But this is a weak objection. Apart from the fact that it is inconsistent with the terms of reference governing the review of preventive detention orders, it ignores the fundamental point that defendants of this type—and indeed dangerous but mentally normal defendants generally—could and should be imprisoned in the normal way under the auspices of a defence of diminished responsibility. In short, the point is not that defendants of this type should not be punished, but that the punishment meted out to them should not be disguised as treatment.

## 4. CRIMINAL LUNATIC ASYLUMS

Prior to 1800 persons acquitted on the grounds of insanity were released back into the community. As a result of the Criminal Lunatics Act of that year they began to be detained in prisons and this practice continued until 1821, when provision was made for

59 [1986] ILRM 244.
60 [1991] ILRM 339.

the transfer of insanity acquittees to district asylums according as accommodation became available.[61] The new transfer arrangements were immediately criticised on the grounds that the criminally insane were a distinct class requiring separate treatment and so should not be confined with the non-criminally insane on whom it was felt they would have an undesirable influence, and this criticism eventually led to the establishment of a special asylum for criminal lunatics in Dundrum, Dublin, in 1850, the first such institution in these islands.[62] Dundrum has since been used as the sole depository in Ireland for persons found guilty but insane or unfit to plead because of insanity.[63] It also houses a number of patients who have committed an indictable offence in another psychiatric hospital.[64] It has a total population of approximately eighty patients.

Dundrum began as an essentially custodial institution and has largely continued in that vein.[65] Like other institutions of its type, the emphasis has been on the secure detention of patients—largely by means of psychotropic medication—rather than the development of therapeutic programmes. In the result, release rates have traditionally been low with the average period of detention—for insanity acquittees and persons found unfit to plead alike—remaining constant at between seven to ten years: the normal length of a life sentence for murder.[66] Indeed, as recently as November 1990, the Director of the Central Mental Hospital, Dr Charles Smith, estimated that as many as 12 to 15 patients, out of a total population of 80, had been detained for even longer periods, and that these patients 'were becoming institutionalised and helpless'. In Dr Smith's opinion, this was partly because 'previously . . . the hospital's administration was too reluctant to move patients away from Dundrum's greater security' and partly because 'other psychiatric hospitals are either unwilling or unable to take [patients on transfer from Dundrum]'.[67]

61 1 and 2 Geo. IV. C. 33 (Lunacy (Ireland) Act), ss. 16-18.

62 'There was, as yet, none in Britain or elsewhere; Broadmoor, the famous English institution, was not founded until 1863': Robins, *Fools and Mad—A History of the Insane in Ireland,* (Dublin, 1986), p. 149. The legislation establishing the asylum—the Central Criminal Lunatic Asylum (Ireland) Act 1845—was passed five years earlier.

63 Mental Treatment Act 1961, s. 39.

64 See the reported remarks of the Director of the Central Mental Hospital in *The Sunday Tribune,* 4 November 1990.

65 Robins, op. cit., pp. 147-51.

66 See the penultimate note.

67 Ibid.

This situation began to change in the 1980s with the gradual introduction of a more therapeutic approach. Largely in response to international developments in forensic psychiatry, greater emphasis came to be placed on the development of treatment programmes designed to help patients to regain their sanity with a view to being released altogether, or at least transferred to less secure psychiatric facilities in order to prepare for release. Indeed, by the end of the 1980s it had become standard practice for the hospital authorities to seek, and for the courts to recommend, the release of patients after four to five years.[68]

This state of affairs is remarkable in view of the fact that research has shown that very few insanity acquittees are severely psychotic by the time of trial, that insanity acquittees generally do not require lengthy commitments on mental health grounds, and that many of them could be treated on an outpatient basis.[69] It should however be emphasised that Dundrum is typical of hospitals for the criminally insane in ignoring these findings, as there is abundant research evidence that the length of insanity acquittal commitments is generally positively correlated with the seriousness of the crime charged rather than the acquittee's psychiatric condition.[70]

Moreover, this correlation appears to hold irrespective of the degree of commitment shown by hospitals to the ideal of developing a more therapeutic regime for the criminally insane. Indeed, in the case of Dundrum, the increased therapeutic emphasis of recent years serves as an ironic reminder of the essentially punitive nature of preventive detention. As we have seen, the net effect of the new emphasis has been to reduce the average period of detention from seven to ten years to four to five years. The longer period was clearly punitive given the fact that it vastly exceeded what you would expect on therapeutic grounds and correlated exactly with the normal length of a life sentence for murder; indeed in some civilian systems this correlation is recognized by an express provision that the

68 *Irish Times*, 25 July 1991.

69 Morse, op. cit., at 1048-9; German and Singer, op. cit. at 1075; Monaghan, 'The Psychiatrization of Criminal Behaviour: A Reply' (1973) *24 Hospital and Community Psychiatry* 105-7; Monaghan and Splane, 'Psychological Approaches to Criminal Behaviour' in Bittner and Messinger (eds.) *The Criminology Yearbook* (Beverly Hills, 1980), pp. 17-47; and see generally Beran and Toomey (eds.) *Mentally Ill Offenders and the Criminal Justice System: Issues in Forensic Services* (New York, 1979); Thornberry and Jacoby, op. cit.; Steadman and Cocozza, op. cit.

70 Ibid.

period of preventive detention may not normally exceed ten years.[71]

By parity of reasoning, the shorter period is also punitive. Given that most insanity acquittees are not seriously disordered and that short-term hospitalisation in any event usually suffices for the treatment of acute serious disorders, it too exceeds what you would expect on therapeutic grounds.[72] Moreover, it is striking that the shorter period more or less coincides with the normal range of custodial sentences for manslaughter. Indeed, it is submitted that this points to the operation of an informal system of 'sentencing' discounts on the grounds of mental disorder rather than to the existence of a programme designed to ensure that preventive detention does not exceed the necessary therapeutic minimum. In other words, if the issue of preventive detention was being decided on purely therapeutic considerations, we should expect to find the widespread release or transfer of insanity acquittees within a year of hospitalisation rather than the four to five years actually required.

To be fair to the authorities at the Central Mental Hospital, these criticisms require qualification. First, there is the difficulty, referred to above, that ordinary psychiatric hospitals have traditionally been reluctant to accept transfers from, or to re-admit patients who have spent a period in, Dundrum. To some extent this is a reflection of the ignorance and prejudice that has always bedevilled the disposition and treatment of the criminally insane both within the psychiatric profession and in society generally. Ironically, it is also partially due to the suddenness of the change of emphasis at Dundrum. Forensic psychiatrists have traditionally taken it for granted that the high-security, essentially custodial, arrangements there were essential to the proper management of the criminally insane, so it is hardly surprising that their recently proclaimed belief that ordinary psychiatric hospitals can play a useful role in this regard should be greeted with a certain amount of scepticism, particularly on the part of the psychiatric authorities who run the hospitals likely to be affected by the new policy.[73]

71 See the discussion of the Italian law of insanity in chapter 9.3.

72 See the penultimate note.

73 Thus in a recent case the authorities at St Brendan's psychiatric hospital in Grangegorman were widely reported as saying that they did not accept that that hospital, despite the fact that it has a closed unit, was sufficiently secure to house a patient arrested on suspicion of murder and found to be certifiably insane until such time as he was well enough to be formally charged. The proper place for patients of this type, according to a spokesperson for the hospital, was the Central Mental Hospital in Dundrum, notwithstanding the

Yet it is undoubtedly true that the evident scepticism from those quarters acts as a potent constraint on attempts to fashion a more therapeutic regime at the Central Mental Hospital. As the Director of the Hospital has ruefully observed,[74] the new policy of seeking the transfer of patients to less secure facilities as a step towards eventual release cannot work without the cooperation of other psychiatric hospitals; yet the idea of forcing other hospitals to take patients from Dundrum is out of the question, if only because it would jeopardize the good relations—between forensic psychiatrists and their psychiatric colleagues generally—essential to the day-to-day operation of the mental health services. In other words, real change is unlikely to occur unless and until legislative provision is made for a scheme of designated hospitals for the reception of the criminally insane—of the kind recommended in the Henchy Report[75] nearly fifteen years ago.

Second, since they do not live on the moon, it has to be acknowledged that there is a limit to what forensic psychiatrists can do, even with the best will in the world, if their efforts are not adequately resourced. A legislatively based scheme of designated mental hospitals for the reception and treatment of the criminally insane is certainly a necessary condition of progress in this area. But unless the hospitals included in the scheme are properly staffed and equipped, progress is likely to be more apparent than real. In practice this means that unless sufficient funds are made available, *via* the Department of Health, to enable the affected hospitals to mount and run the required assessment and treatment programmes, including adequate outpatient facilities, there is a real danger that they too could develop a subculture of custody and security of the kind so long associated with Dundrum; and, consequently, that patients could end up being transferred from one long-term, therapeutically under-resourced hospital to another, without any significant improvement in their chances of recovery and release. Nor is this an alarmist scenario, given the widespread public ignorance of the needs of the criminally insane, and the concomitant failure of political will—as evidenced by the fate of the Henchy Report—that this induces in politicians and governments.

technical difficulty that, as it is a hospital for the criminally insane, patients can only be sent there if they have first been charged with a criminal offence: *Irish Times*, 30 January 1992.

74 *Sunday Tribune*, 4 November 1991.

75 *Report*, pp. 17, 43-51.

### 5. THE DISORDERED PRISONER

Where a prisoner is found to be disordered at the end of his term of imprisonment the government must use the ordinary procedures for civil commitment if it wishes to continue his confinement with hospitalization.[76] As Morse has remarked, the logic of this arrangement is compelling:

> [A]t the end of a prison term a prisoner has been freed and thus enjoys the same civil status as other free citizens. If the state then decides to deprive him of liberty and stigmatize him with involuntary hospitalization, the ex-prisoner should be entitled to the same protections granted other citizens.[77]

This logic did not commend itself to the Henchy Committee, which recommended that the President of the High Court should be empowered to order the continued detention in a 'designated centre' of a prisoner whose sentence was about to expire on proof that he would 'be dangerous to himself or to others' if released in the normal way.[78] The Committee also recommended that the President be given a comparable power in relation to prisoners found to have 'a violent personality disorder' in the period preceding their projected date of release.[79]

These recommendations have not been acted upon and, it is submitted, should not be resuscitated. Since the Supreme Court has held[80] that an unconvicted defendant cannot be denied bail on the grounds that he is likely to commit further offences if released, it seems unlikely to look with favour on the argument that a convicted defendant who has already served his sentence may have his detention continued on the grounds that he may be a danger to himself or others if released. If preventive detention is unlawful in the first case, it seems to follow, *a fortiori*, that it is also unlawful in the second.

Nor should the fact that a prisoner has been found to be mentally ill or to have 'a violent personality disorder' immediately prior to release affect this conclusion. Since evidence of mental illness does not imply dangerousness and is a notoriously unreliable predictor of

76 Following the decision of the Supreme Court in *Baxtrom v. Herold* [1966] 383 US 107, this is also the position in the United States of America.

77 Op. cit., p. 1049.

78 *Report,* p. 47.

79 Ibid., p. 48.

80 *AG v. O'Callaghan* [1966] IR 501; *Ryan* [1989] IR 399.

future violence,[81] it is submitted that there is no compelling reason why it should be allowed to override a defendant's normal constitutional rights. Moreover, as we saw in chapter 4, the concept of 'violent personality disorder' is a euphemism for someone with a (usually criminal) record of violence, but does not denote mental illness or disorder in the standard diagnostic sense of cognitive impairment and does not appear to be amenable to treatment. And while a criminal record of violence is a reasonably accurate predictor of future violence,[82] it is well established that what Hart[83] called 'the principle of retribution in the distribution of punishment' requires that a defendant must have broken the criminal law before he is liable to be punished under it.[84]

81 See supra, 6.2.
82 See Monaghan and Splane, op. cit.; Rabkin, op. cit.
83 *Punishment and Responsibility* (Oxford, 1968), p. 9.
84 Nor, for that matter, restrained. For a discussion of the scope of this principle see MacCormick, *H.L.A. Hart* (London, 1981) pp. 143-8.

# [7]

# Fitness for Trial

When the issue of insanity is raised as a defence to a criminal charge or the trial judge, either acting alone or at the suggestion of the prosecution, rules that the issue has been raised on the evidence, the question is whether the accused was insane at the time he committed the act or omission that forms the basis of the charge against him. The fact that he was insane before or after the event is irrelevant. This rule, which is reflected in the wording of the M'Naghten Rules,[1] follows from the fact that criminal law defences function as answers to a charge of wrongdoing not as statements about an accused's physical or mental condition. Naturally evidence of insanity before or after the event may be relevant when determining the accused's state of mind at the time of the incident but it is not relevant *per se.*

## 1. GENERALLY

Insanity may also be raised as a plea in bar of trial. In these circumstances, the question is whether the accused is insane at the time of trial.[2] Section 2 of the Criminal Lunatics Act 1800[3] provides that:

1 Rule 3 states that 'to establish a defence on the grounds of insanity, it must be clearly proved that, *at the time of committing the act'* etc: supra, ch. 2.2 (italics added).

2 *R v. Padola* [1960] 1 QB 325 (CA). See generally Chiswick, 'Fitness to Stand Trial and Mutism and Deafness' in Bluglass and Bowden (eds.) *Principles and Practice of Forensic Psychiatry* (London, 1990); Larkin and Collins, 'Fitness to Plead and Psychiatric Reports' (1989) *29 Med. Sci. and Law* 26. For the position in Scots law, see Chiswick, 'Insanity in Bar of Trial in Scotland: A State Hospital Study' (1978) *132 B J Psychiat* 598; Normand, Unfitness for Trial in Scotland: Proposed Adjudication of the Facts and the Right to Reprosecute' (1984) *7 Int. J Law and Psychiat* 415.

3 As adapted by the Lunacy (Ireland) Act 1821.

> . . . if any person indicted [in Ireland] for any offence shall be insane, and shall upon arraignment be found to be by a jury lawfully empanelled for that purpose, so that such person cannot be tried upon such indictment, or if upon the trial of any person so indicted such person shall appear to the jury charged with such indictment to be insane, it shall be lawful for the court before whom any such person shall be brought to be arraigned or tried as aforesaid to direct such finding to be recorded, and thereupon to order such person to be kept in strict custody until [the pleasure of the Lord Lieutenant or other Chief Governor or Governors of Ireland] shall be known . . .[4]

Section 2 does not indicate how or by whom the question of the accused's insanity is to be raised, 'but it is now well established that the question may be raised either by the prosecution or by the defence or by the court itself.'[5] If a court becomes aware, either before or during a trial, that the accused's person's sanity is doubtful, it is the duty of the court[6] to have the doubt resolved before beginning or continuing the trial. A special jury may be empanelled for the purpose of hearing the issue or the trial judge may leave it to the jury before whom the general issue is being heard.[7] The procedure before a jury empanelled (or charged) to decide whether a person is 'insane . . . so that he cannot be tried upon the indictment' is an inquiry and not a trial. Thus if evidence of the alleged insanity is not contested, 'the question of onus of proof is not a live issue': the jury must simply be satisfied on that evidence that the accused person is insane 'so that he cannot be tried upon the indictment.' But if the contention that the accused is insane is put forward by the defence and contested by the prosecution, the defence must prove the issue of insanity on the balance of probabilities.[8] Conversely, if the prosecution alleges and the defence disputes insanity, the prosecution must prove its case beyond all reasonable doubt.[9]

4 See Appendix 1 for the full text of the Act.
5 [1960] 1 QB at 325; per Lord Parker CJ.
6 'It should also be observed that it is for the court that has seisin of the matter [and not the executive] to determine whether or not the accused is suffering from insanity of such a character as renders him unfit to stand his trial': *The State (Coughlan) v. The Minister for Justice and Another* (1968) ILTR 177 at 186 (SC); per O'Daly CJ.
7 [1960] 1 QB 325.
8 [1960] 1 QB 325.
9 *Robertson* [1968] 1 WLR 1767 (CA).

## 2. THE PROBLEM OF TIMING

The rule that the question of fitness to plead is to be determined as soon as it arises is open to the criticism that it exposes defendants to the risk of indefinite detention in respect of crimes for which they have not been tried by a court. This criticism is obviously unanswerable in cases where the accused may be acquitted on foot of a substantive defence were the trial to proceed. But it is equally apt in cases where the accused is unable to raise a substantive defence, since the effect of the rule is to put the unfit defendant in the same position as one who has been found 'guilty but insane', i.e., as someone who has been shown to have committed the relevant *actus reus* in a severely disordered mental state. Someone who is sufficiently disordered to be unfit to plead is admittedly also likely to be eligible for involuntary civil commitment to a mental hospital, but since his detention in these circumstances must be shown to be necessary for his own or others' safety, it seems wrong that he can be *automatically* detained in the more restrictive setting of a criminal lunatic asylum in the absence of proof that he has either committed an offence or is dangerous.[10]

One solution to this problem would be to make consideration of the issue of unfitness to plead dependent on conviction, as it was held to be in *R. v. Roberts*[11] and *R. v. Pickstone.*[12] This approach has been recommended in a recent report of the Law Reform Commission of Canada.[13] But it is open to the serious objection that a defendant's fitness is a necessary condition of his trial on the substantive issue of guilt or innocence. In the common-law tradition, part of what it means to try someone on a criminal charge is that he has an opportunity to reply to the charge preferred against him: to plead guilty or not guilty and to instruct counsel accordingly. The defendant's ability to understand and participate in the proceedings as a rational and autonomous agent is therefore an essential component of the trial, not a merely contingent feature that can be dispensed with as the occasion demands.[14] Indeed, an adjudication of the issue of guilt or innocence that excluded the defendant *qua* participant would not be a criminal trial, and so could (or at least should) not lead to an acquittal, much less a conviction, notwithstanding that it

10 See Duff, *Trials & Punishments,* (Cambridge, 1991), p. 31.
11 [1954] 2 QB 329.
12 [1954] *Crim LR* 565.
13 Law Commission Report, *Mental Disorder in the Criminal Process* (1976) pp. 16-9.
14 See Duff, op. cit., ch. 4, for an interesting discussion of this point.

took place before a judge in a properly constituted criminal court.

Another solution would be to allow the court a discretion to postpone consideration of the question of fitness to plead until any time up to the close of the prosecution case if it is in the accused's interest to do so, i.e., where there is a reasonable chance that the prosecution case will be successfully challenged. If postponement occurs and the prosecution does not prove its case, the court could then direct the jury to acquit. This was the position in English law as a result of the enactment of section 4 of the Criminal Procedure (Insanity) Act 1964.[15] However, this solution does not meet the case of the defendant who is unable to mount a challenge to the prosecution case but who might be able to do so were he fit to plead. As already indicated, it is not clear why defendants of this type should be treated in the same way as those who have been found 'guilty but insane'. If there is sufficient evidence that they are a danger to themselves or others, they can and should be detained under the ordinary law of civil commitment. But in the absence of such evidence, it seems right that they should be released.[16]

Perhaps the most compelling solution would be to insist that the issue of unfitness should be determined as soon as it arises, but that the court must be satisfied that the facts can be proved before making any order detaining an accused on the grounds of unfitness, as was suggested by the Thomson Committee in Scotland[17] and as is now the position in English law.[18] This solution meets all of the difficulties we have been discussing. Since it involves an inquiry and not a trial, and so cannot result in a conviction, it does not matter that the accused is unable to participate in the proceedings *qua* defendant; although it goes without saying that he would have a right to be heard by the court and that his participation in the proceedings would be desirable.

If the result of the inquiry is negative, the accused should be released unconditionally, thereby obviating the risk of detaining defendants whose unfitness cannot be anchored in any wrongdoing

15 *Webb* [1969] 2 QB 278; but cf *Burles* [1970] 2 QB 191 where Parker LCJ said that 'the case for the prosecution may appear so strong and the suggested condition of the prisoner so disabling that postponement of the trial of the issue would be wholly inexpedient.'

16 See infra, 7.6.

17 *Second Report of the Committee on Criminal Procedure in Scotland* (1957), Cmnd. 6218, para 52.18.

18 By virtue of section 4A of the Criminal Procedure (Insanity and Unfitness to Plead) Act 1991, amending The Criminal Procedure (Insanity) Act 1964.

on their part. On the other hand, if the result is positive, the court should be free to make an order detaining the defendant at least until fitness has been regained, thereby obviating the risk of defendants feigning unfitness as a way of escaping the law's clutches. However, since a finding that the facts can be proved is not a conviction, it is submitted that detention in these circumstances should be governed by the principle of involuntary civil commitment, i.e., it should be ordered if and only if there is evidence that the defendant is a danger to himself or others.[19]

## 3. THE LEGAL TEST

When insanity is raised as a preliminary issue, the question is whether the accused is fit to stand trial, the underlying principle being that, if he is found to be unfit, the trial should be halted on the grounds that, as one of its *dramatis personae,* his involvement is essential to the proper conduct of the proceedings. In other words, the issue is not merely that it would be unfair to the defendant to continue with the trial once he has been found unfit to plead, or that it would be unsafe to convict someone who cannot plead to the indictment, but rather that it is in the nature of a criminal trial that the defendant is capable of playing a rational part in the proceedings. This is clear from the leading case of *R. v. Pritchard* where the jury were told to consider:

> First, whether the prisoner is mute of malice or not;[20] secondly, whether he can plead to the indictment or not; thirdly, whether he is of sufficient intellect to comprehend the course of

19 Infra, 7.6.

20 This phrase harks back to one of the key problems faced by the criminal courts in medieval and Tudor times: that of the defendant who refused to plead 'guilty' or 'not guilty' to the charge against him. A defendant who refused to plead could not be convicted or executed, nor could his property be forfeited by the Crown. Accordingly, the courts had to decide whether he was mute of malice or by visitation of God. If the jury found that he was mute by visitation of God, a plea of 'not guilty' was entered and the trial went ahead, usually with a relative of the mute person communicating the significance of the proceedings to him in makeshift sign-language. An example of this procedure can be seen in *R v. Steel* [1787] 2 Leach 507, where, notwithstanding a finding that she was mute by visitation of God, the defendant was convicted of larceny and sentenced to seven years transportation; although this case is not typical of the period in which it was decided, as deaf mutes began to be found unfit to plead from the 1750's onwards: Walker, op. cit., p. 222. Alternatively, if the accused was found to be

> proceedings on the trial, so as to make a proper defence—to know that he might challenge any of you to whom he might object—and to comprehend the details of the evidence, which in a case of this nature must constitute a minute investigation. Upon this issue, therefore, if you think there is no certain mode of communicating the details of the trial to the prisoner, so that he can clearly understand them, and be able properly to make his defence to the charge; you ought to find that he is not of sane mind. It is not enough that he may have a general capacity of communicating on ordinary matters.[21]

Nor is this a distinction without a difference. For even if it is clear that the defendant would be convicted if he were fit to stand trial, the fact remains that he can neither be tried nor convicted without being fit to plead. In a word, lack of fitness to participate in the proceedings is a fundamental and insuperable obstacle to a properly conducted common-law criminal trial.[22]

The word 'insane' as used in section 2 of the Criminal Lunatics Act 1800 is not to be confined to its psychiatric meaning or the meaning given to it under the traditional interpretation of the M'Naghten Rules. It includes any condition, whether mental or physical, which prevents an accused from following the proceedings

mute of malice, he was subjected to the *peine forte et dure* (which involved tying each of his limbs to separate stakes situated in the four corners of a punishment cell and pressing him to death with a heavy weight) unless and until he uttered the sacred formula. The prize for remaining mute was that his property would not be forfeit and his family would be saved from penury: Langbein, *Torture and the Law of Proof* (Chicago, 1977), pp. 74-7. Under section 80 of the Criminal Justice Act 1928 the judge alone determines the nature of a defendant's muteness.

21 [1836] 7 C&P 303 at 304. Attempts to fashion a test of unfitness to plead go back at least to Hale, who wrote that 'If a man . . . commits a capital offence, and before his arraignment . . . becomes absolutely mad, he ought to be remitted to prison until that incapacity be removed; the reason is, because he cannot advisedly plead to the indictment . . .': *1 PC*, ch. 4. But Walker has shown that it was not until the middle of the eighteenth century that an insane prisoner had any real chance of being found unfit for trial: op. cit.

22 *The State (Coughlan) v. The Minister for Justice and Another* [1968] ILTR 177 at 185 (SC); per O'Daly CJ. Reviewing the question of unfitness in summary proceedings, Walsh J added, *obiter,* that a finding of unfitness by a District Justice in that context meant 'that he cannot proceed with the hearing of the matter while the accused is in that condition and if he did so in a case where the evidence was such that no other reasonable view was open save that the accused was unfit to plead the proceedings would be quashed': ibid., at 190. See also Duff, op. cit., chs. 1 (3) and 4 (6).

in the sense laid down in *Pritchard*.[23] Thus in the modern Scottish case of *H.M. Advocate v. Wilson*,[24] Lord Wark, relying on the nineteenth century authority of *Jean Campbell*,[25] left the plea in bar to the jury in respect of a deaf mute, with the direction that a defendant was unfit to plead if he was:

> unable either from mental . . . or physical defect, or a combination of these, to tell his counsel what his defence is and instruct him so that he can appear and defend him; or if, again, his condition of mind and body is such that he does not understand the proceedings . . . and cannot intelligibly follow [them].[26]

However, defendants suffering from hysterical amnesia with respect to the events that form the basis of the prosecution case but who are otherwise normal are not insane within the meaning of section 2. The question is whether the accused can follow the proceedings not whether he can remember the incident alleged against him. In *Russell v. H.M. Advocate*[27] the defendant sought to rely on hysterical amnesia with respect to a series of frauds that she was alleged to have committed some years earlier. Lord Sorn rejected her plea in bar of trial on the grounds that there was no doubt that she could understand the charges, follow the proceedings and instruct counsel notwithstanding that she may not have been able to remember the incident. This view was upheld on appeal to the Criminal Appeal Court and followed by the Court of Appeal in England, in *R. v. Padola*.[28] It is open to the criticism that someone who cannot remember the incident might be precluded from instructing counsel as to evidence of accident or alibi. Yet it seems preferable to allowing

23 'Stated in general terms the test to be applied is, has the prisoner sufficient intellect to comprehend the course of the proceedings of the trial, so as to make a proper defence, to challenge a juror to whom he may wish to object, and to understand the details of the evidence': [1968] ILTR 177 at 185 (SC); per O'Daly CJ.
24 [1942] JC 75.
25 [1817] Hume i. 45.
26 1942 JC at 79. Indeed Pritchard was himself a deaf mute who had been indicted for bestiality. And section 2 had earlier been applied to a deaf mute indicted for beheading her 'illegitimate' child in *R v. Dyson* [1831] 7 C&P 305; 1 Lew 64. The application of section 2 to deaf mutes was also upheld in the modern English case of *R v. Governor of Stafford Prison* [1909] 2 KB 1.
27 1946 JC 37.
28 [1960] 1 QB 325.

evidence of amnesia to support a plea in bar of trial to the extent that this arrangement would jeopardise the prosecution of offences where the defendant's loss of memory was caused by drunkenness or concussion resulting from dangerous or reckless driving.

## 4. FITNESS IN PRACTICE

The practical significance of the legal test of unfitness for trial should not however be exaggerated. Research evidence shows that, at best, the legal criteria of unfitness are not systematically applied; and, at worst, are ignored altogether. In a recent survey of 229 findings of unfitness in England and Wales, it was found that the psychiatric reports on which assessment was based almost never invoked all five of the criteria laid down in *Pritchard*:[29] viz., the ability 1) to plead to the indictment, 2) to understand the course of the proceedings, 3) to instruct counsel, 4) to challenge jurors and 5) to understand the evidence. Generally speaking, assessment seemed to turn on the accused's ability to instruct counsel and follow the proceedings; with the remaining criteria being relied on in a minority of cases.[30]

This approach to the formally recognized criteria of unfitness would not matter if, as many forensic psychiatrists appear to assume,[31] the latter were interchangeable, individually sufficient conditions or measures of fitness for trial. But this assumption seems doubtful. A schizophrenic defendant who insanely believes that the legal profession is part of a conspiracy to destroy him may well be capable of following the proceedings and understanding the evidence against him, but he may not be in a position to advise his lawyers in his best interests; indeed he may shun legal representation altogether.[32] Similarly, a defendant who insanely believes that God will protect him from legal punishment may be perfectly fit to plead to the indictment and advise his lawyers, but in what sense can

29 Supra, 7.3.

30 Mackay, 'The Decline of Disability in Relation to the Trial' (1991) *Crim. LR* 87 at 92; see also Grubin, 'Unfit to Plead in England and Wales 1976-86: A Survey' (1991) *158 BJ Psychiat* 277.

31 See Mackay, op. cit.

32 See *People v. Hayes*, *Irish Times*, 1 December 1967, where the defendant, who was not legally represented and conducted his own defence, was acquitted of murdering his wife on the grounds that he insanely believed that she may have been involved with a group of local solicitors in a conspiracy against him.

someone who believes in divine intervention in the criminal process be said to understand the proceedings? These examples suggest that the *Pritchard* criteria are better seen as a set of cumulative indicia of a defendant's fitness for trial; and that a purely selective approach to them is apt to subvert the fundamental principle they are designed to secure: namely, that no one should be tried on a criminal charge unless he is capable of rational participation at *all* levels of the trial process.[33]

While there is some authority for the proposition that the court can refuse to put the issue of fitness to plead to the jury on the grounds that there is insufficient evidence to support it,[34] it does not appear that there is any equivalent of the rule in *Din*,[35] whereby the court is obliged to ensure that the prosecution has probed the soundness of the medical evidence relating to the plea of insanity as a defence.

In practice this sometimes means that a finding of unfitness to plead depends on whether the prison medical authorities are prepared to testify that the accused is certifiably insane, i.e., suffering from a psychosis such that he is a danger to himself or others or has refused treatment necessary for his condition. In other words, if it is clear that the accused is certifiably insane, the courts sometimes act on the *assumption* that he is also unfit to plead, notwithstanding the fact that the psychiatric report on which the assessment of unfitness was based may have made no reference to *any* of the criteria formally recognized in *Pritchard*.[36]

Nor is the partial eclipse of the legal test of unfitness for trial surprising. The traditional criterion of unfitness, like the traditional test of legal insanity *simpliciter*, was based on the assumption that an accused might be severely mentally deranged with respect to one matter and yet perfectly sane with respect to everything else; whereas the modern tendency is to view insanity as a pervasive disorder affecting the accused's reasoning powers *tout court*. As we saw in earlier chapters, the tension between the traditional and modern

33 The distinction between fitness to plead and fitness to participate was recently relied on by the defence, but rejected by the (Special Criminal) Court, in the *Murray* case—infra, 7.5. I am grateful to Dr James Behan, the psychiatrist who testified for the defence, for this information.

34 *Russell v. H M Advocate* 1946 SC (J) 37.

35 Supra, ch. 5.4.

36 I am grateful to the Director of Public Prosecutions for this information. It has recently been estimated that this is true of approximately 30 per cent. of unfitness findings in England and Wales: Mackay, op. cit.

conceptions lies at the heart of the ongoing debate about the proper scope of the defence of insanity; and will be seen to dramatic effect in the discussion of the civilian experience of the defence in chapter 9. Like the broadening of the criterion of insanity to include the inability to make sound judgements on the basis of the relevant available evidence, or the relaxation of the requirement that there must be a strict causal link between the accused's mental disorder and his act, the tendency to equate the notion of fitness for trial with a medical diagnosis that the accused is certifiably insane reflects the growing ascendancy of the hypothesis that serious mental disorder is an indivisible condition affecting the entire personality.

Moreover, findings of unfitness for trial are now relatively rare; since the 1950s the total annual number of persons found unfit or acquitted on the grounds of insanity has seldom exceeded five.[37] Indeed, the global average has declined to less than two cases per year since the mid-1970s. Given that there has been a huge increase in the number of indictable offences brought to trial since the 1950s,[38] the numbers in each category are much smaller than you would expect on statistical grounds. In the case of findings of unfitness, this is most probably at least in part the result of the development of tranquillisers in the treatment of schizophrenia in the early 1950s. Broadly speaking, the new drug treatment significantly reduced the level of thought and communication disorder characteristic of schizophrenia, thereby eliminating, or at least suppressing, the symptoms traditionally associated with a diagnosis of certifiable insanity and/or a finding of unfitness to plead.[39]

Another likely reason for the low frequency of unfitness findings is the fact that, irrespective of the crime charged, they lead to automatic indeterminate detention in the Central Mental Hospital[40]—which must be a clear disincentive for defence counsel who might otherwise raise the issue of fitness. The obvious solution to this problem is for parliament to follow the English example of increasing the powers of disposal available to trial judges in unfitness cases.[41] Once the threat of indefinite psychiatric detention is removed it seems safe to assume that the incidence of unfitness pleas

37 See the epilogue.

38 Ibid.

39 I am grateful to the Director of the Central Mental Hospital, Dr Charles Smith, for drawing this possibility to my attention. Walker has noted a similar trend in the English figures for the same period: op. cit., p. 233.

40 See infra, 7.6.

41 See infra n. 69.

is likely to rise. Other reasons for the low number of unfitness (and insanity) pleas are discussed in the epilogue.

## 5. THE *MURRAY* CASE

Findings of unfitness for trial do however still occur. In *Murray*[42] the trial of a man accused of armed robbery was adjourned for a *second* time as a result of a finding of unfitness to plead. On the first occasion the (Special Criminal) court heard medical evidence that the accused was a psychotic—who suffered from the delusion that his food was being tampered with and whose delusion worsened the nearer he got to Dublin from his home in Derry—and remanded him in custody for further medical treatment. The second adjournment occurred nine months later on foot of similar evidence, although on this occasion the trial was postponed for three months.[43]

The case is unusual as the trial of persons found unfit to plead in practice only takes place if there is a suspicion that the symptoms of unfitness were feigned[44] and because, in the nature of things, the findings of unfitness were made by the court—rather than a jury, as required by the Act of 1800.[45] It does however illustrate the modern tendency of the courts to equate evidence of certifiable insanity with unfitness to plead as the report contains no reference to the classic legal test of unfitness as laid down in *Pritchard*.[46] Indeed the second adjournment—which, like the first, was sought by the *prosecution*—appears to have been granted without going into the question of whether the medical evidence disclosed an inability to follow the proceedings or advise counsel for the defence —thereby tending to confirm the hypothesis, suggested earlier, that there is no specific rule in Irish law requiring the court to satisfy itself as to the relevance of the medical evidence to the issue of unfitness for trial.

The case also raises doubts about the status of the rule in *Padola*[47] in Irish law. For if the courts are prepared to accept that a defendant

42 *Irish Times*, 28 June 1991.
43 The defendant was finally convicted as charged on the 4th December 1992; *Irish Times*, 5 December 1992. See supra, n. 33.
44 I grateful to the Director of Public Prosecutions for this information.
45 Supra 7.1.
46 Supra 7.3.
47 [1960] 1 QB 325.

is unfit to be tried for armed robbery on the grounds that he suffers from the delusion that the prison authorities are interfering with his food!—and in the absence of any other evidence of inability to follow or participate in the proceedings, it is not obvious why someone who cannot remember anything about the incident alleged against him, and who therefore 'cannot advisedly plead to the indictment',[48] should be precluded from raising the issue of unfitness, at least in cases where the amnesia was not brought on by voluntary intoxication or negligent driving on his part. An exception entitling defendants of this type to a finding of unfitness would seem to be required by the general principle underlying the rule in *Pritchard*:[49] namely, that a defendant to a criminal charge is entitled to a fair trial. If the courts are worried about defendants feigning unfitness,[50] the obvious solution is to pay more rather than less attention to the classic legal criteria of unfitness, and certainly more than the Special Criminal Court appears to have given them in *Murray*.[51]

It is submitted that a variant of the rule in *Din*[52] obliging the prosecution to probe the soundness of medical evidence, whether of psychosis or amnesia, specifically in the light of these criteria would greatly assist the courts in this regard. There may well be a case for ceding the question of fitness for trial to a panel of medical experts appointed by the court, as has been suggested by some commentators,[53] but, in view of the drastic consequences of a finding of unfitness for defendants,[54] it seems inappropriate that this matter should in effect be settled by doctors, whether testifying for the defence or the prosecution. As the discussion of the concept of mental disease illustrates,[55] common-law courts have traditionally resisted the equation of the legal with the medical criteria of insanity, largely as a result of an abiding commitment to the fundamental principles of criminal responsibility, and it would be ironic if the courts were unwittingly to renege on that commitment by mismanaging a preliminary procedure designed to ensure that the issue of responsibility is properly considered when a defendant is threatened with virtual indeterminate detention in a criminal lunatic asylum.

48 The phrase is taken from Hale's definition of unfitness for trial: supra, 7.3.
49 [1836] 7 C&P 303.
50 A worry prevalent even in Hale's time: *1 PC* ch. 4.
51 *Irish Times,* 28 June 1991.
52 [1962] 42 Cr App Rep 116.
53 For example, Walker, op. cit., p. 121.
54 Infra, 7.6.
55 Supra, ch. 4.

The proposed solution to this difficulty would certainly conflict with the statement in *Padola*[56] that the burden of proof should not be regarded as a live issue where evidence of unfitness is not being challenged by the prosecution. However, apart from the fact that that statement was *obiter*, the decision in *Padola* has no more than persuasive authority in Irish law and, it is submitted, should not be regarded as an impediment to the reforms being argued for here.[57]

## 6. DISPOSITION AND DETENTION

The disposition and detention of persons found unfit to plead is governed by section 2 of the Criminal Lunatics Act 1800.[58] Unlike section 1[59] which provides that, where a defendant has been acquitted on the grounds of insanity, 'the court . . . *shall* order such person to be kept in strict custody . . . until His Majesty's pleasure shall be known', section 2 merely provides that '*it shall be lawful*' for the court to order the detention of persons found unfit to plead 'until his Majesty's pleasure shall be known.'[60] The marginal note to section 2 notwithstanding,[61] this suggests that judges are not obliged to order the detention of persons found unfit to plead; indeed the language of the section implies that they have a residual discretion not to make a committal order where it would be unnecessary or inappropriate to do so. As it happens, section 2 has always been interpreted, possibly in the light of the marginal note, as requiring mandatory committal,[62]

56 [1960] 1 QB 325.

57 In a recent case before the Central Criminal Court defence counsel sought an adjournment on the grounds that his client was unfit to plead as a result of the consumption of an illicit prison distillation ("hooch"), probably in the prison toilets after breakfast and prior to leaving to attend his trial for rape. Carney J immediately ordered an inquiry before the jury was sworn and adjourned the case for one month following its findings. The case is interesting as there was no suggestion that the accused's alleged unfitness arose from any of the causes normally associated with a plea of unfitness and because the trial judge took it upon himself to decide the issue (rather than leaving it to the jury): *Irish Times*, 5 May 1992.

58 As adapted by the Lunatics (Ireland) Act 1821; see 7.1, supra.

59 And s. 2 (2) of the Trial of Lunatics Act 1883, which replaced it; see appendix 2.

60 Italics added. The same phrase is used in the Lunacy (Ireland) Act 1821.

61 This runs as follows: 'If any person indicted for any offence, shall upon arraignment or trial be found to be insane, &c, the court shall order him to be kept in custody till his Majesty's pleasure be known.'

62 See White, 'The Criminal Procedure (Insanity and Unfitness to Plead) Act' (1992) *Crim. LR* 4; Prevezer, 'Fitness to Plead and the Criminal Lunatics Act 1800', (1958) *Crim L R* 144 at 146.

and in practice this means that persons found unfit to plead are automatically detained in the Central Mental Hospital until the medical authorities there decide that fitness has been regained or that they are well enough to be sent to a less secure mental facility. Thus approximately one third of the total of about eighty patients detained in the Central Mental Hospital at any given time have been found unfit to plead.[63]

The dangers inherent in this arrangement have recently been highlighted by the Director of the Central Mental Hospital, Dr Charles Smith.[64] According to Dr Smith, persons found unfit to plead have traditionally been the most disadvantaged group of patients housed in the Central Mental Hospital, both because they have not been tried and because of a tendency to forget about them precisely because they have not been tried.[65] These patients gradually 'merged into the chronic hospital environment and were unable to break out of that mould', with the result that 'the hospital tended to confirm [the original finding of unfitness] to the courts at intervals and not to seek the patient's transfer.'

In the doctor's view, this has resulted in some dramatic cases of injustice, sometimes involving periods of detention in excess of twenty years; although he claimed that the hospital now has a policy of seeking the withdrawal of charges against unfitness to plead patients thought to be suitable for transfer to less secure facilities. Apparently this tactic has been used successfully on a number of occasions in recent years. In one case mentioned by Dr Smith, a man had a 21-year-old charge of murdering his mother withdrawn in 1990 and was then transferred to St Patrick's hospital. In another charges were withdrawn against two patients accused of sexual offences who had spent seven years at the hospital. Be that as it may, Dr Smith's remarks underline the inadequacy of the arrangements governing the disposition and detention of persons found unfit to plead.[66]

63 According to the Director of the Central Mental Hospital, as reported in the *Sunday Tribune*, 4 November 1990.

64 Ibid.

65 This accords with the findings of the Royal Commission on Capital Punishment, which was told that 'persons who have been found insane on arraignment and ordered to be detained during H.M. pleasure sometimes exhibit a strong sense of grievance on the ground that they have not been proved to have committed any crime and ought not therefore to be detained in an institution for 'criminal lunatics': *Report (1949-53)*, Cmd. 8932, p. 78.

66 The improved situation of persons found unfit for trial described by Dr Smith also appears to obtain in England and Wales. In a recent study carried out by Grubin, op. cit., it was found that the proportion of defendants found unfit who

Two changes seem to be required in order to meet the problem of the low visibility of unfitness to plead patients identified by Dr Smith. First, the courts should be given the power to order the immediate release, with or without conditions, of persons found unfit to plead where the evidence discloses that they do not need to be detained in the public interest.[67] A recommendation to this effect was included in the Henchy Report,[68] in the form of section 25 (4) of the attached Draft Criminal Justice (Mental Health) Bill 1978.[69] Given that this recommendation was made after a thorough investigation of conditions at the Central Mental Hospital, it is difficult to understand why the government has not acted on it. If the government continues to drag its feet on the matter, it is submitted that the courts should consider re-activating the residual discretion that appears to be vested in them by virtue of section 2 of the Criminal Lunatics Act 1800, on the assumption that it has not fallen into complete desuetude.

were subsequently remitted for trial rose steadily from 15 per cent in 1975 to 60 percent in 1988; see also Grubin, 'Regaining Fitness: Patients Found Unfit to Plead Who Return for Trial' (1991) *2 J Foren Psychiat* 140.

67 Some United States jurisdictions, for example, provide for the treatment of persons found unfit to plead on an outpatient basis: see generally Kaplan, 'The Mad and the Bad: An Inquiry into the Disposition of the Criminally Insane' (1977) *2 J Med and Phil* 244-304; Bernan et al. (eds.) *Mentally Ill Offenders and the Criminal Justice System: Issues in Forensic Services,* (New York, 1979); Burt, 'Of Mad Dogs and Scientists: The Perils of the 'Criminal-Insane'' (1977) *123 U Pen L Rev* 258-96.

68 Third Interim Report of the Interdepartmental Committee on Mentally Ill and Maladjusted Persons. *Treatment and Care of Persons Suffering from Mental Disorder Who Appear before the Courts on Criminal Charges* (Dublin, 1978), p. 45 (hereinafter the *Report*).

69 A similar recommendation was included in the *Report of the Committee on Mentally Abnormal Offenders* (The Butler Report), (1975), Cmnd. 6244, paras. 10.27-10.29. The Law Reform Commission of Canada has also recommended that the disposition of accused persons found unfit to plead should be treated as a judicial rather than an administrative matter, and that the present regime of automatic indeterminate detention should be replaced by a wide range of alternatives. These include an order for release subject to recall for trial if fitness is regained, an order for treatment as an out-patient, and an order for mandatory hospitalization until the accused has regained his fitness or until six months has elapsed: *Mental Disorder in the Criminal Process* (1976), pp. 16-9. In England and Wales the matter is now governed by The Criminal Procedure (Insanity and Fitness to Plead) Act 1991, which provides that, in cases where the sentence is fixed by law—in effect, murder cases—the court must make a hospital order without limit of time; but that in all other cases *it has a choice between* 1) a hospital order with or without limit of time, 2) an order of absolute discharge, 3) a supervision and training order under the 1991 Act, or 4) a guardianship order under the Mental Health Act 1983.

Alternatively, it is arguable that the power to order the detention of persons found unfit to plead, rather than being left to the discretion of trial judges, should be made subject to the condition that detention is required in the public interest. An arrangement of this kind would help to ensure that unfit defendants like Glenn Pearson, who are neither mentally ill nor dangerous, are not compulsorily hospitalized. Pearson was a thirty-three-years-old deaf mute of limited intelligence who was cared for satisfactorily by his parents with whom he lived. He was found unfit to plead to a charge of (minor) burglary and detained in a hospital for the mentally handicapped notwithstanding the fact that he was subsequently discharged (on the recommendation of a Mental Health Review Tribunal) at the earliest opportunity on the obvious ground that the degree of his mental impairment was not sufficient to justify his compulsory detention in hospital and would not have allowed his civil commitment to hospital in the first place.[70] Glenn Pearson's was an English case, but to the extent that trial judges cannot be trusted to ensure that defendants of his type are not compulsorily hospitalised, there would seem to be good grounds for legislation requiring them to do so. It is submitted that the relevant legislative provision should confine compulsory hospitalization to defendants found unfit to plead to serious crimes of violence who are also eligible for civil commitment.[71]

A natural corollary of these proposals is that the courts should have the power to select—on the advice of the psychiatrist(s) engaged to investigate the question of fitness—the kind of psychiatric facility or treatment (not excluding outpatient community care) best suited to a particular defendant's condition, as this would help to solve the problem of the committal of unfit defendants not thought to pose a danger to themselves and others to the high-security setting of the Central Mental Hospital. As this power is implicit in the Henchy Committee's recommendation that there should be a range of 'designated centres' for the reception and treatment of persons found unfit to plead,[72] it is worth noting that it is perfectly consistent with the Supreme Court's decision in *Gallagher.*[73] That case

70 See Emmins, 'Unfitness to Plead: Some Thoughts Prompted by *Glenn Pearson's Case*' (1986) *Crim. LR* 604; Bacon, 'Unnecessary Detention: The Criminal Procedure (Insanity) Act' (1989) *86 Law Society's Gazette* 19 (19 April).

71 See White, 'The Criminal Procedure (Insanity and Fitness to Plead) Act' (1992) *Crim. LR* 4 at 5.

72 *Report*, p. 17.

decided that the courts (as opposed to the executive) have no role in deciding whether a person acquitted on the grounds of insanity should be detained or whether his detention should be continued, but said nothing about the *kind* of detention appropriate in such cases or, *a fortiori*, in cases where the finding is one of unfitness rather than insanity.[74]

Second, the Henchy Committee's recommendation that a Review Body should be established to monitor all aspects of the detention of persons in the Central Mental Hospital and other 'designated centres' should be implemented.[75] The chief medical officers of these facilities should then be required by law to furnish the Review Body with details of the conditions of detention and mental state of every person entrusted to their care, and thereafter to update the Review Body on these matters at regular intervals. Persons detained as a result of a finding of unfitness to plead and subsequent recommendation of the Review Body should have a right to apply and, at intervals of not less than six months, to re-apply to the Review Body for a review of their detention. The Henchy Committee recommended that the interval between review applications should be one year,[76] but it is submitted that the shorter period would be more appropriate in view of what was described above as the relatively low visibility of unfit to plead patients.

These recommendations are consistent with the fact that it is now generally recognized that 'with proper medication and management, most disordered defendants can be restored to competence within six to eight weeks';[77] and with the broadly-based finding that hospitals for the criminally insane are generally ill-equipped for therapeutic purposes and unable to provide the type of treatment necessary for short-term fitness to plead patients.[78] As these hospitals

73 [1991] ILRM 339; supra, ch. 6.3.

74 Prior to the enactment of the Criminal Procedure (Insanity and Fitness to Plead) Act 1991, a person found unfit to plead in England and Wales was sent, by order of the court, to a hospital specified by the Home Secretary, where he could 'be detained without limitation of time, the power to discharge him being exercisable only with the Home Secretary's consent': Smith and Hogan, op. cit., p. 195; Criminal Procedure (Insanity) Act 1964, s. 5 (1) (c) and Sch. 1; Mental Health Act 1983, ss. 23 and 41 (as amended by the Mental Health (Amendment) Act 1982. The changes wrought by the 1991 Act are described supra at n. 69.

75 *Report*, pp. 39-43.

76 *Report*, p. 41; these remarks also apply to detainees who have been acquitted on the grounds of insanity.

77 Morse, 'Mentally Disordered Offenders' *International Encyclopedia of Criminal Justice* (New York, 1983), 1046 at 1048.

78 Kaplan, op. cit.

are usually administered by justice or prisons departments rather than departments of health,[79] the accent is firmly on security rather than treatment. Thus in the United States the Supreme Court has held, in *Jackson v. Indiana*,[80] that persons found unfit to plead may only be detained for a reasonable period of time, i.e, for the period necessary for an appropriate course of treatment, and that if competence is not restored within a reasonable period either release or civil commitment was required.

Incidentally, the United States experience in this regard is particularly instructive as there is some evidence that unfit to plead patients tend to be detained longer than the few months necessary for successful treatment notwithstanding the Supreme Court's ruling in *Jackson v. Indiana*. Ironically, this seems to happen, and to be tolerated by the courts, precisely because hospitals for the criminally insane are not geared up for therapeutic purposes and, therefore, can be expected to take longer to organise the appropriate treatment than ordinary mental hospitals![81]

Finally, it is clear from the wording of section 2 of the Criminal Lunatics Act 1800 that a court may order that a person 'be kept in strict custody' if and only if he has been indicted 'and shall upon arraignment be found to be [unfit to plead]'. Moreover, a person may not be transferred from Garda custody to the Central Mental Hospital unless he has been charged with an indictable offence. In practice this appears to mean that a court has no power to order the detention in the Central Mental Hospital of persons who have been arrested on suspicion of having committed a serious offence but who have not yet been charged in respect of it.

This was confirmed in a recent case[82] where a man arrested on suspicion of murder and subsequently diagnosed as certifiably insane before the completion of Garda investigations, was committed to an ordinary psychiatric hospital rather than the more secure Central Mental Hospital notwithstanding the objections of the relevant hospital authorities to the effect that the receiving institution was insufficiently secure to accommodate him. Provision for the direct

79 Section 38 of the Health Act 1970 provided that the The Central Mental Hospital at Dundrum would henceforth be administered by the Eastern Health Board under the aegis of the Department of Health. It had been administered by the Department of Justice since the foundation of the state. Before that it was under the control of the lord-lieutenant's office: Robins, op. cit., p. 151.

80 [1972] 406 US 715.

81 Morse, op. cit.

82 *Irish Times*, 30 January 1992.

transfer of persons of this kind from Garda custody to the Central Mental Hospital was made in the Mental Health Act 1981, but as no ministerial order had ever been signed to bring this measure into force, it was decided, apparently on the advice of the Director of Public Prosecutions, that the suspect should be detained in an ordinary psychiatric facility pending the completion of Garda inquiries and the possible preferment of criminal charges. As the Central Mental Hospital is a *criminal* lunatic asylum,[83] it is submitted that the Director's advice was correct.

It does however have worrying implications. If a suspect is charged and acquitted on the grounds of insanity and subsequently committed to the Central Mental Hospital, he can apply to the government to have his detention reviewed in the event that he recovers his sanity either spontaneously or as a result of treatment. As we saw in chapter 6, the fact that an insanity acquittee has been restored to mental health is no guarantee that he will be released from custody; although, as the *Gallagher* and *Ellis* cases illustrate, it at least ensures that the medical authorities at the Central Mental Hospital will support his application for release and, consequently, that any subsequent decision on the part of the government to continue his detention is difficult to defend on therapeutic grounds. In other words, the policy of activism that has been pursued by the Hospital in recent years has exposed the essentially political character of the decision to continue the detention of insanity acquittees who have been given a clean bill of health by the psychiatric authorities at the Central Mental Hospital.

In contrast, if a suspect is not charged, he runs the risk of being shunted from one mental institution to another with the result that his detention in effect becomes a kind of custodial limbo without the opportunity of review. Indeed, this may well be happening in the instant case. Having been committed to St Brendan's, an ordinary psychiatric hospital, in January 1992, as a person of unsound mind, the suspect was subsequently transferred to the Central Mental Hospital, under section 208 of the Mental Treatment Act 1945, for treatment and security reasons. He responded well to treatment there and was apparently contemplating a legal challenge to his continued detention on the grounds that the doctors at the Hospital were satisfied that he was no longer psychotic. Yet before any such challenge could be mounted, he was returned to St Brendan's as a person of unsound mind in January *1993* on the grounds that, the

83 Supra, ch. 6.4.

opinion of the doctors who had been treating him for a year at the Central Mental Hospital to the effect that he was no longer psychotic notwithstanding, the episodic nature of the illness from which he had been suffering rendered him a security risk![84]

In short, the decision not to charge him has effectively precluded his recourse to the review procedures associated with detention in the Central Mental Hospital, thereby enabling the government to continue his detention in another psychiatric facility, by means of a person of unsound mind order under the Mental Treatment Act 1945. Indeed, it has been suggested that the decision not to charge him represents an attempt by the prosecuting authorities to offset the new willingness on the part of the Central Mental Hospital to encourage (and support) release applications from detainees who have regained their sanity.[85]

Be that as it may, it is submitted that a suspect should generally be charged if there is clear expert evidence that he is medically sane (and, it goes without saying, if there is sufficient incriminating evidence against him to support a charge). In cases where there is a danger that someone who has been acquitted on the grounds of insanity and who is now sane may suffer a relapse such that he would be a security risk if released, the government can always continue his detention by invoking the *Gallagher* precedent. In other words, even in the absence of legislation dealing with the matter, this concern can easily be met without resorting to the ugly expedient of deliberately not charging suspects who were plainly mentally ill when they killed or injured their victims in order to ensure that they do not get the benefit of the insanity defence and, consequently, the opportunity to apply for early release in the event that they make a speedy recovery.

84 *Irish Times*, 11 January 1993.
85 *Irish Times*, 11 January 1993.

# [8]

# Diminished Responsibility

## 1. GENERALLY

The insanity defence has traditionally been concerned with the accused's minimal capacity to act rationally: in general terms, the accused is entitled to the defence if he was suffering from a pathological condition that prevented him from knowing what he was doing or that his actions were wrong. In other words, the threshold of legal insanity in the common-law tradition is defined in terms of perception and basic moral literacy, with the result that the courts have found it virtually impossible to give effect to evidence of illness or disorder that did not undermine the individual's ability to perceive reality or grasp the rudimentary distinction between right and wrong.

Broadly speaking, there have been two more or less successful attempts to solve this problem. As we saw in chapter 2, the first involves recasting the definition of insanity in epistemological terms, as the inability to relate to the world according to the ordinary laws of logic and evidential reasoning. The principal advantage of this solution is that it effectively closes the gap between the legal and psychiatric conceptions of insanity, thereby bringing those forms of serious mental disorder that had hitherto been excluded (by the traditional interpretation of the M'Naghten Rules) within the ambit of the insanity defence. Its main disadvantage is that it shackles the disposition and treatment of the seriously mentally disordered defendant to the regime of automatic indeterminate detention associated with the insanity defence,[1] and appears to exclude the non-psychotic disorders from its purview.[2]

1 See chapter 6.2.

2 See chs. 2 and 3; the plea of volitional insanity, discussed in chapter 3, is also a solution to the problem posed by the traditional interpretation of the M'Naghten Rules.

The second solution involves the creation of an entirely new defence of diminished responsibility designed to cater for the mentally disordered killer who does not qualify for the insanity defence. The defence is typically confined to murder and, where successful, results in a conviction for manslaughter rather than a complete acquittal. Its main advantage is that it enables the court of trial to take account of evidence of mental disorder without disturbing the hornet's nest of the classical criterion of insanity and without prejudice to its decision as to disposition and treatment. The obvious disadvantage of the plea is that it is tied to the crime of murder, and creates problems of definition and limitation no less vexing than those besetting the insanity defence.[3]

Although it is commonly referred to as *the* defence of diminished responsibility, at least three different models of the plea can be identified: the minimalist, maximalist and *mens rea* models, respectively. The minimalist model, which has its origins in Scots law, defines diminished responsibility as a kind of quasi-insanity. The maximalist model, which is based on section 2 of the English Homicide Act 1957, takes the broader view that diminished responsibility consists of any mental abnormality that substantially impairs a defendant's responsibility for his actions, irrespective of whether or not it approximates to legal insanity. The *mens rea* model, which was developed by the California Supreme Court, identifies diminished responsibility with the erosion through mental illness of the defendant's capacity to entertain the requisite malice aforethought for murder. In what follows each of these models is considered in turn, with a view to exploring the case for adapting it to Irish conditions.

## 2. SCOTS LAW: THE MINIMALIST APPROACH

The origins of the defence of diminished responsibility in Scots law go back to the mid-eighteenth century. The earliest cases show that it began as a plea in mitigation,[4] that it was originally based on the principle that some forms 'of mental weakness should be dealt with by way of a conviction accompanied by a recommendation to mercy',[5] and that it applied to non-capital as well as capital offences.[6]

3 See infra, 8.2-3.
4 Keith, 'Some Observations on Diminished Responsibility' (1959) *JR* 109 at 110.
5 Gordon, op. cit., p. 386.
6 See the cases cited by Lord Justice-General Normand in *Kirkwood v. H.M. Advocate* [1939] JC 36.

A good example of the early operation of the plea is *Bonthorn,*[7] a case of assault by a smuggler on a revenue official, where the jury found that 'the intellects of the pannel are most remarkably weak, irregular and confused, and therefore recommend him to the mercy of the Court'. The material difference in capital cases was that the jury emphasised such mental weakness as would 'recommend the pannel to the Royal mercy.'[8]

Diminished responsibility as a defence *stricto sensu* began in 1867 with the decision in *Dingwall.*[9] The defendant, a member of the Scottish aristocracy and an alcoholic, fatally stabbed his wife with a carving knife because she had hidden his whiskey and his money after he came home from a drinking spree on Hogmanay. There was evidence that the defendant had suffered 'a stroke of the sun in India', where he had served with the Indian Army, that he had suffered repeated attacks of epilepsy and *delirium tremens;* and, in the form of her dying declaration, that he had always been kind to his wife when sober. But there was no evidence of 'furiosity' or insane delusions. He was acquitted of murder but convicted of culpable homicide after a strong direction by Lord Deas. His Lordship, who according to Lord Keith was apt to show leniency to gentlemen and handsome women,[10] told the jury that they should consider the following circumstances:

> 1st, the unpremeditated and sudden nature of the attack; 2nd, the prisoner's habitual kindness to his wife, of which there could be no doubt, when drink did not interfere; 3rd, there was only one stab or blow; this, while not perhaps like what an insane man would have done, was favourable for the prisoner in other respects; 4th, the prisoner appeared not only to have been peculiar in his mental constitution, but to have had his mind weakened by successive attacks of disease. It seemed highly probable that he had had a stroke of the sun in India, and that his subsequent fits were of an epileptic nature. There could be no doubt that he had had repeated attacks of delirium tremens, and if weakness of mind could be an element in any case in the question between murder and culpable homicide, it seemed difficult to exclude that element here. [It could not

7 [1763] Hume i. 38.
8 Alison, i. 652.
9 [1867] 5 Irv. 466.
10 Op. cit.

> therefore be excluded] from the consideration of the jury here, along with the whole other circumstances, in making up their minds whether, if responsible to the law at all, the prisoner was to be held guilty of murder or of culpable homicide.[11]

The effect of Lord Deas' initiative was that juries could henceforth bring in a verdict of culpable homicide where there was evidence of 'weakness of mind' falling short of insanity, thereby obviating the risk that a mere recommendation to mercy might not be granted and giving the courts the power to vary the sentence accordingly. It should however be noticed that Lord Deas did not regard the accused's mental weakness as the only basis for a verdict of diminished responsibility; it was rather one of a number of grounds which he thought might justify such a verdict—a view which he continued to espouse until his retirement in 1887.[12] But his initiative did point up the need for a specific doctrine of diminished responsibility. As Gordon has argued:

> The anomalous position of the fixed penalty for murder meant that the effect of diminished responsibility on sentence had to be 'justified', to be 'rationalized' and to be given some conceptual basis in the law of murder which would explain how it could operate to produce an acquittal, and so apparently to affect responsibility. The way this was done was by reference to the mens rea of murder, not in the modern sense of intention or recklessness, but in the old sense of malice, wickedness or wilfulness, of 'general mens rea', in the same way as in the nineteenth century intoxication was regarded as a factor justifying the reduction of murder to culpable homicide.[13]

Initially, the new doctrine was flexibly defined. For example, in *Tierney*[14] Lord Ardmillan told the jury that they could return a verdict of culpable homicide if 'the man's control over his own mind might have been so weak as to deprive the act of that wilfulness which would make it murder'. On this view, 'diminished responsibility, like provocation, operates where there is an intention to kill

11 [1867] 5 Irv. at 479-80.
12 For example, see *McLean* [1876] 3 Couper 334; *Granger* [1878] 4 Couper 86; *Ferguson* [1881] 4 Couper 552.
13 *Gordon,* op. cit., p. 382.
14 [1875] 3 Couper 152.

but the intention arises from a particular circumstance—weakness of mind . . .which deprives it of the heinousness which is necessary for murder.'[15] In this respect, nineteenth century Scots law anticipated the approach to diminished responsibility adopted by the California Supreme Court nearly one hundred years later.[16] But the early twentieth century cases evince a narrower view, fuelled in part by a fear that the doctrine might weaken the deterrent efficacy of the criminal law and in part by a distrust of modern psychiatry.[17] Thus in *H.M. Advocate v. Savage,* now regarded as a leading case on the subject, Lord Alness defined diminished responsibility as follows:

> It is very difficult to put it in a phrase, but it has been put in this way: that there must be aberration or weakness of mind; that there must be some form of mental unsoundness; that there must be a state of mind which is bordering, though not amounting to, insanity; that there must be a mind so affected that responsibility is diminished from full responsibility to partial responsibility—in other words, the prisoner in question must be only partially accountable for his actions. And I think one can see running through the cases . . . that there must be some form of mental disease.[18]

There was no basis in the case law for Lord Alness' claim 'that there must be a state of mind which is bordering on, though not amounting to, insanity'. Yet the definition as a whole, including the requirement of quasi-insanity, was quickly adopted as the standard way of directing juries on the issue of diminished responsibility. Thus in *H.M. Advocate v. Braithwaite,* Lord Cooper said that '[t]here must be something amounting or approaching to partial insanity and based on mental weakness or aberration'.[19] To this extent the Scots law plea would appear to be narrower in scope than its English law counterpart. Indeed, the Court of Appeal in England has recently held that it is a misdirection to tell the jury that diminished responsibility amounts to 'borderline insanity'.[20]

The restrictive effect of the modern emphasis on partial insanity reached its apotheosis in *Carraher v. H.M. Advocate,* where it was held,

15 Gordon, ibid.
16 Infra, 8.4.
17 See Blake (ed.), *Trials of Patrick Carraher* (Edinburgh, 1951), p. 225.
18 [1923] JC 49 at 51.
19 [1945] JC 55 at 58.
20 *R v. Seers* [1985] *Crim LR* 85.

by a Full Bench, that 'the plea of diminished responsibility, which . . . is anomalous in our law, should not be extended or given wider scope than has hitherto been accorded to it in the decisions'; and that psychopathic personality disorder should henceforth not be regarded as a species of diminished responsibility.[21]

*Carraher* has been criticised on the grounds that the exclusion of psychopathy from the ambit of the plea of diminished responsibility has effectively stunted the development of the defence by insulating it from modern trends in psychiatry.[22] To the extent that this criticism implies that there is a relatively stable psychiatric consensus that psychopathy is a medically diagnosable and curable, or even treatable, condition, it is submitted that it is mistaken. Indeed, it is now widely accepted that psychopathy does not involve any impairment of the reasoning faculties and that psychopaths generally do not have psychiatric problems;[23] and that they should accordingly be sent to prison rather than to a mental hospital.[24] Thus the safer view—as we saw in chapter 4—is probably that, as used in the context of the criminal law, the label 'psychopath' does little more than describe offenders with a personality type that lies somewhere in the range from deviant to seriously depraved.[25]

However, this does not entail the conclusion, embraced by Lord Justice-General Normand in *Carraher*, that the defence of diminished responsibility should not be extended to psychopaths. On the contrary, given that psychiatrists *are* agreed that psychopaths probably have greater difficulty controlling their violent impulses than the normal individual,[26] it is submitted that there is no reason *in principle* why they should be denied the defence. They are obviously entitled to it if it turns out that their impaired control is pathologically based, on the general principle that at least some allowance should be made for a medical condition or illness state that appears to affect an accused's ability to control his actions. By parity

21 [1946] JC 108 at 118; per LJ- G Normand.

22 Smith op. cit. p. 160.

23 See Williams, *Criminology* (London, 1991), p. 173 and the references cited therein.

24 See the *Report of the (Butler) Committee on Mentally Abnormal Offenders,* Cmnd. 6244 (London, 1975), ch. 5.

25 Thus in *Carraher* Lord Normand said that it is 'descriptive rather of a typical criminal than of a person of the quality of one whom the law has hitherto regarded as being possessed of diminished responsibility': [1946] JC 108 at 117.

26 Hare, 'A Research Scale for the Assessment of Psychopathy in Criminal Populations' (1980) *1 Personality and Individual Differences* 111; and see the references cited therein.

of reasoning, they are also entitled to it even if it turns out that their impaired control is simply a function of character, since it is equally well established that non-pathological character traits or defects may go to mitigation.

Indeed, this conclusion is strengthened by the fact that a finding of diminished responsibility on the grounds of psychopathy does not prevent the court from treating aspects of a psychopathic defendant's *behaviour* as an *aggravating* factor for the purpose of sentence in an appropriate case. On this view, psychopathy *qua* condition entitles the defendant to a finding of diminished responsibility since we do not normally blame people for their conditions or characters; but since we may and sometimes do blame them for acting in character or for failing to control the predictable effects of a particular condition, there is nothing untoward about refusing a sentencing discount to a psychopathic defendant who appears on the evidence *not* to deserve one.[27]

## 3. ENGLISH LAW: THE MAXIMALIST APPROACH

The defence of diminished responsibility was introduced into English law by section 2 of the Homicide Act 1957. Section 2 provides as follows:

> (1) Where a person kills or is party to a killing of another, he shall not be convicted of murder if he was suffering from such abnormality of mind (whether arising from a condition of arrested or retarded development of mind or any inherent causes or induced by disease or injury) as substantially impaired his mental responsibility for his acts or omissions in doing or being a party to the killing. (2) On a charge of murder, it shall be for the defence to prove[28] that the person charged is by virtue of this section not liable to be convicted of murder. (3) A person who but for this section would be liable, whether as principle or as accessory, to be convicted of murder shall be liable instead to be convicted of manslaughter.

27 This point is also considered in relation to Californian law infra, 8.4; and see ch. 1.5.

28 On the balance of probabilities: *R. v. Campbell* [1987] 84 Cr App Rep 255 at 257 (CA).

The principal effect of the section is that, as a successful defence of diminished responsibility leads to a conviction for manslaughter rather than murder, the courts now have an absolute discretion with respect to the sentencing of defendants who get the benefit of it. Whereas formerly the courts had no option but to impose a sentence of death in homicide cases where evidence of incapacity fell short of legal insanity, they can now choose from a wide range of measures: viz., life imprisonment, imprisonment for a fixed term, a non-custodial measure, a therapeutic measure, or an absolute or conditional discharge. Initially the courts tended to underuse their new freedom by generally opting for a fixed term of imprisonment, but since the mid-nineteen-sixties they have gradually moved to the reverse position and are now twice as likely to impose measures other than imprisonment on defendants who successfully raise the defence.[29]

Section 2 appears to be based on the latter-day Scots law assumption that diminished or impaired mental responsibility is a specific psychopathological state, and not just a convenient label for the disparate psychological factors that might limit a defendant's legal accountability for his actions, much less a procedural device for obviating the need to impose a fixed penalty in murder cases. Hence the definition of diminished responsibility as a product of an underlying inherent condition—as 'such abnormality of mind *(whether arising from a condition of arrested or retarded development of mind or any inherent causes or induced by disease or injury)* as substantially impaired [the defendant's] mental responsibility'.[30] Indeed, a defendant is not entitled to the defence of diminished responsibility unless there is medical evidence of an abnormality arising from one of the causes specified in the parenthesis in section 2.[31]

The anomalous position of the fixed penalty for murder meant that the legislature had to frame the new plea in a way that went to conviction and not merely to mitigation, and the idea that there was

29 Walker, op. cit. p. 163; Gibson, *Homicide in England and Wales 1967-1971* (Home Office Research Study No. 31, 1975), chap. 26; Williams, *Textbook of Criminal Law* (London, 1978), p. 625.

30 Italics added. Thus abnormalities of mind induced by reactive depression: *R v. Morris* [1961] 2 QB 237; paranoia: *R v. Din* [1962] 46 Cr App Rep 269; epilepsy: *R v. Price* [1962] 47 Cr App Rep 21; schizo-affective illness: *R v. Russell* [1964] 2 QB 596; and hysteria: *R v. Harrison, The Times,* 19 September 1957, come within the ambit of the defence. But those caused by hate, jealousy, or intoxication do not: *R v. Fenton* [1975] 61 Cr App Rep 261.

31 *R v. Byrne* [1960] 2 QB 396 at 402; *R v. Dix* [1981] 74 Cr App Rep 306 at 311.

an intermediate psychopathological state of diminished responsibility—between full responsibility and complete irresponsibility—that rendered the accused guilty of a less serious offence, was the device chosen to justify this move. Unfortunately, the device was clothed in vague, somewhat circular, language: the defendant was entitled to the new defence of diminished responsibility if he could show that his responsibility had been impaired, i.e., diminished, by any of the conditions mentioned in parenthesis! Not surprisingly, it fell to the courts to say what this meant, in the form of a reliable test or doctrine of diminished responsibility that could be uniformly applied by juries.

The first problem was to decide whether the Crown could accept the plea of diminished responsibility (where the psychiatric reports were unanimous) or whether the issue had to be left to the jury? The early cases indicate that the courts initially favoured the second option and insisted that the prosecution was obliged to probe the soundness of the psychiatric evidence in cross-examination.[32] By as early as 1964, however, the vast bulk of diminished responsibility pleas were openly accepted by the Crown without the court insisting on this requirement.[33] In view of the difficulties associated with the evaluation of psychiatric testimony in the context of the criminal process,[34] it is submitted that the earlier posture of scepticism in the face of such evidence is the more appropriate.

There was originally some doubt as to whether the prosecution could ask for an acquittal on the grounds of insanity where the defence sought to rely on diminished responsibility, or for a verdict of diminished responsibility on foot of evidence designed to establish insanity,[35] but it is now well established that they may do so[36]—the rationale being that the prosecution should be free to argue for the verdict that best fits the medical evidence.

32 *R v. Din* [1962] 42 Cr App Rep 116; the rule in *Din* is evaluated supra ch. 5.4. But in *R. v. Cox* [1968] 52 Cr App Rep 130, the Court of Appeal approved the procedure whereby the plea of diminished responsibility could be accepted at the discretion of the trial judge where the medical evidence was uncontested; the history of the decision is set out in *R v. Vinagre* [1979] 69 Cr App Rep 104.

33 Walker, op. cit., p. 154. In a fairly recent study, Dell found that the proportion of cases in which the plea of guilty of manslaughter on the grounds of diminished responsibility was accepted was as high as 80 per cent: 'Diminished Responsibility Reconsidered' (1982) *Crim LR* 809 at 811-2.

34 See chapter 1.3.

35 Compare *R v. Bastion* [1958] 42 Cr App Rep 75 and *R. v. Price* [1962] 47 Cr App Rep 21.

36 By virtue of section 6 of the Criminal Procedure (Insanity) Act 1964; see also *R v. Nott* [1958] 43 Cr App Rep 8.

The courts were initially reluctant to get involved in the construction of section 2, preferring to leave that to juries. Thus in *R. v. Spriggs* Lord Goddard CJ, delivering the judgment of the Court of Appeal, said that judges should do no more than read the section to juries and ask them to decide what it meant.[37] The trouble with that approach is that it sometimes left juries in the position of having to choose between two competing interpretations of section 2, notwithstanding the established principle that the interpretation of statutes is strictly a matter of law for the courts. Indeed, this was one of the problems in *Spriggs*, where the jury had to choose, without any help from the judge, between the prosecution's contention that since the defendant was highly intelligent he could not be suffering from an 'abnormality of mind', and the defence's claim that his 'abnormality of mind' consisted in an inability to control his emotions!

This problem was resolved by the decisions in *DPP v. Byrne*,[38] which has become the *locus classicus* on the defence, and *DPP v. Terry*.[39] In *Byrne* the appellant was charged with the murder of a young woman whom he had strangled and whose dead body he had mutilated. He admitted the facts of the killing but pleaded that he was suffering from diminished responsibility and was, accordingly, not guilty of murder but of manslaughter. There was uncontested psychiatric evidence that the accused was a sexual psychopath, i.e., that he suffered from violent perverted sexual desires which he found it difficult or impossible to control. Moreover, all three doctors who testified to this effect said that sexual psychopathy was an 'abnormality of mind' which arose from 'a condition of arrested or retarded development of mind or . . . inherent causes'. The trial judge told the jury that difficulty or even inability on the part of an accused to exercise will-power to control his actions could not amount to such abnormality of mind as substantially impaired his mental responsibilities within the meaning of section 2 and the defendant was convicted of murder.

Delivering the judgment of the Court of Appeal, Lord Parker CJ said that this was a misdirection and that:

> 'Abnormality of mind', which has to be contrasted with the time-honoured expression in the M'Naghten Rules, 'defect of

37 [1958] 42 Cr App Rep 69 at 75.
38 [1960] 2 QB 396, [1960] 3 All ER 1 (CA).
39 [1961] 2 QB 314, [1961] 2 All ER 569.

> reason', means a state of mind so different from that of ordinary human beings that the reasonable man would term it abnormal. It appears to us to be wide enough to cover the mind's activities in all its aspects, not only the perception of physical acts and matters and the ability to form a rational judgment whether an act is right or wrong, but also the ability to exercise will-power to control physical acts in accordance with that rational judgment.[40]

This direction was expressly approved in *Terry* where the Court of Appeal held that it was no longer proper merely to read the section to the jury, as Lord Goddard had done in *Spriggs,* 'but that a proper explanation of the terms of the section as interpreted in *Byrne* ought to be put before [them]'.[41] In view of the final clause in the passage just cited, this suggests that, unlike its Scots law counterpart, the English plea of diminished responsibility definitely embraces psychopathic personality disorder, although it could be argued that this result does not strictly follow from the reasoning in *Byrne.*

Referring to the problem of the aetiology of abnormalities of mind, i.e., to the question of whether a given abnormality arose from one of the conditions mentioned in parenthesis in section 2, Lord Parker CJ said in that case that this was a matter to be determined on the expert evidence;[42] and while most psychiatrists are likely to view psychopathy as a product of 'arrested or retarded development', it sometimes happens that an expert witness may incline to the more sceptical view that the notion of psychopathy is too vague to support an unequivocal diagnosis. When this occurs, there is nothing to stop a jury denying the defence to a psychopathic defendant,[43] since juries are only required to follow the psychiatric evidence where it is clearly all one way (and where there is no other evidence which can displace or throw doubt on it).[44]

The notion of 'substantially impaired . . . mental responsibility' as used in section 2 also requires elucidation. As we have seen, 'mental responsibility' includes volitional control as well as the cognitive

40 [1960] 2 QB at 403, [1960] 3 All ER at 4.
41 [1961] 2 All ER at 574.
42 [1960] 2 QB at 403.
43 *Walton v. R* [1978] 1 All ER 542.
44 *R v. Matheson* [1958] 2 All ER 87, [1958] 1 WLR 474, 42 Cr App Rep 145 (CA); *R v. Bailey* [1961] *Crim LR* 828 (CA).

ability to perceive and judge reality.[45] But 'substantially impaired . . . mental responsibility' is not the same as a state of irresistible impulse, which suggests the complete impairment of volitional control.[46] Nor does it mean a real as opposed to illusory loss of control.[47] But it is something more than trivial or minimal impairment, although precisely how much more is hard to say.[48] In *R v. Simcox*[49] the Court of Appeal appears to have held that even a moderate impairment would not be substantial, which suggests that the term implies that the degree of impairment must be marked and, more importantly, that the expert witnesses must be prepared unequivocally to testify to that effect. Thus Simcox's plea failed because although four expert witnesses agreed that he was suffering from paranoia, and that this condition arose from inherent causes and made it difficult for him to control his actions, they could not bring themselves to say that it had *substantially* impaired his ability in this regard.

It is however clear that the defendant is not required to prove borderline insanity, the remarks of the Privy Council in *Walton v. R*[50] notwithstanding. In *Rose v. R*[51] the Board had earlier said that diminished responsibility could be defined as borderline insanity provided the latter term was used 'in its broad popular sense' but that this would be a serious misdirection if the term was used in its technical legal meaning.[52] In *Walton* the Board failed to emphasise this distinction in a *dictum* to the effect that a jury would be entitled to reject the defence if it 'thought that there was nothing in the evidence indicative of a man whose mental state bordered on insanity',[53] thereby potentially restricting the scope of the defence to cases of quasi-legal or quasi-medical insanity, respectively. Clarification came with the decision of the Court of Appeal in *Seers* where it was re-affirmed that if the term insanity was included in a direction on the issue of diminished responsibility the word must be used in its broad popular sense.[54]

The court also concluded that it was inappropriate to mention

45 See s. 2 (1) of the Homicide Act 1957 and the quotation from *Byrne* [1960] 2 QB at 403, [1960] 3 All ER at 4, supra.
46 Smith and Hogan, op. cit., p. 213.
47 *R v. Lloyd* [1967] 1 QB 175 at 179.
48 [1967] 1 QB 175 at 180.
49 [1964] *Crim LR* 402.
50 [1978] 1 All ER 542.
51 [1961] AC 496.
52 [1961] AC 496 at 508.
53 [1978] 1 All ER 542 at 547.
54 [1984] 79 Cr App Rep 261 at 264.

insanity where the defendant was relying on a depressive illness to support a plea of diminished responsibility, apparently on the assumption that since depressives generally know what they are doing and that it is wrong, juries would be unlikely to regard them as partially insane from a legal point of view; and because there are many cases in which the type of abnormality (such as reactive depression, from which the defendant in the instant case was suffering) relied on cannot be related to any of the generally recognized heads of *medical* insanity.[55] It is submitted that this conclusion is right and should be applied across the board in cases of diminished responsibility, given the narrow cognitive definition of insanity that has dominated common-law thinking; although it should be conceded that, for obvious reasons, judges are far more likely than jurors to conceptualise insanity in narrow legal terms.

Finally, there is recent authority for the view that alcoholism qualifies as one of the conditions capable of giving rise to an abnormality of mind within the meaning of section 2 of the Homicide Act 1957.[56] In *R v. Tandy*[57] the Court of Appeal accepted that if the defendant could show that she was suffering from an abnormality of mind induced by alcoholism, and that the abnormality thus induced substantially impaired her ability to control her actions, she would be entitled to the defence of diminished responsibility. The defence would fail, however, if the abnormality of mind resulted from the voluntary consumption of alcohol.

The first proposition is unexceptionable as it is logically consistent with the analogous rule that a 'defect of reason ' induced by *delirium tremens* affords a good defence of insanity.[58] If the second proposition means that drunken defendants cannot generally rely on the defence of diminished responsibility, it too is unexceptionable. But if it means that a defendant whose drinking induces an illness state, which in turn causes an abnormality of mind, cannot rely on the defence of diminished responsibility if his initial consumption of alcohol was voluntary, it seems suspect. If the logic of the analogous insanity rule is that the defendant has a good defence because his defect of reason was caused by a supervening illness, rather than the

55 [1984] 79 Cr App Rep 261 at 265.

56 Where however there is evidence of both diminished responsibility and intoxication unaccompanied by alcoholism, the jury should disregard the latter when deciding whether or not the defendant is entitled to the defence: *R v. Gittens* [1984] QB 698; *R v. Atkinson* [1985] *Crim LR* 314.

57 [1989] 1 All ER 267. See also *R. v. Fenton* [1975] 61 Cr App Rep 261 (CA).

58 *R v. Davis* [1881] 14 Cox CC 563 at 564; *DPP v. Beard* [1920] AC 479 at 501.

drinking that gave rise to the illness,[59] it seems to follow that a *Tandy*-type defendant whose abnormality of mind was similarly induced should have a good defence of diminished responsibility notwithstanding the fact that the supervening illness was brought on by the voluntary consumption of alcohol. Since it is clear that a defendant who drinks in order to get himself into a state in which he knows he will kill is guilty of murder if he kills in that state,[60] it is submitted that there is no need for a special rule barring the defence in cases where the defendant's illness was triggered by voluntary intoxication.

Two main criticisms can be levelled against the defence of diminished responsibility as it has been operated by the English courts. The first is that the defence discriminates against the mentally sane but abnormal defendant who denies any involvement in the alleged killing.[61] If a defendant of this type introduces evidence of mental abnormality in support of a defence of diminished responsibility, he runs the risk of undermining the credibility of his claim that he had nothing to do with the killing. On the other hand, if he decides for this reason not to introduce evidence of mental abnormality before the verdict, he cannot raise the issue of diminished responsibility after it in view of the existence of the fixed penalty of life imprisonment for murder. While there has been no detailed empirical investigation of this problem, Dell found that all of the 11 such cases (6 per cent. of her total sample) she studied resulted in a conviction for either murder or manslaughter.[62]

The second criticism arises from the fact that section 2 of the Homicide Act 1957 requires the defendant to prove that he was suffering from such abnormality of mind as substantially impaired his 'mental responsibility' for his actions. As the Butler Committee pointed out, 'mental responsibility' in this context is an ethico-legal rather than a psychiatric matter, and is therefore not something on

59 '[D]runkenness is one thing and the diseases to which drunkenness leads are different things; and if a man by drunkenness brings on a state of disease which causes such a degree of madness, even for a time, which would have relieved him from responsibility if it had been caused in any other way, then he would not be criminally responsible': *R v. Davis* [1881] 14 Cox CC 563 at 564; per Stephen J; approved by the House of Lords in *DPP v. Beard* [1920] AC 479 at 501.

60 *A-G for Northern Ireland v. Gallagher* [1963] 349 at 382.

61 Dell, op. cit., at 810-11.

62 Ibid.

which doctors have any special competence to testify.[63] Yet the statistics suggest that the defence of diminished responsibility enjoys a success rate of around 80 per cent; and that there is an almost perfect correlation between the success of the plea and the fact that the courts are willing to accept it without trial if it is supported by uncontradicted medical evidence.[64] Moreover, it has been found that where psychiatrists disagree on whether diminished responsibility had been made out, they are as likely as not to disagree on the moral rather than psychiatric aspects of the plea, i.e., on whether the accused's responsibility was impaired rather than on whether he was suffering from a recognized mental abnormality.[65]

In other words, the conspicuous success of the plea seems to depend on the fact that the expert witness has been allowed to usurp the function of the jury: if the experts agree that responsibility has been impaired, the defence is virtually certain to succeed; and virtually certain to fail if they disagree on this point—notwithstanding that there appears to be no clinical basis for an expert conclusion on the matter one way or the other!

One solution to this problem would be to amend section 2 to the effect that the defence of diminished responsibility is available if, on a charge of murder, it is proved that the accused 'was suffering from such abnormality of mind (whether arising from a condition of arrested or retarded development of mind or any inherent causes or induced by disease or injury) as, *in the opinion of the jury (or fact finder)*, substantially impaired his mental responsibility for his acts or omissions in doing or being a party to the killing'.[66] It is submitted

63 'It seems odd that psychiatrists should be asked to agree to testify as to legal or moral responsibility. It is even more surprising that courts are prepared to hear that testimony': *Report of the Committee on Mentally Abnormal Offenders,* Cmnd. 5698 (London, 1975), para. 19.5. This is also the view of the American Bar Association: *First Tentative Draft. Criminal Justice Mental Health Standards* (Washington, 1983), p. 283. But cf Hayes, 'Diminished Responsibility: The Expert Witness' Viewpoint' in Meng Heong Yeo, *Partial Excuses to Murder* (Sydney, 1991), pp. 145-57. The significance of this point has been heightened by the passage of s. 1 (2) of the Criminal Procedure (Insanity and Fitness to Plead) Act 1991, which provides that a verdict of insanity or diminished responsibility (or a finding of unfitness to plead) cannot be returned without the evidence of two doctors, one of whom must have proven expertise in the diagnosis or treatment of mental illness; see ch. 5.4.

64 Dell, op. cit. at 813.

65 Dell, ibid.

66 Italics added. Cf the changes of wording recommended by the Butler Committee, Cmnd. 5698 (1975), para. 19.17; the Criminal Law Revision Committee, *Fourteenth Report: Offences Against the Person,* Cmnd. 7844 (1980),

that this form of words would produce a marked improvement on the present division of labour between experts and non-experts in the operation of the defence.[67] Not only would it make it clear that the question of responsibility is ultimately one of fact for the jury, rather than one of science or medicine that can be safely resolved by the trial judge in light of the expert testimony of psychiatrists, but it would also underline the fact that the logically prior question of whether the defendant was suffering from an abnormality of mind of the kind contemplated in the parenthesis in section 2 is one for psychiatrists.

A clear division of labour along these lines would be particularly helpful where the defendant is seeking to rely on evidence of psychopathy as a basis for the defence of diminished responsibility. As things stand, the fact that the expert witnesses are agreed that a psychopathic defendant probably found it substantially more difficult to control his actions than an ordinary person would have done in the same circumstances is generally enough to secure the defence[68]—the governing assumption apparently being that this level of difficulty in controlling one's violent impulses entails the conclusion that the agent's responsibility for failing to control them must have been diminished or impaired, and that it would be perverse for a jury to decide otherwise. By contrast, in the revised arrangement, it would be incumbent on the jury to satisfy itself, on a review of the evidence as a whole, that the defendant's uncontested difficulty in controlling his behaviour actually amounted to diminished responsibility.

Nor is this a distinction without a difference. If responsibility in this context means the minimal capacity to control one's impulses,[69] and it is difficult to see what else it could mean, it seems clear that it is a mistake to assume that a marked degree of difficulty in controlling one's impulses is the same thing as diminished or impaired capacity to control them. On the contrary, a man may experience extreme difficulty doing something without his minimal capacity to do it in any way being impaired. For example, a very small athlete is likely to find it abnormally difficult to play basketball or compete in the high jump, and on that account to attract more praise and less

paras. 92-94; and the Law Commission, *Codification of the Criminal Law—A report to the Law Commission. Law.* Com. No. 143: Draft Criminal Code Bill, cl. 58.

67 Cf Griew, 'The Future of Diminished Responsibility' (1988) *Crim LR* 75.

68 See the discussion of *Byrne* [1960] 2 QB 396, [1960] 3 All ER 1 (CA), supra.

69 And thus 'to conform to the requirements of the law': Griew, op. cit., p. 81.

criticism for his successes and failures, respectively, in these disciplines than the medium-sized or tall athlete. But this does not mean that his minimal capacity to engage in either sport is thereby diminished or impaired with respect to his taller colleagues, or that this is why we (should) take a more indulgent view of his performances than we are accustomed to taking of theirs. All it means is that he has considerably more difficulty, and therefore has to try considerably harder, than they do in doing something that he is basically capable of doing.

Similarly, the fact that a defendant has been 'diagnosed' as psychopathic, and that the psychiatric description of his condition includes an uncontested statement that he killed while under the influence of violent urges which he found it extremely difficult to control, does not entail the conclusion that his capacity to control the impulses in question was impaired. Once again, the critical issue is not the strength of the man's urges or the degree of difficulty he experienced in taming them, but whether his ability to tame them was seriously affected by his underlying personality disorder. Given that the defendant may not have tried to control his impulses, may have given in to them when he could have fought them, or may have planned the crime in a way that seems incompatible with the hypothesis that he was in the grip of extremely powerful urges, it seems appropriate that juries should be given the chance to decide this issue in light of the evidence as a whole. At all events, it is submitted that this solution is preferable to the existing arrangement whereby the matter is effectively left to the judge as guided by expert witnesses who often appear to take it for granted that extreme difficulty and impaired ability in the matter of checking one's violent impulses are one and the same thing.

The proposed revision of section 2 does not solve the problem of what exactly counts as diminished responsibility, in the sense that it does not provide juries with a clear criterion for deciding when responsibility has been substantially impaired. On the contrary, the old circularity of definition is preserved: diminished responsibility consists in those abnormalities of mind that substantially impair, i.e. diminish, the defendant's responsibility for his actions; the only difference being that, in the revised version, it falls to the jury, rather than the judge as guided by (in)expert opinion, to decide if and when responsibility has been substantially impaired.

However, it is submitted that the difficulties occasioned by the logically circular nature of section 2 should not be exaggerated. On the assumption that diminished responsibility means substantially impaired minimal capacity, it seems reasonable to suppose that the section contemplates two kinds of defendants: those with serious cognitive and those with serious volitional difficulties, respectively. As regards the first kind of defendant, it is suggested that the jury should be directed that the test is whether the accused had serious difficulty understanding his actions in terms of the basic principles of logic and evidential reasoning,[70] even if his intellectual capacity in that regard was not completely destroyed. In effect this would mean that the section would cover those forms of psychosis excluded by the traditional interpretation of the M'Naghten Rules and, therefore, much the same ground as the liberal criterion of volitional insanity discussed in chapter 3.

As regards the second type of defendant, it is suggested that it is enough to ask the jury whether the evidence as a whole showed, on the balance of probabilities, that, as a matter of ordinary human evaluation, the accused's ability to comply with the law's requirements was markedly affected by any of the conditions or causes mentioned in the parenthesis in section 2. This question may still leave jurors in a quandary when faced with uncontested evidence of psychopathic personality disorder, but, by inviting them to examine the expert evidence in the broad context of the defendant's behaviour as described to the court, it at least forces them to confront the essentially common-sense, inferential character of judgments about responsibility.

The dictates of common sense and inference are often all juries have to go on when assessing the relationship between mind and behaviour. For example, they are as much as they have to rely on when deciding whether a defendant intended or foresaw consequences which he denies he intended or foresaw, or whether his conduct was voluntary in circumstances in which he claims he was acting as an automaton. So there is nothing inherently odd about leaving the issue of diminished responsibility to juries as a common-sense matter, or about expecting them to handle it in a common-sense way. Moreover, this conclusion is consistent with the fact that, unlike serious cognitive impairment, volitional impairment is not normally regarded as an entailment of mental disorder.[71] In other words, it is submitted that, at least as far as the issue of volitional impairment is concerned, ordinary common-sense analysis of the defendant's conduct in the light of what is commonly known and

70 See the discussion of this criterion in ch. 2.6-7.

71 This point is discussed at length in ch. 3.2 et seq.

understood about human behaviour is the only reliable bridge between expert testimony and responsibility judgments.

### 4. THE *MENS REA* MODEL: A CALIFORNIAN EXPERIMENT

The Californian experience of diminished responsibility is especially interesting. Unlike its English law counterpart, the Californian plea was created by judicial legislation rather than by parliament. Partly because of this and partly as a response to the narrowness of the insanity defence in Californian law, it underwent considerable development in the course of its thirty-year history.[72] Indeed, by the mid 1960s, it had been widened to the extent that it bore only a superficial resemblance to the plea originally carved out by the California Supreme Court in 1949. Having begun as a plea designed to give effect to psychiatric evidence that mental abnormality falling short of legal insanity prevented the accused from forming the requisite intent for the crime charged, it had evolved into a claim that the defendant, notwithstanding that he was legally sane and had *mens rea,* was not fully responsible for his actions as mental abnormality had rendered him less capable of entertaining the requisite intent than the ordinary individual.

The history of the plea in California falls into three stages: recognition, expansion and abolition, respectively. Recognition came with the decision of the Supreme Court in *People v. Wells.*[73] Section 1026 of the California Penal Code provides that, when insanity is raised as a defence, the state must prove the elements of the offence, including *mens rea* and *actus reus,* before the issue of insanity can be considered. In *People v. Troche*[74] the California Supreme Court held that this meant that evidence of mental abnormality went exclusively to the issue of insanity and could not be introduced to show that the accused lacked *mens rea.* Wells was charged with the capital offence of assaulting a prison guard 'with malice aforethought', contrary to section 4500 of the California Penal Code. Counsel for the defence tried to introduce medical evidence that the defendant was suffering from a 'state of tension' such that he mistakenly believed that he was

72 See generally, Arenella, 'The Diminished Responsibility and Diminished Capacity Defenses: Two Children of a Doomed Marriage' (1977) 77 *Colum L Rev* 827.

73 [1949] 33 Cal 2d 330, 202 P 2d 53; 338 US 836.

74 [1928] 206 Cal 35, 273 P 767, [1929] 280 US 524.

defending himself against an unlawful attack when he assaulted the guard, and so lacked the requisite *mens rea* for the crime charged.[75] The trial judge ruled that this evidence was inadmissible on the principle laid down in *Troche*.[76]

On appeal a majority of the California Supreme Court found that this was a misdirection and that *Troche* had been wrongly decided. In the opinion of the majority, section 1026 merely required that the basic elements of culpability must be established before the issue of insanity can be decided. It was therefore a mistake to assume, as the Supreme Court had done in *Troche*, that psychiatric testimony bearing on the question of *mens rea* was inadmissible when the primary issue of culpability was being decided; that limitation only applied where such testimony bore on the accused's capacity to form the requisite intent, since then and only then did the issue of insanity come into focus.[77] Moreover, the majority concluded, since it was well established that evidence of intoxication was relevant to the question of whether or not the defendant had *mens rea* where the crime charged was one of specific intent, it followed that any other evidence, not excluding psychiatric evidence, tending to show that he did not entertain the requisite specific intent was also admissible.[78] To hold otherwise would be inconsistent with the basic principle that the prosecution was required to prove the elements of the offence charged beyond all reasonable doubt.

The scope of the plea established by *Wells* was therefore extremely limited: psychiatric evidence tending to show that the accused lacked the requisite intent was admissible provided it did not go to the question of his capacity to entertain such intent. In other words, the defence was confined to cases where there was psychiatric testimony that some non-pathologically induced emotional state such as fear, panic or anger prevented the formation of the requisite intent. Moreover, since the Supreme Court's reliance on the analogy with voluntary intoxication was subsequently interpreted to mean that the new plea was confined to crimes of specific intent, to the express exclusion of crimes of general intent, i.e., to the exclusion of crimes

75 [1949] 33 Cal 2d at 344-5, 202 P 2d at 62.

76 [1949] 33 Cal 2d at 339, 202 P 2d at 59.

77 [1949] 33 Cal 2d at 351, 202 P 2d at 61. '[I]f the proffered evidence tends to show not merely that [the defendant] *did* or *did not*, but rather that because of legal insanity he *could not*, entertain the specific intent or other essential mental state, then that evidence is inadmissible under the [diminished capacity] plea': ibid.

78 [1949] 33 Cal 2d at 357-58, 202 P 2d at 70.

where, in the absence of rebutting evidence, the element of intent can be inferred from the doing of the act charged, the effect of the plea was that a successful defendant was invariably convicted of a lesser included offence—which in practice meant a lesser degree of homicide.[79] Indeed, where the crime charged was one of specific intent that did not contain a lesser included offence, the courts adopted the fiction of treating it as a crime of general intent, on the grounds that it would be illogical if a defendant could secure a complete acquittal on the basis of a partial defence (of diminished capacity)![80]

The expansion of the plea began in *People v. Gorshen*.[81] The defendant shot and killed his foreman after a fight on the docks where they both worked. He had reported for work in an intoxicated condition and been asked to go home by the deceased on that account. A struggle ensued and the defendant was knocked to the ground. He then left the scene, promising to return with his gun and kill the deceased. On his return to the docks, he was searched by police but no weapon was found, whereupon he produced his gun and fired the fatal shot in the presence of the officers who had unsuccessfully searched him!

In reply to a charge of first-degree murder, it was claimed that the defendant was suffering from a mental abnormality that undermined his capacity to commit a premeditated killing. According to the psychiatrist that testified on his behalf, the defendant was a chronic paranoid schizophrenic who suffered from auditory delusions and visual hallucinations to the effect that he had gradually been deprived of his sexual powers by a company of devils. In the expert's opinion, these paranoid beliefs had led him to attach such exaggerated significance to his work that he had come to see it as a badge of his virility. In the result, the expert concluded, he had understood the order to leave work as an attack on the last vestige of his sanity, and accordingly felt constrained to launch the homicidal attack 'as an alternative to total disintegration'.[82]

The trial judge held that this raised the defence of diminished responsibility and the defendant was duly convicted of second-degree murder. On appeal the Supreme Court of California followed suit

79 See, for example, *People v. Noah* [1971] 5 Cal 3d 469, 487 P 2d 1009, 96 Cal Rptr. 441.

80 *People v. Hood* [1969] 1 Cal 3d 444, 462 P 2d 370, 82 Cal Rptr. 618; *People v. Nance* [1972] 25 Cal App 3d 925, 102 Cal Rptr. 266.

81 [1959] 51 Cal 2d 716, 336 P 2d 492.

82 [1959] 51 Cal 2d at 722, 336 P 2d at 496.

and upheld the trial judge's decision as a straightforward application of the rule in *Wells*.[83] This was surprising given that the rule in that case governed the admissibility of psychiatric evidence designed to negate the element of specific intent, whereas the psychiatric evidence in the instant case—that the defendant felt he had to kill his victim in order to preserve his own sanity—tended to confirm rather than negate the hypothesis of a deliberate, premeditated killing. In other words, the effect of the decision in *Gorshen* was to broaden the defence articulated in *Wells* into the much wider principle that a legally sane killer was entitled to be convicted of second-degree murder if mental illness impaired his capacity to engage in the process of premeditation and deliberation required for first-degree murder.[84]

This was confirmed in *People v. Wolff*[85] and *People v. Anderson*.[86] In *Wolff* the defendant was a schizophrenic who, by his own account, brutally killed his mother with an axe so that he could take women to his house and rape them. Reducing his conviction for murder from the first to the second degree, the California Supreme Court held that a defendant was not guilty of first degree murder even though the killing was carefully planned in advance if the evidence disclosed that there was a 'limited extent to which [he] could maturely and meaningfully reflect upon the gravity of his contemplated act'.[87] In similar vein, the court in *Anderson* stated that 'clearly we cannot hold defendant responsible for a crime which requires as one of its elements the presence of a state of mind which he is incapable of achieving because of subjective abnormality or impaired volitional powers'. Indeed, in that case the court went on to change the designation of the defence from diminished responsibility to diminished capacity, thereby signalling that the defence now turned on a defect in the defendant's ability to conform with the law's requirements rather than on a mere want of *mens rea*.[88]

The process of expansion culminated in *People v. Wetmore*.[89] There the defendant was charged with burglary. The case against him was that he broke into an apartment and proceeded to treat it as

83 [1959] 51 Cal 2d at 735, 336 P 2d at 504.
84 Arenella, op. cit., at p. 841.
85 [1964] 61 Cal 2d 795, 394 P 2d 959, 40 Cal Rptr. 271.
86 [1965] 63 Cal 2d 351, 406 P 2d 43, 46 Cal Rptr. 763.
87 [1964] 61 Cal 2d at 821, 394 P .2d at 975, 40 Cal Rptr. at 287 (italics in original).
88 [1965] 63 Cal 2d 351, 406 P 2d 43, 46 Cal Rptr 763.
89 [1978] 22 Cal 3d 318, 583 2 P 2d 1308, 149 Cal Rptr. 265.

his own—to the extent of cooking and eating the occupant's food, wearing his clothes, re-arranging the furniture and appropriating a number of personal effects. There was evidence that the defendant had a long history of psychosis and had been homeless since his release from mental hospital a short time before the incident. According to the psychiatric reports submitted on his behalf, his psychosis had led him to believe that he 'owned' property and that he had been 'directed' to the complainant's apartment. There was also evidence that he was shocked and embarrassed when the police arrived at the scene and convinced him that he was really a trespasser.

In reply to the charge of burglary, defence counsel submitted that the accused's belief that he owned the apartment and its contents showed that he lacked the element of specific intent—i.e., the ulterior intent to commit a felony whilst in the apartment—required for that offence.[90] Relying on *Wells,* the trial judge ruled that this evidence was inadmissible on the issue of diminished capacity as it tended to show that the defendant was legally insane. But the California Supreme Court, overruling *Wells* on this point, held that psychiatric testimony of diminished capacity is admissible when determining a defendant's guilt whether or not it also goes to the issue of insanity.

For good measure, the court also rejected its earlier view that the defence of diminished capacity was confined to crimes where the defendant could be convicted of a lesser included offence. In the words of Torbriner J, delivering the judgment of the court: '[t]he prosecution must prove all elements of the crime beyond a reasonable doubt; we do not perceive how a defendant who has in his possession evidence which rebuts an element of the crime can logically be denied the right to present that evidence merely because it will result in his [complete] acquittal'.[91] In the result, the process of transformation from a defence to the issue of *mens rea* for the crime of murder in the first degree to a general defence of incapacity to entertain *mens rea* by reason of mental abnormality was completed.

Nor was the court prepared to countenance the argument that the defence of diminished capacity, given that it normally led to a reduced prison term and could lead to a complete acquittal, was unsuitable for defendants who were mentally ill and dangerous, and therefore inconsistent with the criminal law's fundamental concern

90 [1978] 22 Cal 3d at 318, 583 2 P 2d at 1308, 149 Cal Rptr. at 265.
91 [1978] 22 Cal 3d at 327, 583 2 P 2d at 1317, 149 Cal Rptr. at 274.

with public safety. It was up to the legislature to provide suitable confinement and treatment for persons found to be of diminished capacity as a result of mental illness or defect![92]

It is widely accepted that the decision to abolish the defence of diminished capacity was triggered by the verdict in the notorious *Dan White* case.[93] White asked the Mayor of San Francisco to reappoint him to the office of City Supervisor, from which he had recently resigned. When the Mayor declined and appointed another person to the position, White went to City Hall with a loaded gun and shot him dead. He then reloaded his gun and went to another room in the building where he shot and killed his replacement, Mr Harvey Milk, who was one of his political opponents and a leader of the San Francisco homosexual community. White was charged with two counts of first degree murder. His defence was that he should be convicted of manslaughter on the grounds of diminished capacity. The plea of diminished capacity was supported by psychiatric evidence that the defendant's violent reaction was a result of stress occasioned in part by the loss of political office and in part by his habit of gorging himself on convenience food with a high sugar content when under stress.[94]

The defence was successful on both counts (and the defendant was released from prison after serving four years for the two killings), but '[t]he intense public reaction in California to the [manslaughter] verdict united liberals and conservatives in opposition to the diminished capacity defence' to the extent that, 'in a rare unanimous vote, the California Legislature repudiated the expanded definitions of premeditation and malice aforethought which the state courts had created' and abolished the defence altogether.[95]

In the result, evidence of incapacity in Californian law now goes solely to the question of insanity: according to section 25 (b) of the California Penal Code, enacted in 1982, in the wake of the *White* decision, a defendant is guilty as charged unless it is established that he was 'incapable of knowing or understanding the nature and quality of his or her act and [sic] of distinguishing right from wrong at the time of the commission of the offence'. In other words, the *White* case had the ironic outcome that a defence that had been

92 [1978] 22 Cal 3d at 329, 583 2 P 2d at 1319, 149 Cal Rptr. at 276.

93 For a full account of the case, see Johnson, *Criminal Law* (New York, 1985), pp. 377-8.

94 Ibid.

95 Johnson, op. cit., p. 378.

invented to ameliorate the harshness of the M'Naghten Rules led eventually to the adoption by the legislature of an even narrower definition of criminal incapacity by reason of insanity than that sanctioned by the Rules. The Rules provided for a defence of insanity where mental disorder prevented a person *either* from knowing the nature and quality of his act *or* from knowing that it was wrong,[96] whereas section 25 (b) requires that it does *both* of these things.

It is submitted that there are three lessons to be drawn from the California experiment. The first is that it is a mistake to tie the defence of diminished responsibility to the issue of *mens rea*. Most mentally ill defendants are perfectly capable of purposive action. As the bulk of the California decisions discussed in this section show, the psychotic killer typically plans his actions carefully and often carries them out exactly as he planned them. What he wants to do may be bizarre, and his motives for wanting to do it highly irrational, but there is no doubt that he usually intends to do what he wants to do and does what he intends to do in a way that gives effect to his prior intentions.[97] The contrary assumption requires a suspension of disbelief that, in the end, is likely to prove unacceptable to juries and to undermine public confidence in the diminished responsibility defence.

The second lesson is that a legal system which recognizes the plea of diminished responsibility should endeavour to draw a clear line between it and the defence of insanity. As its name suggests, the point of the plea is to cater for legally sane defendants who, by reason of mental abnormality, are not fully responsible for their actions. Thus it should not be possible to rely on diminished responsibility in cases where the evidence discloses that the defendant lacked the minimal cognitive capacity necessary to 'test reality', i.e., to assess his actions, and the motives or reasons for them, in the light of the relevant available evidence.[98] A defendant who cannot do this is legally insane, or would be in a rational legal system, and therefore requires treatment rather than a reduction of punishment of the kind normally associated with a plea of diminished responsibility. Nor is it an answer to this point to say that the necessary treatment can always be provided in prison. Apart from the fact that punishment *tout court* is inappropriate in the case of legally insane defendants, it is widely accepted that the facilities for psychiatric

96 See chapter 2.2.
97 This point is discussed at length in chapter 3.2-4.
98 See ch. 2.6 et seq.

treatment in most prisons are virtually non-existent.[99] As the California experience shows, these distinctions are apt to be overlooked when the defence of diminished responsibility is viewed primarily as a covert means of getting round the unwanted consequences of an excessively narrow definition of insanity.

The third lesson to be drawn from the California experience, although not unique to it, is that the availability of the defence of diminished responsibility may weaken the deterrent efficacy of the criminal law. Admittedly, this is not a danger if the scope of the defence is confined to mental illnesses, like psychosis, that impair a defendant's ability to 'test reality' in the sense just described, since there is plainly no deterrent advantage in punishing a defendant for a (partial) lack of capacity he could not help and which others can see he manifests. But it is a real possibility if the defence is modelled on the formula adopted by the Supreme Court of California in *Wolff*: viz., if it is extended to cases where there was a 'limited extent to which [the defendant] could maturely and meaningfully reflect upon the gravity of his contemplated act'.[100]

This form of words is so vague that it can be applied to just about any defendant whose upbringing and/or involvement in crime and deviance has coarsened his moral responses to the extent that he has become indifferent to the suffering of others, including his victims, and heedless of society's disapproval of his behaviour. Indeed, on this criterion, the more alienated from ordinary human values a defendant has become—i.e, the more depraved he has become—the more he would be entitled to the defence of diminished responsibility! Moreover, a formula of this kind, or indeed any formula couched in terms of mental *abnormality*, would effectively mean that any defendant who had been diagnosed as psychopathic would be automatically entitled to the defence notwithstanding that he may be more dangerous and no less culpable than the ordinary offender.

This is not to suggest, following Arenella,[101] that mental abnormality giving rise to dangerousness should invariably be treated as an *aggravating* circumstance, or that the idea of diminished responsibility should be abandoned on the grounds that it automatically treats mental abnormality as a formal mitigating factor. The problem of how to dispose of the legally sane but mentally impaired

99 See Morse, 'Mentally Disordered Offenders', *International Encyclopedia of Criminal Justice* (New York, 1983), 1046 at pp. 1047-48, and the references cited therein.

100 [1964] 61 Cal 2d at 821, 394 P 2d at 975, 40 Cal Rptr. at 287 (italics in original).

101 Op. cit., at pp. 857, 863.

defendant who is also dangerous certainly does highlight a serious flaw in the system of automatic sentencing discounts associated with the plea of diminished responsibility as it operated in California: namely, that a defendant of this type may need more, not less, custody than the normal offender.[102] Yet it is submitted that the solution to this problem is, following Scots law, to exclude psychopathy from the ambit of the defence where the evidence discloses that the defendant is incorrigibly dangerous, rather than to abandon the plea altogether. Given that many legally sane but mentally ill, and some legally sane but mentally abnormal, defendants are not incorrigibly dangerous, abandoning the defence altogether would be to throw the baby out with the bathwater.[103]

Alternatively, as the English experience of the defence illustrates, the problem can be solved at sentencing stage by imposing a life or long fixed term of imprisonment where this seems appropriate on the grounds of dangerousness, without prejudice to the many cases where a short custodial. or even non-custodial, sentence would be sufficient for retributive and/or therapeutic purposes. After all, one of the principal reasons for the adoption of diminished responsibility was to give the courts a sentencing discretion in homicide cases where there is evidence of mental illness or defect falling short of criminal incapacity.

## 5. CONCLUSION

It has been suggested that the ideal solution to the problems thrown up by the defence of diminished responsibility would be to abolish the fixed penalty for murder.[104] The fixed penalty means that judges cannot take evidence of diminished responsibility into account at the sentencing stage, but if it was removed they would be free to do so, with the result that there would be no need for a special defence of diminished responsibility or any of the doctrinal refinements associated with it. In other words, the argument is that since murder is not a homogeneous offence, it should attract a maximum, rather than a minimum, penalty of life imprisonment, as this would enable judges to give effect to extenuating circumstances, like diminished

102 As the California Supreme Court acknowledged in *Wetmore* [1978] 22 Cal 3d at 329, 583 2 P 2d at 1319, 149 Cal Rptr. at 276; see also Arenella, op. cit.

103 See *Wetmore* [1978] 22 Cal 3d at 329, 583 2 P 2d at 1319, 149 Cal Rptr. at 276.

104 The *Butler Report*, paras. 19.8-19.14; and see Advisory Council on the Penal System, *Sentences of Imprisonment* (HMSO, 1978), ch. 12.

responsibility and provocation, without having to negotiate the cumbersome superstructure of a formal plea in mitigation.

On the grounds of simplicity and efficiency, this view has much to commend it. Yet it has at least one serious flaw: as the Butler Committee has pointed out,[105] if implemented, it would mean that defendants who are now convicted of manslaughter on the grounds of provocation or diminished responsibility would henceforth be convicted of murder and consequently stigmatized as murderers in the public mind. Dell has made light of this criticism on the grounds that 'a person convicted of homicide will inevitably be set apart and stigmatized by that fact, whatever legal name is given to [his act]'.[106] But this hardly meets the objection that murder is generally regarded as the most heinous form of homicide, involving a significantly greater degree of moral turpitude than manslaughter. Alternatively, Dell has argued,[107] *pace* Lord Kilbrandon,[108] this problem could be solved by substituting a comprehensive offence of homicide for the existing offences of murder and manslaughter, thereby leaving it to the judge to give effect to differences of gravity, including culpability, at the sentencing stage. But this proposal also seems flawed, if only because the widespread popular view of murder as more serious than manslaughter is likely to be seen as an argument for the *retention,* rather than the abolition, of these crimes in their present form.

If this reasoning is correct, it follows that the defence of diminished responsibility *stricto sensu* represents the best, and certainly the most realistic, solution to the problem posed by the sane but mentally partially impaired defendant; and, consequently, that the real question is not whether, but in what form, it should be introduced in Ireland? As already indicated, the California model of the defence seems fatally flawed by the distortions engendered by its identification of diminished capacity with the negation of *mens rea.* The Scottish model also seems unsuitable, given that it appears to exclude psychopathy from the ambit of the defence on *a priori* grounds. In light of the Supreme Court's view, as stated in *O'Mahony,*[109] that psychopaths are entitled to the defence of insanity in Irish law, it is submitted that the sensible course of action would be to bring psychopathy within the scope of diminished responsibility.

105 Op. cit., para. 19.16.
106 Op. cit., p. 816, n.
107 Ibid.
108 In *Hyam v. DPP* [1975] AC 55 at 98.
109 [1986] ILRM 244 at 248; per Finlay CJ, delivering the judgment of the court.

This points to the adoption of the English model of the defence, although it should be emphasised that care needs to be taken to ensure a clean division of labour between experts and jurors on the issue of diminished responsibility. As suggested above, the former should be confined to questions of diagnosis and aetiology, so that the latter can be given exclusive dominion over the central question of diminished responsibility.[110] This arrangement is unlikely to please the prosecuting authorities, as it would preclude the English practice[111] of accepting a plea of diminished responsibility where the psychiatric evidence led by the defence was not being contested by the state, thereby increasing the overall cost of managing the plea.

However, it can scarcely be gainsaid that administrative efficiency is not the guiding aim of the criminal process and should never be pursued to the point where it conflicts with the core values of the criminal trial. In the common law tradition, it is a well established principle that the purpose of expert evidence is to assist the fact finder, not to usurp his role;[112] and since the English evidence suggests that trial judges, when left to their own devices, cannot be relied on to ensure that this principle is routinely applied in diminished responsibility cases, it is submitted that there is a good argument for requiring them to apply it by means of a positive rule of statute law.

110 This was originally the position in English law: *R v. Matheson* [1958] 42 Cr App Rep 145 (CA).

111 Introduced in the early 1960's and approved by the Court of Appeal in *R v. Cox* [1968] 52 Cr App Rep 130; see also *R v. Vinagre* [1979] 69 Cr App Rep 104.

112 *R v. Matheson* [1958] 42 Cr App Rep 145 (CA).

[9]

# The Civilian Experience

The problems associated with the insanity defence are not confined to the common law. Apart from issues like burden of proof and fitness to plead, which are peculiar to the adversarial structure of the common-law criminal trial, virtually all of the problems we have been discussing have long been at the centre of concern in civilian legal systems. In particular, the issue of the proper scope of the insanity defence has been a vexed question since the era of codification began in the early nineteenth century. Each civilian system has had to grapple with it, and the technical problem of definition to which it gives rise. Similarly, most civilian systems have long experience of the problems relating to the disposition and detention of insanity acquittees, especially insofar as these matters are affected by the presumption of dangerousness.

Yet it is impossible to speak of a dominant civilian conception of insanity, in the sense that there is no civilian equivalent of the M'Naghten Rules. The notoriety and influence of Article 10 of the Code Napoléon notwithstanding,[1] at least three distinct approaches to the problems of scope and definition can be identified: the psychopathological or psychiatric approach which equates insanity with mental illness; the psychological approach which defines it as a radical defect of reason; and the interactionist approach which seeks to combine these two perspectives by focusing on how the element of psychopathology affects the accused's cognitive functions, respectively.[2] As we shall see, there are many illuminating similarities and differences between these approaches and their common-law

1 See 9.2, infra.

2 See Bertolino, *L'Imputabilità e il Vizio di Mente nel Sistema Penale* (Milan, 1990), pp.143-9.

counterparts. Moreover, it should be emphasised at the outset that there are also striking variations within each approach from one legal system to another; and that a minority of civilian systems eschew all three approaches, having abolished the insanity defence altogether.[3]

## 1. THE PSYCHOPATHOLOGICAL APPROACH: FINLAND, NORWAY, GREECE AND SPAIN

The psychopathological approach reduces the issue of insanity to a diagnosis of mental illness or deficiency: the guiding question is was the accused suffering from a clinically diagnosed mental illness or deficiency when he did the act that forms the basis of the charge against him? The question of what constitutes mental illness or deficiency is settled by reference to psychiatric nosology, and a finding that the accused was mentally ill or deficient in the psychiatric sense leads automatically to a finding of insanity. In other words, a finding of mental illness or deficiency is a necessary and sufficient condition of a successful insanity defence, there being no residual question—of the kind familiar in the common-law world and in civilian systems that adhere to the mixed or interactionist approach—as to whether and to what extent the defendant's psychiatric condition may have impaired his reasoning powers or his ability to comply with the law's requirements. Moreover, there is no equivalent of the causal requirement familiar under the Durham Rule.[4] Once it is established that the defendant was mentally ill or deficient when he committed the wrongful act, there is a conclusive presumption of law that his act was a causal product of his illness or deficiency.

The psychopathological approach has been adopted in Finland, Norway, Greece and Spain. For example, article 3 of the Finnish Penal Code provides for a verdict of insanity where it has been established that the defendant was 'mentally ill or mentally deficient when he committed the act', and the Finnish courts have consistently held that the decision as to whether a particular defendant is men-

3 For a discussion of the Swedish experience of abolition see, Antilla, 'Conservative and Radical Criminal Policy in the Nordic Countries' in Christie et al (eds.) *Scandinavian Studies in Criminology* (London, 1971), p. 9 et seq.; Cornils, 'Neuere Entwicklung der Kriminalpolitik in den nordishen Landern (1987) *ZStW* 876.

4 See ch. 1.5.

tally ill or deficient is a psychiatric and not a legal question.[5] A similar situation obtains in Norway where article 44 of the Penal Code provides for a defence of insanity where it has been established that the accused was suffering from 'a morbid psychic disorder when he committed the act'.[6] The relevant provision in the Greek Penal Code is more narrowly drawn, being confined to cases of schizophrenia and depressive psychosis, respectively.[7]

The Spanish experience is especially interesting as the legislature has recently re-affirmed its commitment to the principle that proof of mental illness is *per se* enough to secure the insanity defence. This principle was originally adopted as article 8 of the Penal Code of 1822, which made the insanity defence available to 'el enajenado y el que se halle en situación de trastorno mental transitorio . . .', i.e., to the defendant who is shown to be 'alienated' or 'temporarily deranged'. The concepts of 'alienation' and 'temporary derangement' were not defined in article 8 and have not been legislatively defined since 1822. Indeed, the government defended its decision not to define them as part of the legislative reforms of 1983 on the grounds that they had always been associated with the concept of mental illness and that the definition of mental illness was a matter for psychiatrists.[8]

Academic writers have been more sceptical about the merits of treating insanity as a strictly medical issue, and have repeatedly criticized the psychopathological approach on penological and constitutional grounds.[9] The principal criticism has been that, as it trades on the essentially fluid concept of mental illness, article 8 is

5 See generally Koskinen, 'Strafrechtsreform in Finland: Zielsetzung und Stand' in Eser and Cornils (eds.) *Neuere Tendenzen der Kriminalpolitik* (Freiburg, 1987), p. 83; Backman et al, *Finnish Criminal Policy in Transition* (Helsinki, 1979). Article 3 also provides for cases of 'temporary derangement': *The Finnish Penal Code,* trans. Antilla and Joutson (London, 1987).

6 See Bjerke, 'Zielsetzung und Stand der Strafrechtsreform in Norwegen' in Eser and Cornils (eds.), op. cit., p. 124 et seq.; Matheson, 'Norwegen' in Eser and Huber (eds.) *Entwicklungstendenzen in Europa* (Freiburg, 1988), p. 1037 et seq.; Ancel et al, *Le Droit Pénal de Pays Scandinaves* (Paris, 1969), p. 51 et seq. The situation in Danish law is broadly similar: Ancel et al, ibid., p. 53.

7 Kareklas, 'Griechenland' in Eser and Huber (eds.), op. cit., p. 593; *The Greek Penal Code,* trans. Lolis and Mangakis (London, 1923), especially the references to articles 36-8; Mezger et al., *Das Ausländische Strafrecht der Gegenwart* (Berlin, 1959), p. 294.

8 Cobo del Rosal and Vives de Antón, *Derecho Penal* (Valencia, 1984), p. 466 et seq.; Mir Puig, *Derecho Penal* (Barcelona, 1984), p. 487 et seq.

9 Cf Carbonell Mateu et al., *Enfermedad Mental y Delito: Aspectos Psiciátricos* (Valencia, 1987), p. 169 et seq.

too vague to satisfy the constitutional requirement of legality, yet too wide to secure the preventive aims of the criminal law.[10] The courts have responded to this criticism in three interrelated ways. First, they have contrived a rigorously restrictive interpretation of the concept of 'alienation' as used in article 8, thereby limiting its application to cases of psychosis and schizophrenia—to the specific exclusion of personality and neurotic disorders.[11] Second, they have struck at the heart of the psychopathological approach by insisting that the psychotic condition on which the defendant is seeking to rely must be shown to have undermined his appreciation of what he was doing and his ability to act in accordance with that appreciation—thereby importing a common-law type causal requirement into the insanity defence.[12] Third, they have held that psychopathy is not a 'temporary derangement' within the meaning of article 8 as it neither affects a defendant's reasoning powers in the way just described nor qualifies as a mental illness in terms of psychiatric nosology.[13] Finally, they have defined 'alienation' as a pathological condition and a 'temporary derangement' as a pathological condition of temporary duration—to ensure, *inter alia,* that the purely emotional disorders do not attract the insanity defence.[14]

Taken together these developments suggest that the Spanish courts have all but abandoned the psychopathological approach in favour of a mixed or interactionist approach that combines psychiatric diagnosis with an assessment of the impact of mental disorder on the accused's reasoning powers. The advantage of this move is that it more or less solves the problems of vagueness and porousness traditionally associated with the psychiatric formula set out in article 8. Yet the outcome seems less than ideal. As one leading commentator has observed, if the requirement that mental illness must be pathologically based is taken literally to mean that the accused's alleged condition must be rooted in an *organic* pathology, the effect

10 For example, see Devesa, *Derecho Penal Espanól* (Madrid, 1986), p. 588; Torío Lopez, 'Las Fórmulas Legislativas Sobre la Enfermidad Mental: Discusión del Concepto de 'Enajenación' ', in *Torío Lopez (ed.) Estudios Jurídicos en Honor del Profesor Octavi Pérez-Vitoria* (Barcelona, 1983), p. 970 et seq.

11 See the list of authorities cited by Devesa, op. cit., p. 589, n. 16.

12 See Córdoba Roda and Mourullo, *Comentarios al Código Penal* (Barcelona, 1976), p. 206.

13 The case law is virtually unanimous on these issues: Carbonell Mateu et al, op. cit., p. 234 et seq.

14 For a discussion of the jurisprudence on this point, see Devesa, op. cit., p. 604 et seq.

will be to exclude the functional psychoses and schizophrenias from the ambit of the insanity defence.[15] In other words, the result will be an insanity defence as unacceptably narrow as article 8 was thought to be unacceptably wide.[16]

### 2. THE PSYCHOLOGICAL APPROACH: FRANCE, BELGIUM AND HOLLAND

The psychological approach equates insanity with unsoundness of mind—which is typically defined in broad, non-technical language to include any condition that radically impairs an accused's reasoning powers. The classic example of the psychological approach is contained in article 64 of the French Penal Code which provides that 'Il n'y a ni crime ni delit, lorsque le prévenu était en etat de démence au temps de l'action.'[17] Other examples include article 71 of the Belgian Penal Code, which allows the insanity defence to anyone who was in 'a state of *démence* at the time of the act or who committed the act under the influence of an impulse he was unable to resist';[18] and article 37 of the Dutch Penal Code, which defines insanity as a 'a morbid disorder of [the accused's] mental capacities.'[19] The concepts of *démence* and 'morbid disorder of the mental faculties' are not themselves defined in these provisions but the French[20] (and Belgian)[21] and Dutch[22] courts, respectively, have repeatedly declared

15 See Carbonell Mateu et al, op. cit., p. 280 et seq.

16 Notwithstanding these criticisms, Article 19 of the new Draft Penal Code (*Anteproyecto de Código Penal;* última versión, 30 Diciembre 1991) retains the key concepts and essential structure of Article 8.

17 Article 64 is a restatement of article 10 of the Code Napoléon. Prior to the enactment of article 10 the insane defendant was punished more severely than the ordinary criminal. For an account of the successful attempt—led by the pioneering forensic psychiatrists Pinel and Esquirol—to get the old law changed, see Aussel, *Les Délinquants Aliénés et Anormaux Mentaux* (Paris, 1966). See generally Brousolle, *Délinquance et Déviance* (Toulouse, 1978).

18 Article 10 of the Code Napoléon was applied in the province of Belgium until the Belgian Penal Code was enacted in 1876. The *démence,* but not the irresistible impulse, provision in the latter was directly copied from it. I am grateful to Professor Christine Van den Wyngaert of the University of Antwerp for this information.

19. The Dutch Penal Code came into force in 1886.

20 See Adda and Benezech, *L'irresponsabilité Pénale des Handicapés Mentaux* (Paris, 1978) p. 28 et seq.

21 See Costant, *Traité Élementaire de Droit Pénal* (Liege, 1965), p. 398 et seq; *Précis de Droit Pénal* (Liege, 1975), p. 240 et seq; Van den Wyngaert, *Strafrecht en Procesrecht,* Boek 1 (Antwerp, 1991), p. 248 et seq.

22 See Kruger, *Kante van Imputasie in die Nederlandse en Suid-Afrikause Strafreg*

that they are not psychiatric terms, in the sense that they should not be taken to denote a particular psychiatric illness or diagnosis or even a group of illnesses or diagnoses. This move has resulted in a jurisprudence-driven definition of insanity in which the issue of whether or not the accused was mentally ill gives way to the question of whether his condition has undermined his autonomy as a moral agent.[23] In other words, the emphasis is placed on the psychological effects of the accused's condition as determined by the courts, as opposed to a diagnostic assessment of the symptoms of his condition by psychiatrists.

Not surprisingly, this formula has not been easy to apply as its effect has been to replace one set of contentious ideas (the categories of clinical psychiatry) with another (the philosophical concepts of personal autonomy and moral agency). The principal difficulty has been to give concrete legal form to the abstract notion of personal autonomy. Broadly speaking, the courts have attempted to do this by identifying the concept of personal autonomy with the intellectual and volitional capacities associated with intentional action: viz., the ability to understand what one is doing and the ability to control one's actions, respectively.[24] The notion of being able to understand what one is doing has not received anything like the detailed treatment associated with its common-law counterpart, but there is general agreement that it is confined to the strictly cognitive aspect of understanding and therefore does not include a properly developed *moral* sense or perspective.[25] This refinement is usually invoked to justify the exclusion of the psychopathic and neurotic disorders from the ambit of the insanity defence,[26] although it may not actually entail that conclusion—since it is arguable that the neuroses at least partially affect the ability to think rationally about the effect of one's actions, and an insanity criterion that embraces the neuroses, albeit theoretically, is open to the charge of overinclusiveness. Alternatively, the courts sometimes insist, in the manner of pre-M'Naghten English law, on the total negation of the accused's powers of understanding as a prerequisite of the insanity

(Leiden, 1972), p. 295 et seq; Waling, *Enstehung und Entwicklung des Niederlandisches Strafgesetzbuches,* Research Paper, Max Plank Institute (Freiburg, 1986), p. 21.

23 Merle and Vitu, *Traité de Droit Criminel* (Paris, 1987), p. 739; Stefani et al, *Droit Pénal Général* (Paris, 1978), p. 328.

24 Stefani et al, ibid., p. 400 et seq.

25 See Stefani et al, ibid., p. 411.

26 See Merle and Vitu, op. cit., p. 740.

defence.[27] But this criterion seems equally unsatisfactory since, if sharply applied, it would be seriously underinclusive as it would remove the insanity defence from many psychotic defendants.

The courts have also found it difficult to develop a satisfactory criterion of the volitional aspect of personal autonomy. This is largely because they have tended to treat volitional control as synonymous with free will, i.e., with the ability to identify alternative courses of action and choose between them; and this tendency has been reinforced by some academic commentators.[28] For example, the Belgian Supreme Court has consistently held that loss of volitional control entails the destruction of free will to the point where the accused was completely powerless to resist the desires and impulses which led to the wrongful act.[29] As the analysis of the rule in *Doyle* illustrates, the literal application of this criterion removes from the ambit of the insanity defence those forms of psychosis—such as paranoid schizophrenia and depressive psychosis—that entail the exercise of choice on the defendant's part.[30] Indeed, the only way that Belgian trial judges have been able to get round this difficulty is by ignoring the free will requirement altogether, or by treating it as a loose metaphor for the loss of personal autonomy associated with serious mental illness.[31]

On the assumption that both paranoid schizophrenia and depressive psychosis ought to attract the insanity defence, both of these strategies can be defended on the grounds that they produce the desired result. Yet it is difficult to reconcile either of them with the constitutional (legality) principle that the limits of criminal liability should be clearly fixed by law and uniformly adhered to by the courts. Moreover, the fact that the courts have found it necessary to resort to strategies of this kind in order to guarantee a workable insanity defence exposes the contradiction at the heart of the psychological approach: the fact that its emphasis on the destruction of free

27 See Stefani et al, op. cit., p. 418; Merle and Vitu, op. cit., p. 735.

28 For example, according to Schuind, the concept of *démence* means 'unsoundness of mind' and only applies to a defendant whose mental condition 'rendered him incapable of doing otherwise or of bringing his behaviour into conformity with the law': *Traité Pratique de Droit Criminel*, Bd 1, (Bruxelles, 1980), p. 165.

29 For an exhaustive review of the relevant jurisprudence, see Schäfer, 'Belgien' in Eser and Huber (eds.) *Entwicklungstendenzen in Europa* (Freiburg, 1988), p. 32 et seq. See also Cass. 28 Fév. 1955, in Pas. 1955, I, 709; Cass. 8 Sept. 1983, ivi 1983, I, 33.

30 See ch. 3.3-4.

31 For a detailed account of the case law on this point, see Schuind, op. cit., p. 167 et seq.

will leads to a seriously inadequate account of the psychological aspects of serious mental illness.

Articles 64, 71 and 37 of the French, Belgian and Dutch Penal Codes, respectively, do not require proof of a causal link between the accused's state of mind and his alleged offence: it is enough that he was in a condition that qualifies as 'a state of "démence" *at the time of the act.*'[32] This arrangement is consistent with the assumption that since serious mental disorder is a pervasive defect of reason affecting the whole personality, the question of causation is otiose and so should not be allowed to determine the availability of the insanity defence. Yet it seems likely that its survival is due in no small measure to the fact that the courts have limited the insanity defence to cases of severe psychosis involving the negation of reason and/or freedom—i.e., to cases where it would be jesuitical to argue that there was no connection between the disorder and the act.[33] Whether it would survive a more liberal interpretation of the concept of *démence* —for example, one that embraced cases of paranoia where the defendant's victim was not obviously one of his fancied persecutors— is an open question.

A striking feature of the psychological approach is that a successful insanity defence leads to an unconditional acquittal: the courts have no power to order the mandatory detention of successful insanity defendants in a mental hospital. Once an acquittal has been secured, it is up to the accused person himself to decide if he needs psychiatric treatment. The question of whether he needs to be hospitalized is a matter for his family and is governed by the ordinary law of civil commitment. Thus in France even in cases where there is evidence that a person who has successfully relied on the insanity defence is dangerous, that person cannot be removed to a mental hospital unless and until a relative takes steps to have him committed, or involuntary commitment is sought by the prefect of police. This arrangement is consistent with the basic premise of the psychological approach that the insanity defence is confined to the issue of criminal responsibility for alleged wrongdoing; but it has been heavily criticized as unrealistic.[34]

The unconditional acquittal of insane defendants was also the

32. Italics added. This is the wording actually used in articles 64 and 71 of the French and Belgian codes, respectively. Article 37 of the Dutch Penal Code is similarly phrased.

33 Walker also makes this point in his discussion of the French position: op. cit., p. 90.

34 See Stefani et al., op cit., pp. 408, 557.

norm in Belgium until 1964, when the social defence law of that year gave trial judges the power to order the hospitalization of insane defendants whom they believed to be in need of inpatient psychiatric treatment.[35] A similar reform was introduced in Holland in 1986, according to which the courts can order the compulsory treatment (including hospitalization) of defendants suffering from any form of mental illness—even in cases where no causal link has been established between the accused's illness and his alleged wrongdoing—provided there is clear evidence that he is a danger to person and property.[36]

Legal systems that adhere to the psychological approach have traditionally eschewed the concept of diminished responsibility: a defendant is either fully responsible for his actions and therefore eligible for punishment or not responsible at all and therefore completely exempt from punishment or (until the reforms discussed in the preceding paragraph were introduced) restraint of any kind. There is no intermediate category of partial responsibility catering for hard cases of mental or emotional disturbance that do not qualify as instances of *démence* or 'disordered mental capacity'. Thus in French law evidence of mental or emotional disorder that fails to disclose a state of *démence* is irrelevant both to the grade of offence of which a defendant may be convicted and the verdict of the court. The harshness of this rule has been ameliorated in practise by the fact that the courts routinely accept evidence of this kind at the sentencing stage as grounds for reducing the *quantum* of punishment appropriate in an individual case.[37] For example, evidence of mental deficiency, neurosis, hysteria, epilepsy and psychopathy is almost invariably regarded as an extenuating circumstance in this regard.[38]

This arrangement has been widely condemned by academic commentators on the grounds that mentally disordered defendants require treatment rather than a diminution of punishment and that the courts should be empowered to order psychiatric treatment

35 See Doucet, *Précis de Droit Pénal Général* (Liege, 1965), p. 199; Costant, op. cit., p. 404. The new arrangements have themselves been criticized on the grounds that they are inconsistent with the codified position and the principles on which it is based: Costant, ibid., p. 410.

36 See Waling, op. cit., p. 933; Brand-Koolen, 'At the Government's Pleasure. Trends and Developments in the Compulsory Treatment of Mentally Disturbed Offenders in the Netherlands', (1987) *Int J Law and Psychiat* 339.

37 See Adda and Benezech, op. cit., p. 36.

38 See Stefani et al., op. cit., p. 410 et seq., for a review of the relevant jurisprudence.

(including hospitalization) where the medical evidence shows that it would be appropriate to do so. This proposal has not been acted on by the French legislature, probably in deference to the principle—implicit in the psychological approach—that since punishment is the only justifiable response to a finding of criminal responsibility, a reduction of punishment is the appropriate response to a finding of diminished responsibility.[39]

The Belgian solution to this dilemma is contained in the social defence law of 1964, which provides trial judges with a discretionary power to order the detention and treatment in a mental hospital of defendants suffering from 'mental weakness' or 'serious mental disequilibrium' falling short of a state of *démence* but significantly affecting their ability to control their actions. This arrangement, which is usually employed in cases where there is medical evidence of psychopathy, is tantamount to a defence of diminished responsibility. Unlike its English counterpart of that name, however, it applies to offences generally (and not just to murder) and does not lead to a conviction of a lower grade of offence than that with which the defendant was originally charged.[40] Similar arrangements were put in place by the Dutch legislature in 1986, although the discretionary power to substitute treatment for punishment seems to have been more tightly drawn in the Dutch case: the court of trial must be satisfied that the accused was suffering from some form of mental illness not excluding psychopathy (although there is no requirement that the illness be shown to have caused the alleged wrongdoing); and that compulsory hospitalization is necessary to ensure the safety of persons and property.[41]

### 3. THE INTERACTIONIST APPROACH: GERMANY, AUSTRIA, ITALY AND SWITZERLAND

The difficulties of fashioning a satisfactory criterion of insanity within the parameters of the psychological approach will be familiar to common lawyers. Broadly speaking, they reflect the fact that the basic tenets of that approach—as encapsulated in the idea that insanity completely destroys understanding and/or freedom—were derived from eighteenth century rationalism and therefore pre-date

39 See Merle and Vitu, op. cit., p. 742.
40 See Costant, *Traité*, p. 104; Précis, p. 243; Schäfer, op. cit., p. 32.
41 See Brand-Koolen, op. cit., p. 349.

the development of modern psychiatry. As in the case of the common-law world, this gave rise to a false antinomy between the legal and psychiatric conceptions of insanity in which the former acquired the status of a fixed, *a priori* criterion controlled by the courts, against which psychiatric claims about the impact of mental illness on human behaviour could be assessed (and, more often than not, rejected). Rather than being seen as an important resource for the development of a criterion of insanity that reflected the realities of serious mental disorder, modern psychiatry thus came to be regarded as an interloper that had no intrinsic connection with the principles of criminal liability and that threatened the very idea of moral responsibility. This in turn spawned a definition of insanity that excluded some conditions—such as paranoid schizophrenia and depressive psychosis—that are universally recognized by psychiatrists as serious mental disorders, while including others—such as irresistible impulse and volitional insanity—that have no basis in psychiatric nosology.[42]

The interactionist approach seeks to redress this imbalance by incorporating the findings of modern psychiatry into the definition of insanity. The approach proceeds in two stages. The first stage is concerned with the question of whether or not the accused is suffering from a serious mental illness. This issue is regarded as a psychiatric matter, although it falls to be determined by the courts in the light of a codified criterion of serious mental disorder. The second stage is concerned with deciding whether the agreed mental disorder prevented the accused from understanding the significance of his actions or from acting in accordance with such understanding. This issue is regarded as a legal matter, although the criteria actually employed by the courts when determining it coincide with the psychiatric understanding of the psychological effects of serious mental disorder. Thus stage two ensures that the inquiry is based on a realistic assessment of the impact of serious mental disorder on the accused's reasoning powers, while at the same time avoiding the equation of insanity with psychiatric diagnosis characteristic of the psychopathological approach.

The interactionist approach has been adopted in Germany, Italy, Austria and Switzerland.[43] The German experience is particularly

42 See chapter 3.7.

43 It has also been adopted in Hungary where article 24 of the Penal Code allows the insanity defence to anyone who 'commits the action in a state of mental deficiency, in particular a state of insanity, of mental weakness, of intellectual degeneration, of schizophrenia or personality disorder, that renders him

interesting as the relative merits of the approach have been hotly debated since the 1930s, and were exhaustively reviewed in the run-up to the enactment of the new Criminal Code in 1975.[44] Article 51 of the old Code of 1871 limited the types of disorder that could support a finding of insanity to 'disorders of consciousness', 'pathological disorders of mental functioning' and 'mental weakness', respectively; and the courts accepted the prevailing wisdom of contemporary forensic psychiatry that these categories referred exclusively to organically-based disorders, i.e., to disorders that could be traced to an underlying physical pathology.[45] Furthermore, a finding of insanity depended on proof that the alleged mental disorder had completely obliterated the accused's freedom of choice.[46] This latter rule, which excluded all but the most severe forms of hallucinatory psychosis from the ambit of the insanity defence, was modified in 1933 by the substitution of a requirement that it was sufficient that the accused's mental disorder prevented him 'from realizing that his actions were wrong or from acting in accordance with that understanding.'

Since it was designed specifically to take account of the discovery that serious psychiatric illness can profoundly affect an accused's capacity to act rationally without impairing his freedom of choice,

incapable of understanding the consequences of his actions or of acting in accordance with that understanding': Gonczol, 'Mentally Abnormal Offenders in Hungarian Criminal Procedure', cited by Bertolino, op. cit., p. 289n. The Hungarian and Austrian Penal Codes follow the German model of classifying the varieties of mental condition capable of supporting the insanity defence at stage one of an insanity inquiry.

44 See generally Mrozynsky, 'Krankheit—Hang—Schädliche Neigungen' (1985) *GA* 2; Maurach-Zipf, *Strafrecht, Allg.* (Heidelberg, 1983) p. 450 et seq.

45 See Hippel, *Deutsches Strafrecht* (Berlin, 1925), p. 125 et seq. The German Code of 1975 also adheres to the principle of classifying the types of disorder capable of supporting the insanity defence (although it modifies the boundaries of the traditional categories and adds a new one: Mrozynsky, op. cit.; Maurach-zipf, op. cit., p. 452); as do the modern Austrian and Hungarian Criminal Codes: Triffter, *Österreichisches Strafrecht* (Vienna, 1985) p. 75 et seq.; *Bertolino,* op. cit., respectively. By contrast, article 89 of the Italian Penal Code merely requires proof that the defendant was suffering from a clinically diagnosed illness at stage one of an insanity hearing, there being no requirement that the illness fits into a given psychiatric or medical category: Bertolino, op. cit., p. 376 et seq. The rationale for insisting on an underlying pathology at stage one of the interactionist approach can probably be traced to the influence of the medical model of insanity on German legal thinking about the insanity defence: Blau, 'Prolegomena zur Strafrechtlichen Schuldfähigkeit' (1982) *Jura* 401.

46 See Blau, op. cit. p. 400.

the revised arrangement should have broadened the insanity defence to include all of the psychoses and schizophrenias. However, its effect was blunted in this regard by the fact that the courts initially continued to espouse the traditional orthodoxy that only organically-based disorders could support the insanity defence within the meaning of article 51.[47] In other words, the liberalization of stage two of the interactionist approach (the autonomy criterion) was effectively offset by insisting on the narrowest possible interpretation of stage one (the diagnostic criterion).

This difficulty eventually receded as the courts grew to accept the idea that the purely functional psychoses—such as paranoid schizophrenia—should be brought within the ambit of the insanity defence notwithstanding the fact that the language of article 51 appeared to exclude them.[48] However, a fresh difficulty appeared as a direct result of this change in judicial attitudes: in the form of an ever-widening gap between the codified definition of insanity and the decisions of the courts. Indeed, by the late 1960s, this gap had widened to the point where neurosis and psychopathy (and even some personality disorders falling short of psychopathy) were sometimes accepted by the courts as capable of supporting the insanity defence,[49] a state of affairs that would have been unthinkable ten years previously.

A solution to this problem was finally worked out in the context of the re-codification debate of the early 1970s. One side in that debate had argued for a broad definition of mental illness that would add a fourth category—defined as 'other mental abnormalities'—to the list of disorders traditionally regarded as capable of supporting the insanity defence, on the grounds that this move would provide the necessary statutory basis for the established practice of extending the insanity defence to non-organic disorders.[50] The other side conceded that this was a desirable objective but rejected the proposed means of achieving it, on the grounds that it would also give legislative approval to the minority practice of treating psychopathy as a recognized mental disorder for the purposes of the insanity defence. The argument was that since there is widespread disagreement on

47 See Blau, ibid., p. 401.
48 See Blau, ibid.
49 See Schmitt, 'Die "schwere andere seelische Abartigkeit" in par. 20 und 21' (1980) *ZStW* 346 et seq.
50 This side of the debate is summarised by Rasch, 'Die Zuordnung der psychiatrisch-psychologischen Diagnosen zu den vier psychischen Merkmalen der par 20 und 21 StGB' (1984) *Strafverteidiger* 265 et seq.

the question of whether psychopathy is a mental illness, there could be no guarantee that a legislative provision extending the insanity defence to psychopathic defendants would be uniformly applied; and that the ensuing uncertainty would weaken the deterrent force of the criminal law and could not be justified on retributive grounds.[51]

The solution eventually adopted as article 20 of the new Criminal Code of 1975 was a compromise between these two positions: the functional psychoses were comprehended by the concept of 'psychic disorders of a pathological nature' (which replaced the old category of 'pathological disorders of mental functioning') and the proposed fourth category was limited to 'other *serious* mental abnormalities.'[52] The latter qualification means that the courts cannot exclude psychopathy at stage one of an insanity inquiry on the *a priori* ground that it is not rooted in an organic pathology and is not generally regarded as a mental illness.[53] By the same token, it ensures that the courts will accept evidence of psychopathy at this stage if and only if it discloses that the accused's condition was so severe as to approximate to one of the other conditions specifically provided for under article 20, which in practice means that the only cases that get past stage one are those where the evidence discloses that the accused was so alienated from ordinary morality that he had little or no appreciation of the significance of his actions.[54]

However, it should be remembered that even if an accused's condition qualifies as a 'serious mental abnormality' at stage one of an insanity hearing, it must still pass the autonomy criterion which

51 For example, see Krümpelmann, 'Die Neugestaltung der Vorschriften über die Schuldfähigkeit durch das Zweite Strafrechtsreformgesetz vom 4 Juli 1969' (1976) *ZStW* 6 et seq.

52 Italics added. For a detailed description and analysis of the four categories of mental disorder/abnormality embraced by article 20, see Glatzel, *Forensische Psychiatrie* (Stuttgart, 1985), p. 37 et seq.

53 See Meyer, 'Psychiatrische Diagnosen und ihre Bedeutung für die Schuldfähigkeit im Sinne der par. 20/21' (1976) *ZStW* 54.

54 The courts take this requirement to be logically entailed by article 20: Witter, 'Die Beurteilung der Schuldfähikeit bei Belastungsreaktionen, Neurosen und Persönlichkeitsstörungen am Beispiel der Affektdelikte' in Witter (ed.) *Die psychiatrische Sachverständige im Strafrecht* (Berlin, 1987), p. 175 et seq. Approximation is judged by whether or not the relevant abnormality produces effects similar to those normally associated with serious mental illness: Witter, ibid. By contrast, article 11 of the Austrian Criminal Code of 1975, which is virtually identical in both form and content with article 20 of its German counterpart, expressly requires 'other serious mental abnormalities' to be 'equivalent' in their effects to serious mental illness: Triffter, op. cit., p. 75.

article 20 carries over from the 1933 legislation before it will attract an acquittal. Article 20 defines this criterion as a requirement that the accused's condition must have prevented him from 'understanding that his actions were wrong or from acting in accordance with that understanding'.[55] Moreover, although it is well established that this requirement amounts to a legal test of culpability (as opposed to a question of psychiatric diagnosis),[56] the courts have generally interpreted it to mean that the accused must have been so deranged that he was unable to assess his actions in the light of ordinary human motives and reactions.[57] In other words, they have effectively equated the autonomy criterion with the psychiatric concept of 'reality testing.'[58]

The upshot of this arrangement is that most cases of psychosis and schizophrenia—both organic and functional—qualify for the insanity defence on the autonomy criterion laid down in article 20, since the inability to test reality is a characteristic feature of these conditions. By contrast, most cases of psychopathy fail the autonomy criterion, since a high degree of moral alienation (coupled with a strong desire

55 Thus the autonomy criterion in Article 20 implicitly requires proof of a causal link between the accused's deranged mental state and his wrongful act. The position is similar in regard to the corresponding article (11) of the Austrian Criminal Code: Eder and Rieder, *Die freiheitsentziehenden vorbeugenden Massnahmen* (Vienna, 1985), p. 35 et seq. The position in Italian law is less clear. Article 88 of the Penal Code provides that a defendant is entitled to the insanity defence if 'at the moment he committed the act he was, as a result of illness, in such a state of mind as to exclude *la capacità d'intendere o di volere*'—which strongly suggests a causal requirement since *'la capacità d'intendere o di volere'* has traditionally been defined as the ability to understand the significance of one's actions or to act in accordance with such understanding: Fiandaca and Musco, *Diritto Penale* (Bologna, 1991), p. 162. On the other hand, there are those who argue that there is no need to prove a causal link between the accused's mental condition and his act if there is clear evidence that he was suffering from a condition that typically undermines *'la capacità d'intendere o di volere'*: see the references cited by Fiandaca and Musco, ibid. The problem of causation in the context of the insanity defence is discussed in chapter 1.4-5.

56 Witter, op. cit.

57 See Roxin, 'Schuldunfähigkeit Erwachsener im Urteil des Strafrecht' in *Fest. Spann* (Heidelberg, 1986), p. 466. The autonomy criterion in Article 11 of the Austrian Criminal Code of 1975 has been similarly construed by the courts: Triffter, op. cit., p. 259.

58 Cf Witter, 'Die Grundlagen für die Beurteilung der Schuldfähigkeit im Strafrecht' in Witter, op. cit., p. 37 et seq., who argues that the courts have not gone far enough in this regard—apparently on the assumption that the inability to 'test reality' is *not* confined to the psychoses, and may also include severe psychopathy. The concept of 'reality testing' is explained in ch. 2.7.

to gratify one's impulses and extreme indifference to the plight of one's victims) does not necessarily impair the intellectual ability to grasp that there is no objective justification for unprovoked violence against the person. Where there *is* clear evidence of a cognitive failure of this sort in cases of psychopathy the courts are naturally prepared to accept it as a basis for the insanity defence. However, since evidence of psychopathy unaccompanied by evidence of psychosis generally leads to a conviction, it would appear that it is the element of psychosis rather than the element of psychopathy that determines the availability of the insanity defence in such cases.[59]

There is no defence of diminished responsibility in German law but article 21 of the Criminal Code provides that evidence of any condition that partially impairs an accused's intellectual faculties within the meaning of article 20 may be taken into account when punishment is being apportioned.[60] Reliance on this provision generally, though not invariably, leads to a reduction of punishment in cases where the defendant is able to show that his judgment was

59 See Krümpelmann, op. cit., p. 23. One empirical study has suggested that approximately two out of every ten cases of psychopathy get the benefit of the insanity defence (the bulk of the remainder resulting in a reduction of punishment under article 21 StGB): Schumann, *Psychisch Kranke Rechtsbrecher* (Stuttgart, 1987), p. 72. The position in Italian law is that article 90 of the Penal Code expressly excludes the emotional disorders—including psychopathy—from the ambit of the insanity defence: Pagliaro, 'Colpevolezza e Responsibilità Obiettiva: Aspetti di Politica Criminale ed Elaborazione Dogmatica' (1988) *Riv. It. Dir. Proc. Pen.* 389 et seq.

60 The position is substantially the same in Italian law where article 89 of the Penal Code provides that 'A person who, at the time he committed the act, was, as a result of illness, in such a state of mind as seriously to diminish, without excluding, his ability to understand the significance of his actions or to act in accordance with that understanding, is answerable for his wrongful act; but the punishment is mitigated' The distinction between a finding of insanity *(vizio totale di mente)* under article 88 of the Penal Code and of diminished responsibility giving rise to a reduction of sentence *(vizio partiale di mente)* under article 89 is one of degree rather than kind; even in the latter case the accused's illness must have seriously (as opposed to radically) impaired his reasoning powers: Bertolino, *L'imputabilità e il Vizio di Mente nel Sistema Penale,* (Milan, 1990), p. 388 et seq; Crespi, 'Imputabilità' (Diritto Penale), *Enc. Dir, XX* (Milan, 1970), p. 764. Moreover, article 90 of the Penal Code provides that where the impairment of an accused's reasoning powers is attributable to causes other than an underlying illness, the court may not accept a plea of insanity or a plea in mitigation. Article 90 has been criticized on the grounds that some emotional states—such as severe shock or panic—can undermine an accused's reasoning powers in a way that is comparable with, if not identical to, the psychological effects of clinical psychosis: Fiandaca and Musco, op. cit., p. 163.

clouded by neurosis or in psychopathy cases where there is evidence of severe moral alienation.[61] Although an article 20 verdict leads to a theoretical acquittal and the application of article 21 presupposes a conviction, article 63 continues the arrangement, introduced in 1933, whereby the government can initiate proceedings for the civil commitment of a defendant who gets the benefit of either article if there is evidence of a substantial risk that he might otherwise commit a serious offence and that the resultant loss of liberty would not be disproportionate to the harm caused or threatened.[62] This provision has been repeatedly criticized on the grounds that it leads to a system of arbitrary detention as there are no reliable criteria for deciding when someone who has been 'diagnosed' as dangerous ceases to be so: 'dangerousness' is an administrative prediction, not a condition whose onset and disappearance can be accurately diagnosed like the symptoms of an illness. Moreover, it is in the nature of a self-validating prediction as it cannot easily be falsified as long as the allegedly 'dangerous' person is hospitalized.[63]

Empirical research findings suggest that the risk of arbitrary detention is minuscule as far as article 21 cases are concerned since only a tiny proportion of these result in civil commitment proceedings;[64] but that it cannot be discounted in the case of insanity acquittals as about half of these lead to hospitalization as a result of such proceedings.[65] However, by ensuring that the period of hospitalization cannot exceed the normal period of imprisonment associated with the crime of which the defendant was acquitted, the proportionality requirement in article 63 at least sets a minimum standard of safety in this regard.[66]

Austrian criminal law also recognizes a system of preventive

61 Psychopathy cases account for over seventy per cent of the total number of successful article 21 cases: Schumann, op. cit., p. 72.

62 '. . . es muß eine akute Gefahr für Dritte vorliegen': Baumann and Weber, *Strafrecht* (Bielefeld, 1985), p. 716.

63 See Eicknoff, 'Die Benachteiligung des psychisch kranken Rechtsbrechers im Strafrecht' (1987) *NStZ*, 65; Rasch, 'Die Prognose im Massregelnvollzug als Kalkuliertes Risiko' in *Fest. Blau* (Berlin, 1985) p. 309 at p. 317.

64 One study puts the proportion as low as three per cent: Athen, 'Zur Gegenwärtigen Situation der Behandlung psychisch kranker Rechtsbrecher' (1985) *Mschrkrim* 29.

65 See Athen, ibid.

66 Eicknoff, op. cit., p. 66, has demonstrated that the proportion of successful insanity defendants hospitalized under article 63 would be much higher but for judicial misgivings about the risk of arbitrary detention associated with the criterion of dangerousness.

psychiatric detention for dangerous defendants.[67] Article 21 of the Criminal Code empowers a court of trial to order the *indeterminate* hospitalization of persons acquitted on the grounds of insanity under article 11 or whose sentence was reduced on the grounds of diminished responsibility under article 34,[68] provided it is satisfied (i) that the defendant is dangerous, i.e., *highly likely* to commit other similar offences, (ii) that the offence with which he was charged attracts a prison sentence of more than one year, and (iii) that his 'psychic and intellectual abnormality was particularly grave.'

Although the latter requirement seems to have been conceived by the legislature as additional to the need for a finding of insanity under article 11, it is generally regarded as otiose by the courts in insanity cases.[69] By contrast, in cases where there has been a finding of diminished responsibility under article 34, the courts have insisted on giving effect to it by requiring proof that the defendant's condition is amenable to psychiatric treatment.[70] In practice this means that very few psychopaths are hospitalized under article 21 given that most forms of psychopathy are notoriously untreatable and acknowledged to be so by psychiatrists.[71]

Hospital orders made under article 21 are regarded as indeterminate, there being no proportionality requirement—of the kind included in article 63 of the German Criminal Code—whereby the period of hospitalization may not exceed the normal term of imprisonment for the crime charged. This arrangement was apparently designed to maximize the therapeutic objectives of article 21, but it

67 See Berger, 'Österreich' in Eser and Huber (eds.), op. cit., p.11.

68 Like its German counterpart, Austrian criminal law does not recognize a defence of diminished responsibility: article 34 merely lists the types of mental disorder and abnormality that may be relied on as extenuating circumstances when punishment is being imposed. Moreover, a particular disorder or abnormality will only be treated as an extenuating circumstance in the event that there is evidence that it significantly impaired the accused's ability to understand that his actions were wrong or to act in accordance with that understanding. In other words, article 34 employs the autonomy criterion that governs the insanity defence *simpliciter* under article 11. So, for example, cases of psychopathy and neurosis that present as mere deviations from the behavioural norm unaccompanied by cognitive impairment are not given the benefit of article 34: Probst, 'Die strafgerichtliche Behandlung geistig abnormer Rechtsbrecher aus kriminalpolitischer Sicht', in *AAVV Strafrechtliche Probleme der Gegenwart* (Ottenstein, 1981), p. 177 et seq.

69 See Mayerhoffer and Reider, *Das Österreichische Strafrecht* (Vienna, 1981), para. 21, n. 2.

70 Ibid., par. 21, n. 5.

71 See Walker, op. cit., p. 82.

has been heavily criticized on constitutional and human rights grounds. The absence of a proportionality requirement effectively means that the duration as well as the imposition of a term of therapeutic detention turns on an essentially unverifiable prediction of dangerousness.[72]

The Italian version of the mixed approach is also interesting. Unlike its German counterpart, the Italian Penal Code does not list the types of disorder capable of supporting the insanity defence: article 88 simply provides that a defendant is entitled to the defence if 'at the time he committed the act, he was, as a result of illness, in such a state of mind that he did not understand the significance of his actions or was unable to act in accordance with that understanding'; and article 89 provides for a plea of diminished responsibility in mitigation of punishment in respect of illnesses that partially impair an accused's reasoning powers. Moreover, the concept of 'illness' (infermità) employed in articles 88 and 89 is not confined to mental illnesses; any clinically verifiable illness state, whether physical or mental, which affects the accused's reasoning powers in the appropriate way, is capable of supporting the insanity defence or the plea of diminished responsibility, respectively.[73] Although the authorities are not unanimous on the point, the dominant view is that psychopathy is not an illness within the meaning of articles 88 and 89.[74]

However, Italian law draws a sharp distinction between physical and mental illness in respect of the disposition of persons who have been acquitted on the grounds of insanity under article 88 or whose sentence has been reduced on the grounds of diminished responsibility under article 89. Under articles 219 and 222 of the Penal Code, preventive detention was an automatic consequence in cases

72 Both the critical literature and the jurisprudence are reviewed by Gratz, 'Die Unterbringung geistig abnormer Rechtsbrecher—Ausbruch und Wirklichkeit' (1987) *Öjz* 333.

73 Cass. 16 Marzo 1953, *Giust. Pen.* 1953, II, 991. See Bertolino, op. cit. p. 396 et seq. For a detailed analysis of the meaning and scope of the concept of illness as used in articles 88 and 89, see Pagliaro, *Principi di Diritto Penale* (Milan, 1987), p. 647, who argues, *inter alia,* that it is wider than the concept of sickness: ibid.

74 Cass. 28 Aprile 1986, *Cass. Pen.* 1987, 1767; Cass. 2 Aprile 1988, n. 180234; Cass. 7 Luglio 1989, n. 182181. As we shall see presently, even in cases where it is accepted as an illness within the meaning of articles 88 and 89, the courts are agreed that psychopathy does not go to a defendant's intellectual or volitional capacities. In other words, although evidence of psychopathy is sometimes accepted at stage one of an insanity hearing (the diagnostic stage), it is invariably rejected at stage two (the autonomy criterion).

where a plea of insanity or diminished responsibility, respectively, was based on evidence of a clinically recognized mental illness. In other words, there was an absolute presumption of dangerousness in such cases. In a series of landmark decisions in the early 1980s, the Constitutional Court held that this arrangement was unconstitutional;[75] and, by virtue of article 31 of the law of 10 October 1986,[76] the trial judge is now required to decide the issue of dangerousness in each case before making an order of preventive detention. The length of the period of preventive detention depends on the seriousness of the crime charged and is not subject to review by the courts or the government: offences carrying a sentence of life imprisonment attract a minimum period of ten years, while those carrying a custodial sentence of not less than ten years attract a minimum period of five years. Otherwise the minimum period of preventive detention is two years.

By contrast, where a defendant's alleged insanity or diminished responsibility is rooted in a bout of *physical* illness which is unlikely to recur, it seems that the court has no power to order preventive detention. This interpretation is not obvious from the language of articles 222 and 219, which merely states that a verdict of insanity or partial insanity (i.e., diminished responsibility) is a condition precedent of the imposition of preventive detention and that the latter is an automatic consequence of the former. But it is supported by a long line of authority to the effect that the legislature cannot be said to have intended compulsory psychiatric detention for persons who are neither mentally ill nor dangerous.[77] In the result, there is no equivalent of the *Ellis* problem in Italian criminal law: since mentally normal defendants who get the benefit of the insanity defence (on account of the psychological effects of a transitory physical illness) are not subject to restraint in the first place, the question of whether and when they should be released from custody does not arise.[78]

As in German law, evidence that the accused was suffering from a recognized mental illness when he committed the act is not *per se* enough to secure the insanity defence: article 88 also requires proof

75 Corte Cost. 27 Luglio 1982, n. 141, in *Foro It.*, 1982, I, p. 292; Corte Cost. 15-18 Luglio 1983, n. 249, in *Riv. It. Dir. Proc. Pen.*, 1984, p. 460; Corte Cost. 8-27 Luglio 1982, n. 139, *Riv. It. Dir. Proc. Pen.* 1985, p. 1585.

76 N. 163.

77 See Fioravanti, *Le Infermità Psichiche nella Jurisprudenza Penale* (Padua, 1988), p. 94 et seq.

78 This issue is discussed at length in ch. 6.2.

that the accused's condition was such that he lacked *'la capacità d'intendere o di volere'*. In broad terms, this means that it must be established that the defendant's illness prevented him from understanding the significance of his actions or from acting in accordance with that understanding. *La capacità d'intendere* or the ability to understand what one is doing is not confined to an appreciation of the physical nature and consequences of one's actions or of the fact that they are contrary to law.[79] It is widely accepted that it also embraces 'the ability of the subject to identify and comprehend the reasons for his conduct and, consequently, to evaluate his conduct as it is perceived in the real world and not just in terms of its physical impact and consequences: in short, to appreciate the real value of his actions.'[80] Similarly, *la capacità di volere* is generally regarded as denoting 'the ability to dominate one's impulses to action and to make autonomous and responsible choices.'[81]

Thus the criterion of insanity in Italian law covers all of the psychoses not excluding conditions like paranoid schizophrenia and psychotic depression which neither interfere with the patient's grasp of physical reality nor completely destroy his moral sense.[82] This follows because, like its counterpart in German law, it is virtually identical with the psychiatric criterion of serious mental illness. Both criteria turn on the agent's ability to make an objective assessment of his conduct, including his reasons or motives for acting; and on this basis the defendant who shoots his fancied persecutor in what he insanely believes to be self-defence (the paranoid schizophrenic), or who kills his loved ones in order to spare them the shame of having to live with his failure as a parent or breadwinner (the depressive psychotic), is no less entitled to the insanity defence than the defendant who fatally stabs her husband in the belief that he is King Herod and that she is avenging the death of John the Baptist, i.e., than the hallucinating psychotic who *has* lost contact with physical reality.[83]

By parity of reasoning, the Italian courts have consistently rejected the contention that severe psychopathy goes to *la capacità d'intendere o di volere*. The argument has been that psychopathy is essentially a radical want of fellow feeling, a species of *la follia morale*, that has no

79 See Bertolino, op. cit., p. 393 et seq.

80 Crespi, 'Imputabilità', (Diritto Penale), *Enc. Dir.*, (Milan, 1970), p. 762. See also Antolisei, *Manuale di Diritto Penale* (Milan, 1989), p. 535 et seq.

81 Fiandaca and Musco, op. cit., p. 173.

82 See Bertolino, op. cit., p. 401.

83 See Bertolino, ibid.

bearing on an accused's intellectual capacities.[84] Thus in a typical pronouncement on the matter, the Court of Cassation has stated that:

> [O]f the three mental faculties (feeling, intelligence and will) that characterize action on its subjective side, the penal code—as regards criminal capacity and therefore also mental illness—is concerned only with the last two . . . the various anomalies of character and cases of a lack of ethico-social feeling cannot by themselves be taken to indicate mental illness as they are not pathological disorders of the understanding.[85]

Moreover, since the plea of diminished responsibility provided for by article 89 requires proof of a substantial impairment of *la capacità d'intendere o di volere,* this effectively means that evidence of psychopathy cannot even be relied on as grounds for the mitigation of sentence;[86] and, consequently, that convicted psychopaths cannot be compulsorily detained in a psychiatric institution under article 219. This state of affairs, which is in sharp contrast with the position in German law as described above,[87] has recently been criticized on the grounds that the exclusion of psychopathy from the ambit of articles 88 and 89 is based on an arbitrarily restrictive view of the nature of serious mental illness.[88] Yet it cannot be gainsaid that it is consistent with the classical view of serious mental illness as a cognitive failing and with the empirical evidence that psychopathy does not appear to be amenable to psychiatric treatment.[89]

The abolition of the presumption of dangerousness in relation to successful insanity defendants whose plea was based on a recognized

84 See Mantovani, *Diritto Penale* (Padua, 1988), p. 650.

85 Cass. 26 Giugno 1968, *Cass. Pen,* 1969, p. 1215. See also Cass. 19 Aprile 1986, *Cass. Pen.* 1986, p. 1254; Cass. 24 Marzo 1986, *Cass. Pen.* 1987, p. 1069; Cass. 7 Luglio 1986, *Riv. Pen.* 1987, p. 783; Cass. 2 Aprile 1988, n. 180234; Cass. 7 Luglio 1989, n. 182181; Cass. 28 Aprile 1986, *Cass. Pen* 1987, 1767.

86 The text of article 89 of the Penal Code reads: 'Anyone who, at the moment he committed the act, was, as a result of illness, in such a state of mind as seriously to diminish (scemare), without excluding, *la capacità d'intendere o di volere,* is answerable for the crime committed; but the punishment is reduced.'

87 Article 11 of the Swiss Penal Code also recognizes (severe) psychopathy as a plea in mitigation of sentence: infra.

88 Romano, *Commentario Sistematico del Codice Penale* (Rome, 1991), art. 89/9. Bertolino, op. cit., p. 405 et seq.; Fiandaca and Musco, *Diritto Penale* (Bologna, 1989), p. 253.

89 See ch. 8, n.23 and accompanying text.

mental illness has been widely discussed in the Italian literature.[90] The majority opinion is that the presumption of dangerousness is incompatible with the notion of preventive detention. The argument has been that as the latter is a prophylactic measure, it follows that only those who constitute a real social danger should be subjected to it; and that when dangerousness is automatically presumed, this cannot be guaranteed. Moreover, it has been contended that in cases where the presumption of dangerousness is unfounded, preventive detention imposed pursuant to it amounts to punishment; and that the punishment of defendants who have been acquitted on the grounds of insanity cannot be justified on retributive grounds.[91]

This analysis raises the difficult question of how trial judges are to decide the issue of dangerousness in the absence of the presumption? One solution would be to treat the issue as a diagnostic matter for psychiatrists. However, this approach is beset with difficulty. First, dangerousness is not a diagnostic category in the sense that it is not a recognized symptom of any known mental illness—apart from psychopathy which, as we have seen, many psychiatrists do not regard as a mental illness and most legal systems do not accept as a basis for the insanity defence. Second, there is no known correlation between mental illness and violence; the mentally ill are no more likely to commit crimes of violence that the mentally healthy.[92] Thus there are no grounds for assuming that psychiatrists have a privileged insight into the nature of the potentially dangerous defendant such that they can provide the courts with reliable information on the likelihood of his committing further offences. Third, notwithstanding these difficulties, there is an abundance of evidence that psychiatrists are apt to view defendants who have committed crimes of violence apparently under the influence of mental illness as dangerous.[93] In other words, a trial judge who acts exclusively on psychiatric advice is likely to end up applying the presumption of dangerousness disguised as a diagnostic assessment. For these and other reasons, this approach has not been adopted in practice.[94]

90 See generally, Grevi (ed.) *L'ordinamento Penitenzario dopo la Riforma* (Padua, 1988); Ponti et al. 'L'abolizione delle Prezunzioni di Pericolosità Sociale' (1987) *Riv. It. Med. Leg.* 17; Russo, 'Infermità di Mente e Pericolosità Sociale' (1987) *Riv. It. Med. Leg.* 736.

91 Ibid.

92 Bandini and Gatti, 'Perizia Psichiatrica e Perizia Criminologica: Riflessioni sul Ruolo del Perito nell'Ambito del Processo Penale', (1982) *Riv. It. Med. Leg.* 360.

93 Bandini, Gatti and Traverso, *Omicidio e Controllo Sociale* (Milan, 1983), p. 164.

94 Bertolino, op. cit., p. 483 et seq.

The approach actually adopted by Italian judges is to decide the issue on common sense grounds having listened to all of the evidence including the relevant psychiatric testimony. The core of their solution is the thesis that a defendant is dangerous to the extent that he remains prey to the pathological beliefs and attitudes that produced his violent actions.[95] Thus a paranoid schizophrenic who killed one of his fancied persecutors would be dangerous on this view as long as he felt constrained to defend himself by such drastic means; and, *mutatis mutandis,* the same reasoning would encompass the psychotic whose enduring feelings of worthlessness and despair led him to kill members of his family. This simple criterion begs no questions as to whether violence is an essential feature of paranoid schizophrenia or any other mental illness, or whether the mentally ill are generally more prone to violence than the mentally healthy. Moreover, it offers a firm basis for the unconditional release of defendants who, as a result of treatment or spontaneous recovery, are no longer mentally disordered when the court comes to consider the question of preventive detention. For example, someone suffering from schizophrenia could be released on this basis if the court was satisfied that the symptoms—of thought and communication disorder and loss of intersubjectivity—typically associated with that condition had been successfully brought under control by medication.

It cannot however be gainsaid that this solution is also based on a disguised presumption of dangerousness: the implicit presumption being that a more or less stable set of irrational beliefs and desires that has led to violence on one occasion may do so again; and that the empirical basis for this assumption is highly questionable.[96]

Swiss law also adheres to the interactionist approach to the insanity defence. Thus article 10 of the Swiss Penal Code of 1942 provides that:

> No one is punishable who as a result of mental illness, mental weakness or a serious disorder of consciousness was unable at the time of the act to understand the wrongness of his conduct or to act in accordance with that understanding.

95 Cass. Ord. 28 Aprile 1988, (1988) *Foro It. 11,* p. 713; Cass. 4 Magio 1984, (1986) *Cass. Pen.* p. 273.

96 See chapter 1, n. 13; and generally Mestrovic and Cook, 'The Dangerousness Standard: What is it and how is it used?' (1986) *Int J Law & Psychiat* 444.

Article 11 provides for a plea of diminished responsibility in mitigation of sentence in cases where the accused was, at the time of the act, suffering from mental illness or retardation 'such that his ability to understand the wrongness of his actions or to act in accordance with that understanding was impaired.' It is well established that article 10 comprehends all of the psychoses, and that evidence of severe psychopathy will secure a finding of diminished responsibility within the meaning of article 11.[97]

A highly unusual feature of the Swiss system is the provision in article 43 of the Penal Code which allows for indeterminate preventive detention even in cases where the insanity defence has been *rejected*, provided that the evidence discloses that the accused is (a) mentally ill, (b) dangerous, (c) guilty of the offence as charged and (d) that the latter carries a custodial sentence. Article 43 also makes provision for a psychiatric treatment order (which may specify *out-patient* psychiatric care) in such cases provided the court is satisfied that treatment is necessary and that the defendant is *not* dangerous. Although the period of detention that may be ordered under article 43 is indeterminate, it may not exceed the term of imprisonment for the offence charged. In the nature of things, the vast bulk of *convicted* defendants dealt with under article 43 are suffering from non-psychotic mental illnesses or have been diagnosed as psychopathic. Not surprisingly, these arrangements have been severely criticized on human rights grounds; and there have been numerous, if as yet unsuccessful, proposals for reform.[98]

97 For a detailed discussion of articles 10 and 11 and the jurisprudence associated with them, see Noll and Trechsel, *Schweizerisches Strafrecht* (Zürich, 1986), p. 136 et seq.

98 See Schulz, *Schweizerisches Strafrecht* (Bern, 1989), p. 1067; 'Probleme einer Revision des Allgemeinen Teils des Schweizerischen Strafgesezbuches', in *Fest. Lackner* (Zurich, 1985), p. 890 et seq. See also Bertolino, op. cit., p. 354.

# EPILOGUE

# Statistical Overview

The issue of insanity is rarely raised in criminal proceedings in Ireland; since 1947 it has been successfully raised on indictment on a total of 118 occasions, i.e., in approximately three cases per year. To put this figure in perspective, suffice it to say that it represents a fraction of 1 per cent. of the total number of cases brought to trial on indictment during this period.[1]

Strictly speaking, as the official criminal statistics do not provide information on how often pleas of insanity or unfitness are rejected, we do not know what proportion the figure of 118 represents of the total number of cases in which the issue of insanity was actually raised; although the circumstantial evidence suggests that it is likely to be high. For even if we assume that the issue of insanity was often unsuccessfully raised in murder cases prior to the (virtual) abolition of the death penalty in 1964,[2] this is unlikely to be true of non-murder cases generally or of murder cases after 1964, which, as can be seen from Table 1, together constitute over 80 percent of the total of 118 cases.

Given that the cost of raising the issue in the absence of the death penalty manifestly outweighs any benefit that might accrue from doing so, it is reasonable to assume that there is a near perfect ratio of successful to actual pleas in these cases. Moreover, it should be borne in mind that the total number of murder cases brought to trial on indictment between 1947 and 1963 was only 64, and that the

1 Thus in 1947 there were 506 cases brought to trial on indictment; whereas by 1987 this figure had increased to 837—source: *Report on Crime 1947, 1987* (by the Garda Commissioner to the Minister for Justice). These figures are calculated as three-year sliding averages for the years 1947 and 1987, respectively. The annual *Report on Crime* contains the official criminal statistics for Ireland. See also Table 3, column E.

2 As a result of the Criminal Justice Act of that year.

**Table 1: Insanity cases by offence type**[3]

| *offence type* | *no.* | % |
|---|---|---|
| murder and attempted murder | 28 | 23 |
| wounding and assault | 8 | 7 |
| sexual offences | 15 | 13 |
| malicious damage and arson | 21 | 18 |
| breaking and entering | 21 | 18 |
| larceny and related offences | 25 | 21 |
| *total* | 118 | 100 |

issue of insanity was successfully raised in 18 (28 per cent.) of these.[4] Thus even if we make the unlikely assumption that the issue was *unsuccessfully* raised in *all* of the remaining 48 cases, the proportion of successful to actual pleas for the total period would still be of the order of 70 per cent.

Nor do we know how many of the successful cases involved pleas of unfitness for trial, as opposed to pleas of insanity *simpliciter,* as the official statistics merely provide a global figure for the annual number of cases in which a finding of *either* insanity *or* unfitness was recorded. However, if we assume that the *defence* of insanity is unlikely to be raised beyond the confines of the crimes of murder and capital murder, the proportion of unfitness cases is likely to be well in excess of 50 per cent., and may even be as high as 75 per cent., of the total. As Table 1 illustrates, as many as 66 (56 per cent.) of the 118 cases in which the issue of insanity was successfully raised involved offences against property: typically malicious damage, burglary and larceny; and it seems safe to assume that defence strategy in cases of this kind is unlikely to have included recourse to the insanity *defence.*[5]

This conclusion is bolstered by the fact that the larceny cases

3 Source: all tables in this chapter are based on the official annual *Report(s) on Crime 1947-1990* (by the Garda Commissioner to the Minister for Justice).

4 Source: *Report(s) on Crime 1947-63.*

5 Admittedly, a finding of unfitness also leads to mandatory detention in the Central Mental Hospital; although it might be argued that, since defendants are (at least in theory) returned for trial if fitness is regained, this is less a disincentive for defence counsel than the certainty of *indeterminate* detention following a successful insanity defence; see chs. 6 and 7.

often involved the theft of small amounts of money,[6] articles from motor vehicles[7] and sometimes the vehicles themselves; and even 'pedal cycles'![8] *Mutatis mutandis,* these considerations also apply to the bulk of the 15 sexual and 8 non-sexual assault cases which between them make up 20 per cent. of the total. Moreover, allowance must be made for the fact that many of the murder cases tried after 1964, and even some of those tried before 1964, may have involved pleas of unfitness rather than insanity. In other words, it is not improbable that the insanity defence *stricto sensu* accounts for no more than approximately 25 per cent. of the total number of cases in which the issue of insanity was successfully raised. Contrariwise, allowance should also be made for the fact that the insanity defence can be raised both by the prosecution and the court in the event that the defendant puts his state of mind in issue,[9] and that this is likely to generate at least a trickle of insanity verdicts even in the most trivial non-murder cases.

Finally, it should be remembered that since the official criminal statistics are calculated on the basis of the number of charges brought rather than the number of persons charged, the figure of 118 is likely to exaggerate the real incidence of insanity findings. The margin of exaggeration is difficult to quantify, although it seems safe to assume that atypically high annual total numbers of insanity findings for particular offences in all probability reflect multiple charges against a single defendant. For example, although the official statistics show that there were nine findings of insanity recorded in 1976, the fact that all of these relate to sexual offences against children may mean that they involve a single defendant.[10]

Table 2 shows the distribution of the total population of insanity cases over time relative to the number of indictable offences brought to trial. It can be seen from column B that all the five-year totals prior to 1976 are above, and all bar one well above, the average of 13 cases, but that those for the succeeding periods vary from just under a third to just over a half of that figure. Columns C and D show a similar pattern for the figures relating to non-murder and murder cases, where the averages are 10 and 2.7 cases, respectively. At first glance this suggests that the frequency of insanity

6 For example, the official statistics for 1953 record three cases on insanity involving the alleged larceny of sums less than £5; see Appendix 3.
7 See *Report on Crime 1989;* Appendix 3.
8 For example, see *Report(s) on Crime 1952, 1963*; Appendix 3.
9 See ch. 5.
10 See Appendix 3.

**Table 2: Insanity cases by indictable offences brought to trial**

| A | B | C | D | E | F |
|---|---|---|---|---|---|
| *Period* | *Insanity cases*[11] | | | *Indictable offences brought to trial*[12] | |
| | Generally | Non-murder | Murder | Generally | Murder |
| 1947-51 | **17** | **12** | **5** [23%] | 2533 | 22 |
| 1952-56 | **23** (15) | **20** (11) | **3** (3) [27%] | 1986 (-12%) | 11 (-50%) |
| 1957-61 | **14** (15) | **5** (11) | **9** (6) [43%] | 1982 (-0.3%) | 21 (+91%) |
| 1962-66 | **16** (33) | **13** (24) | **3** (6) [14%] | 4391 (+121%) | 22 (+5%) |
| 1967-71 | **16** (29) | **12** (21) | **4** (10)[11%] | 3439 (-12%) | 38 (+73%) |
| 1972-76 | **15** (44) | **12** (32) | **3** (16) [5%] | 5263 (+53%) | 60 (+58%) |
| 1977-81 | **4** (39) | **4** (28) | **0** (25) | 4117 (-12%) | 94 (+57%) |
| 1982-86 | **5** (41) | **4** (29) | **0** (21) | 4287 (+4%) | 81 (-14%) |
| 1987-91 | **8** (41) | **7** (29) | **1** (18) [1%] | 4235 (-1%) | 69 (-15%) |

cases declined sharply around 1977. However, when the raw figures are viewed in the light of the total number of cases brought to trial on indictment in each period, it can be seen that the sharp downward trend began as far back as the early to mid-1960s.

As column E illustrates, although the number of cases brought to trial on indictment did not vary greatly from 1947 to 1961—the quinquennial average was 2167—it more than doubled to 4391 cases between 1962 and 1966 and has been running more or less at that level ever since. On purely statistical grounds you would expect a proportionate increase in the number of insanity cases over the same period, which would put the quinquennial average since 1961 at approximately 36 cases. As it happens, it has been running as low as 6 cases since the mid-1970s, i.e., at roughly half its 1961 level. In other words, the current actual number of insanity cases is about a sixth of what would be expected on statistical grounds. The expected totals for each five-year period are given in round brackets,

11 The raw figures are shown in bold. The figures given in round brackets in columns B, C and D are statistically expected values, calculated on the basis of the correlative percentage increases shown in columns E and F. The figures in square brackets in column D are percentages of the total number of murder cases brought to trial for each period in the time series.

12 The figures shown in columns E and F are calculated on the basis of three-year moving averages for the entire time series.

beside the actual totals, in columns B, C and D.

The decline in the proportion of insanity-murder cases in the total number of murder cases brought to trial on indictment is even more marked. As can be seen from column F, although there has been a near four-fold increase in the number of murder cases brought to trial since 1961, the number of insanity-murder cases has been at or near zero since 1977. Moreover, the frequency of insanity-murder cases also began to decline earlier than the raw figures in column B suggest. As column D shows, the proportion of insanity-murder to murder cases brought to trial prior to 1961 fluctuated around an average of 30 per cent., whereas it fell to 14 per cent. between 1962 and 1966, to 5 per cent between 1972 and 1976 and has been at less than 2 per cent ever since.

It is tempting to attribute these trends to the virtual abolition of the death penalty in 1964, on the theory that abolition removed the main incentive for raising the issue of insanity either as a plea in bar of trial or as a defence. This hypothesis probably accounts for the sharp drop in the rate of insanity-murder cases after 1964, to approximately half its statistically expected level, although it hardly explains why there was a further slump around 1977 and why the rate has tended to zero ever since. Given that the issue of insanity can be raised by both the prosecution and the court, one would have expected at least a trickle of insanity-murder cases even after abolition. Indeed this may explain why the number of such

**Table 3: Acquittal rate for indictable offences[13]**

| A<br>*Period* | B<br>*Acquittal Rate* |
|---|---|
| 1947-51 | 14 |
| 1952-56 | 17.5 |
| 1957-61 | 18 |
| 1962-66 | 17.5 |
| 1967-71 | 15 |
| 1972-76 | 11 |
| 1977-81 | 5.5 |
| 1982-86 | 3.5 |
| 1987-91 | 5 |

13 The values given in column B are based on five-year moving averages for each year in the time series.

cases continued to run at an average of 10 per cent. of the total number of murder cases brought to trial throughout the decade following abolition. But it adds to the puzzle as to why the trickle virtually dried up after 1977, fully thirteen years after abolition.

*A fortiori,* the abolition of the death penalty can scarcely be invoked to explain why the number of insanity cases not involving a charge of murder also appears to have fallen sharply around 1964, and again precipitously around 1977. One possibility is that both of these shifts are by-products of the huge increase in the backlog of cases awaiting trial that began to build up in the early 1960s. From 1959 to 1969 the number of cases awaiting trial at the end of the year increased from 87 to 403, an increase of over 350 per cent. Moreover, in 1959 the ratio of cases brought to cases awaiting trial was 4.5:1, whereas it had declined to 3.5:1 in 1964, and to 1.5:1 in 1969.[14] In other words, by 1969, not only was there a huge annual backlog of cases awaiting trial, but there were almost as many cases awaiting trial at the end of the year as there were trials during the year. On the assumption that the criminal justice system will always strive to maximise its annual throughput of cases, it might be expected that congestion of this order will lead to greatly increased pressure on defendants to plead guilty, and that this in turn will lead to an increase in the number of guilty pleas and, consequently, to a decrease in the number of cases in which the issue of insanity—or any other defence issue—can be raised.

There is support for this hypothesis in the fact that the acquittal rate for indictable offences went into a steep decline around 1970, as can be seen from Table 3. Having been running at around 17 per cent. since the late 1940s, it began to fall in the late 1960s, declined suddenly to just over 11 per cent. in the early 1970s, fell again to around 5 per cent. in the mid 1970s, and continued its downward spiral to a nadir of 2.4 per cent in 1984. As already indicated, given that a verdict of guilty but insane is an acquittal, and that a finding of unfitness to plead aborts the trial, it is to be expected that the number of insanity cases would fall in proportion to the increase in the number of guilty pleas.[15]

Nor is this conclusion affected by the fact that the acquittal rate did not begin to decline until the late 1960s, whereas, as Table 2 indicates, the decline in the rate of insanity cases is clearly evident in

14 *Report(s) on Crime 1959, 1969.* The ratios are based on five-year moving averages for the years in question.

15 This point is developed in relation to the discussion of Table 4, infra.

the figures for the period 1962 to 1966. As the number of insanity cases is small, and constitutes only a tiny proportion of the number of cases brought to trial, even a sharp decline in the number of insanity acquittals is unlikely to affect the overall acquittal rate. Moreover, if the congestion hypothesis is correct, one would not expect the overall acquittal rate to fall until the backlog of cases causing the congestion began to work its way through the system. In other words, you would expect a time lag of a few years before the effects of an increasing guilty-plea rate would be reflected in the acquittal figures. As Table 3 illustrates, this is exactly what appears to have happened.

Does the congestion hypothesis explain why the rate of insanity cases plunged again around 1977? As we have seen, the congestion hypothesis assumes that the number of cases awaiting trial is increasing faster than the number of cases brought to trial. That is to say, it assumes a worsening ratio of cases sent forward for trial to cases awaiting trial as the trigger mechanism for an increasing guilty-plea rate. Thus, if the congestion hypothesis is true, i.e., if it is true that the criminal justice system abhors a backlog, it follows that the acquittal rate will continue to fall until such time as the backlog begins to clear, i.e., until the number of cases brought to trial starts to grow faster than the number of cases awaiting trial. As can be seen from Table 4, this did not happen until the acquittal rate fell to around 5 per cent, between 1977 and 1981; although the respite was brief given that the ratio of cases sent forward to cases awaiting began to worsen again around 1982, and has been steadily, if gradually, worsening ever since.

Interestingly, although it declined to a low of 2.4 in 1984, the acquittal rate has remained more or less constant at around 5 per cent since 1977. On the assumption that the acquittal rate will not decline to zero, this suggests that we are heading for an inverse ratio of cases brought to trial to cases awaiting trial. In short, it suggests that the criminal justice system will eventually choke on its own caseload unless the capacity of the courts to deal with the total volume of cases fed into the system is dramatically expanded. This prospect is surprising given that the serious crime rate appears to have fallen, albeit slightly, since the early 1980's.[16] As the detection rate normally varies in proportion to the crime rate,[17] you would

16 Between 1961 and 1982 serious recorded crime grew from 14813 to 97626 indictable offences, which is well in excess of a six-fold increase. From 1982 to 1990 the annual total declined to 87658 indictable offences, a drop of about 10 per cent: *Report(s) on Crime 1961-1990.*

17 Thus the proportion of indictable offences cleared up by the police has

expect the total volume of cases with which the courts have to deal also to have fallen and, consequently, that the backlog of cases awaiting trial would be on the decline rather than the increase.

The fact that the opposite appears to be the case is not easy to explain, although at least two possibilities suggest themselves. The first is that there has been a significant increase in the workload of the courts on the *civil* side, as a result of the expansion of the

**Table 4: Ratio of cases brought to trial to cases awaiting trial by acquittal rate**[18]

| A | B | C |
|---|---|---|
| *Period* | *Ratio* | *Acquittal Rate* |
| 1947-51 | 10:1 | 14 |
| 1952-56 | 10:1 | 17.5 |
| 1957-61 | 5:1 | 18 |
| 1962-66 | 4:1 | 17.5 |
| 1967-71 | 2:1 | 15 |
| 1972-76 | 1.5:1 | 11 |
| 1977-81 | 2:1 | 5.5 |
| 1982-86 | 1.5:1 | 3 |
| 1987-91 | 1.2:1 | 5 |

jurisdiction of the Circuit Court in 1981;[19] by virtue of the Courts Act of that year the financial jurisdiction of the Circuit Court was increased from £7000 to £15000. On this view, the courts simply have less time to devote to serious criminal cases than they had before the financial limit affecting the civil jurisdiction of the Circuit Court was raised, with the result that the proportion of criminal cases sent forward for trial has continued to decline notwithstanding that the overall number of criminal cases being fed into the system has also been declining (as a consequence of the decline in the crime rate and the concomitant decline in the *number*—as distinct from the proportion—of cases cleared up by

remained constant at approximately 30 per cent since 1981.

18 The values in columns B and C are based on five-year moving averages for each year in the time series.

19 I am grateful to my colleague, Mr Tom Cooney, for this point; the financial jurisdiction of the Circuit Court was further increased to £30,000 by the Courts Act 1991.

the police). The other possibility is that the declining proportion of cases sent forward for trial is due to delays in preparing the book of evidence occasioned by staff shortages in the State Solicitor's Office, although it has to be conceded that the supporting evidence for this hypothesis is entirely anecdotal.[20]

Be that as it may, it seems safe to assume that the drop in the acquittal rate in the mid 1970s, from just over 11 to just over 5 per cent., was the most likely reason for the corresponding drop in the rate of insanity cases. The argument is that the drop in the acquittal rate drove down the number of insanity *defences* because the insanity defence is itself an acquittal, albeit of a technical sort,[21] and would therefore be expected to fall in proportion to the acquittal rate. Admittedly, this argument needs to be amplified with regard to pleas of unfitness; since they are not acquittals, even in a technical sense, it might be argued that there is no reason to suppose that they would decline in proportion to the acquittal rate.[22]

However, it should be emphasised that (like insanity pleas) they *would* be expected to vary in inverse proportion to the guilty-plea rate, since a rising guilty-plea rate necessarily reduces the overall number of contested trials and, therefore, the number of trials that can be aborted by means of an unfitness plea (or result in an acquittal on the grounds of insanity), just as a falling rate necessarily increases the overall number of contested trials and, therefore, the number of trials that can be aborted by means of an unfitness plea (or result in an acquittal on the grounds of insanity). And since the low acquittal rate is most probably a result of a high guilty-plea rate (if the argument from the congestion hypothesis is true), it is reasonable to assume that it will drive down the number of unfitness pleas no less than the number of insanity defences. Indeed, it is submitted that this conclusion is strengthened by the fact that the number of insanity cases and the overall acquittal rate both declined by approximately the same margin—50 per cent.—at approximately the same time—around 1977. As unfitness pleas are likely to be at least as numerous as insanity pleas, you would not expect this to happen unless the opportunities to plead unfitness

20 As against that, the point has been made to the author by people directly involved in the state prosecution service.

21 See ch. 6.1.

22 But they may well vary with the guilty-plea rate since a rising guilty-plea rate necessarily reduces the opportunities to abort the trial by means of a plea of unfitness; while a falling rate would be expected to produce the opposite effect.

for trial were declining at the same rate as the opportunities to plead insanity.

But doesn't this beg the question as to why the decline in the acquittal rate (and, by implication, in the rate of insanity cases) *accelerated* in the mid 1970s? The answer to this question, it is submitted, is that the sudden acceleration of both trends around that time may well be an indirect effect of the appointment of the Director of Public Prosecutions in 1974. On the assumption that the advent of the Director led to greater quality control of cases from a prosecution point of view, and therefore to fewer weak or doubtful cases being sent forward for trial, one would expect the acquittal rate to fall more or less contemporaneously with his appointment. In other words, the further decline in the acquittal rate in the mid 1970s, together with the concomitant drop in the rate of insanity cases, may be a result of the fact that the Director of Public Prosecutions succeeded in identifying and weeding out of the system most of the cases that would have resulted in an acquittal had they gone to trial.

Nor is this conclusion affected by the fact that the insanity defence, although technically an acquittal, is in reality more like a conviction given that it leads to the indeterminate detention of acquittees rather than their unconditional release—in other words, because of its social protection function. In murder cases this consideration is likely to weigh heavily with the Director of Public Prosecutions when deciding whether or not the issue of insanity should be raised, either as a defence or as a plea in bar of trial. But it is unlikely to be a critical consideration in non-murder cases, which, as it happens, make up 90 per cent. of the insanity cases decided since the Director came into office and which, in the main, consist of offences against property.[23] Moreover, it seems unlikely that the Director would insist on raising the issue of insanity in the face of a guilty plea in cases of this kind.

This explanation also accounts for the fact that the liberalization of the insanity test by the Supreme Court in 1974[24] appears to have had no effect on the frequency of insanity cases. Normally you would expect a more liberal insanity test to lead to more rather than fewer insanity cases—unless one can identify the presence of some other factor, such as a declining acquittal rate, pushing in the opposite direction (and, it goes without saying, unless the test had

23 See Appendix 3.
24 See ch. 3.

already been relaxed in practise before it was formally adopted by the courts).[25] By parity of reasoning, it also explains why the frequency of insanity cases was unaffected by the change of policy at the Central Mental Hospital in the mid 1980s, which effectively reduced the mean length of time persons found guilty but insane or unfit to plead could expect to be kept in detention from 7-10 to 5-7 years.[26] In theory, this change greatly enhanced the attractiveness of the insanity plea as a defence strategy, and therefore should also have led to more rather than fewer insanity cases; but in practice it seems that it too could not compete with the contrary pressure exerted by the downward trend in the acquittal rate.[27]

To what extent is the introduction of diminished responsibility likely to affect the trends and patterns being described here? If we go on the evidence from England and Wales, the answer to this question is 'very little'. As Walker has demonstrated,[28] although the frequency of findings of insanity (and unfitness to plead) declined sharply following the introduction of diminished responsibility in 1957, the overall proportion of cases in which the issue of mental disorder determined the outcome remained more or less as it had been prior to 1957. In other words, the cross-channel evidence suggests that the proposed new defence is unlikely to do more than take over the cases that would otherwise attract the insanity defence (or result in a finding of unfitness to plead).

At first blush it might be thought that the Irish situation is sufficiently different to cast doubt on the likelihood that this pattern would be repeated here. After all the defence of insanity in Irish law is already considerably wider than its English-law counterpart was in 1957 (or is today),[29] and therefore considerably less vulnerable to the kind of 'take-over' described by Walker. However, it should not be forgotten that the insanity defence, irrespective of how generously framed it happens to be, automatically leads to indeterminate detention in a criminal lunatic asylum.[30] As presently constituted, therefore, it is almost certain to be perceived by defendants as a much less attractive option than a defence of

25 This possibility is discussed in ch. 3.1.

26 See ch. 6.4; ch. 7.6; *Irish Times,* 20 July 1991.

27 This point was missed by Carney who mistook a short-term increase in insanity cases in 1989 for a long-term trend: *Irish Times,* 13 January 1990.

28 Op. cit., p. 158 et seq.

29 See ch. 3.

30 See ch. 6.2.

diminished responsibility given the latter's associated regime of fixed prison sentences and relatively short periods of hospitalization.[31]

Equally, however, it would be a mistake to assume that the introduction of a defence of diminished responsibility is likely to lead to a significant increase in the number of cases in which the issue of mental disorder determines the outcome. This *is* likely to happen if, in the event of the defence being introduced, the courts were to decide the length of the period defendants had to spend in prison or hospital on purely therapeutic grounds, i.e, to the exclusion of considerations of retribution and social defence, as this would almost certainly lead to very short sentences and/or periods of detention in the general run of cases and, consequently, to a much greater number of insanity cases. But since the courts are unlikely to do anything of the sort, the prudent expectation is that the level of diminished responsibility cases would not greatly outstrip the existing level of insanity cases in the event of a plea of diminished responsibility being introduced by the legislature. In any event, the introduction of a plea of diminished responsibility would not affect the issue of mental disorder beyond the confines of the crime of murder.

Yet the foregoing analysis does not signal the virtual eclipse of the insanity plea. On the contrary, it is submitted that the frequency of insanity pleas *is* likely to increase significantly in the event of the expansion of the powers of disposal available to the courts when dealing with persons acquitted on the grounds of insanity or found unfit to plead. Were the legislature to follow the English example and abolish the requirement of automatic compulsory hospitalization in such cases, giving courts the option of choosing between a hospital order with or without limitation of time, a guardianship order, a supervision and treatment order and an order of absolute discharge, the effect would arguably be to remove one of the principal disincentives for raising the issues of insanity and unfitness.[32]

This might not of itself lead to a significant increase in the incidence of insanity cases, if only because we cannot discount the possibility that defendants would continue to be deterred by the stigma associated with a finding of insanity or unfitness just as much as they are now deterred by the prospect of compulsory

31 See ch. 9.3.
32 See chs. 6.2 and 7.6.

indeterminate detention in a criminal lunatic asylum. However, if a change of this kind were accompanied by a change in the form of the verdict in insanity cases such that the associated element of stigma was significantly reduced—if, for example, the verdict was changed to one of 'not guilty by reason of mental disorder or disability'[33]—it is hard to imagine that the numbers of defendants pleading insanity would not show a sizeable increase—always assuming, of course, that the courts were prepared to use their discretion to keep defendants who do not pose a danger to themselves or others out of hospital. Similarly, it seems safe to assume that the number of unfitness pleas would also increase significantly in these circumstances if findings of unfitness were expressed in terms of mental disorder or disability rather than insanity.

33 Supra, ch. 6.1.

# APPENDIX I

# Criminal Lunatics Act 1800

AN ACT FOR THE SAFE CUSTODY OF INSANE PERSONS CHARGED WITH OFFENCES [28TH JULY 1800].

Preamble

The jury, in case of any person charged with treason, &c. being proved to be insane, and being acquitted, to declare whether he was acquitted by them on account of insanity; and if so acquitted, the court shall order him to be kept in custody till his Majesty's pleasure be known; and his Majesty may give orders for his safe custody, &c.

Whereas persons charged with high treason, murder or felony, may have been or may be of unsound mind at the time of committing the offence wherewith they may have been or shall be charged, and by reason of such insanity may have been or may be found not guilty of such offence, and it may be dangerous to permit persons so acquitted to go at large: Be it therefore enacted by the King's most excellent Majesty, by and with the consent of the lords spiritual and temporal, and commons, in this present parliament assembled, and by the authority of the same, that in all cases where it shall be given in evidence upon the trial of any person charged with treason, murder or felony, that such person was insane at the time of the commission of such offence, and such person shall be acquitted, the jury shall be required to find specially whether such person was acquitted by them on account of such insanity; and if they shall find that such person was insane at the time of the committing of such offence, the court before whom such trial shall be had shall order such person to be kept in strict custody, in such place and in such manner as to the court shall seem fit, until his Majesty's pleasure shall be known; and it shall thereupon be lawful for his Majesty to give such order for the safe custody of such person during his pleasure, in such place and in such manner as to his Majesty shall seem fit; and in all cases where any person before the passing of this Act has been acquitted of any such offences on the ground of insanity at the time of the commission thereof, and has been detained in custody as a dangerous person by order of the court before whom such person has been tried, and still remains in custody, it shall be lawful for his Majesty to give the like order for the safe custody of such person during his pleasure as his Majesty is hereby enabled to give in the cases of persons who shall hereafter be acquitted on the ground of insanity.

If any person indicted for any offence, shall upon arraignment or trial be found to be insane, &c., the court shall order him to be kept to be kept in custody till his Majesty's pleasure be known.

II. And be it further enacted, that if any person indicted for any offence shall be insane, and shall upon arraignment be found so to be by a jury lawfully empannelled for that purpose, so that such person cannot be tried upon such indictment, or if upon the trial of any person so indicted such person shall appear to the jury charged with such indictment to be insane, it shall be lawful for the court before whom any such person shall be brought to be arraigned or tried as aforesaid to direct such finding to be recorded, and thereupon to order such person to be kept in strict custody until his Majesty's pleasure shall be known; and if any person charged with any offence shall be brought before any court to be discharged for want of prosecution, and such person shall appear to be insane, it shall be lawful for such court to order a jury to be empannelled to try the sanity of such person; and if the jury so empannelled shall find such person to be insane, it shall be lawful for such court to order such person to be kept in strict custody, in such place and in such manner as to such court shall seem fit, until his Majesty's pleasure shall be known; and in all cases of insanity so found it shall be lawful for his Majesty to give such order for the safe custody of such person so found to be insane, during his pleasure, in such place and in such manner as his Majesty shall seem fit.

Proceedings where persons brought up to be discharged for want of prosecution appear to be insane.

# APPENDIX II

## Trial of Lunatics Act 1883

AN ACT TO AMEND THE LAW RESPECTING THE TRIAL AND CUSTODY OF INSANE PERSONS CHARGED WITH OFFENCES. [25TH AUGUST 1883].

Be it enacted by the Queen's most excellent Majesty, by and with the advice and consent of the Lords Spiritual and Temporal, and Commons, in this present Parliament assembled, and by the authority of the same, as follows:

Short title.

**1.** This Act may be cited as the Trial of Lunatics Act, 1883.

Special verdict where accused found guilty, but insane at the date of act or omission charged, and orders thereupon.

**2.** (1). Where in any indictment or information any act or omission is charged against any person as an offence, and it is given in evidence on the trial of such person for that offence that he was insane, so as not to be responsible, according to law, for his actions at the time when the act was done or omission made, then, if it appears to the jury before whom such trial is tried that he did the act or made the omission charged, but was insane as aforesaid at the time when he did or made the same, the jury shall return a special verdict to the effect that the accused was guilty of the act or omission charged against him, but was insane as aforesaid at the time when he did the act or made the omission.

(2). Where such special verdict is found, the Court shall order the accused to be kept in custody as a criminal lunatic, in such place and in such manner as the Court shall direct till Her Majesty's pleasure shall be known; and it shall be lawful for Her Majesty thereupon, and from time to time, to give such order for the safe custody of the said person during pleasure, in such place and in such manner as to Her Majesty may seem fit.

(3). In all such cases any two justices of the peace of the county, city, or place where such person shall have been tried, or shall be kept in custody, shall have the like power as is given by the Act of the third and fourth years of Her present Majesty, chapter fifty-four, in the cases therein mentioned, to inquire into and ascertain the last legal settlement of such person, and also to make the like order or orders for the payment of such person's maintenance and other charges as therein mentioned.

(4). All provisions in any existing Act or in any rules or orders made in pursuance of any existing Act, having reference to a person or persons acquitted on the grounds of insanity, shall apply to a person or persons in respect of whom a special verdict is found under this Act.

Extent of Act.

**3** (1). This Act shall extend to Ireland with the following modifications, that is to say, the words 'the Lord Lieutenant' shall be substituted for 'Her Majesty', and the words 'the pleasure of the Lord Lieutenant' for 'Her Majesty's pleasure.'

(2). This Act shall not extend to Scotland.

## APPENDIX III

# Findings (on Indictment) of Insanity and Unfitness to Plead 1947-1990

| | |
|---|---|
| 1947 | 6 findings: murder (1); malicious damage (1); burglary (1); larceny (2) (one of the charges related to a sum of less than £5); theft from motor vehicle (1). |
| 1948 | 3 findings: murder (3). |
| 1949 | 0 findings. |
| 1950 | 4 findings: murder (1); arson (2); fraud (1). |
| 1951 | 4 findings: breaking and entering (1); indecent assault (1); arson (2). |
| 1952 | 15 findings: burglary (8); larceny (4) (three of the charges related to sums of less than £5); larceny of pedal cycles (1); theft from motor vehicles (2). |
| 1953 | 4 findings: murder (1); arson (2); larceny (of less than £5) (1). |
| 1954 | 4 findings: murder (2); indecent assault (1); obscene libel (1). |
| 1955 | 0 findings. |
| 1956 | 0 findings. |
| 1957 | 5 findings: murder (4); breaking and entering (1). |
| 1958 | 5 findings: murder (1); attempted murder (3); arson (1). |
| 1959 | 1 finding: breaking and entering (1). |
| 1960 | 2 findings: attempted murder (1); rape (1). |
| 1961 | 1 finding: larceny (of more than £50) (1). |
| 1962 | 3 findings: arson (2); larceny (of more than £50) (1). |

| | |
|---|---|
| 1963 | 5 findings: murder (1); wounding (1); breaking and entering (1); indecent assault (1); larceny (of a pedal cycle) (1). |
| 1964 | 2 findings: malicious damage (2). |
| 1965 | 4 findings: murder (1); wounding (1); breaking and entering (1); larceny (1). |
| 1966 | 2 findings: murder (1); indecent assault (1). |
| 1967 | 4 findings: arson (2); larceny (1); obtaining by false pretences (1). |
| 1968 | 2 findings: murder (2). |
| 1969 | 4 findings: attempted murder (1); dangerous driving causing death (2); breaking and entering (1). |
| 1970 | 6 findings: murder (1); assault (1); arson (4). |
| 1971 | 0 findings |
| 1972 | 0 findings |
| 1973 | 4 findings: murder (1); receiving stolen goods (3). |
| 1974 | 0 findings. |
| 1975 | 2 findings: murder (2). |
| 1976 | 9 findings: indecency between males (4); statutory rape (4); indecent assault (1). |
| 1977 | 0 findings. |
| 1978 | 2 findings: assault (on a member of the Garda Síochána) (1); larceny (1). |
| 1979 | 1 finding: bribery (1). |
| 1980 | 1 finding: burglary (1). |
| 1981 | 0 findings. |
| 1982 | 1 finding: burglary (1). |
| 1983 | 1 finding: larceny (1). |
| 1984 | 0 findings. |
| 1985 | 0 findings. |
| 1986 | 3 findings: burglary (3). |
| 1987 | 1 finding: larceny (1). |
| 1988 | 1 finding: malicious damage (1). |
| 1989 | 5 findings: murder (1); assault (1); malicious damage (1); burglary (1); larceny from a motor vehicle (1). |
| 1990 | 1 finding: malicious damage. |

# Bibliography

## ARTICLES AND ESSAYS

*The following is a complete list of the articles and essays referred to in the footnotes to the text. Journal titles are given in full.*


Antilla, 'Conservative and Radical Criminal Policy in the Nordic Countries' in Christie et al., (eds.) *Scandinavian Studies in Criminology* (London, 1971).

Arafat and McCahery, 'The Insanity Defence and the Juror' (1973) *22 Drake Law Review* 538.

Arenella, 'The Diminished Responsibility and Diminished Capacity Defences: Two Children of a Doomed Marriage' (1977) *77 Columbia Law Review* 827.

Athen, 'Zur Gegenwärtigen Situation der Behandlung psychisch kranker Rechtsbrecher' (1985) *Monatschrift Kriminologie* 29.

Bacon, 'Unnecessary Detention: The Criminal Procedure (Insanity) Act' (1989) *86 Law Society Gazette* 19.

Bandini and Gatti, 'Perizia Psichiatrica e Perizia Criminologica: Riflessioni sul Ruolo del Perito nell'Ambito del Processo Penale (1982) *Rivista Italiana di Medicina Legale* 360.

Bartholemew and Milte, 'The Reliability and Validity of Psychiatric Diagnoses in Courts of Law' (1976) *50 Australian Law Journal* 450.

Beck, 'The Development of Depression: A Cognitive Model' in Friedman and Katz (eds.) *The Psychology of Depression: Contemporary Theory and Research* (Washington, 1974).

Becker, 'Durham Revisited: Psychiatry and the Problem of Crime: Part II' (1973) *Psychiatric Annals* 1.

Berger, 'Österreich' in Eser and Huber (eds.), *Entwicklungstendenzen in Europa* (Freiburg, 1988).

Bjerke, 'Zielsetzung und Stand der Strafrechtsreform in Norwegen' in Eser and Cornils (eds.), *Neuere Tendenzen der Kriminalpolitik* (Freiburg, 1987).

Blau, 'Prolegomena zur Strafrechtlichen Schuldfähigkeit' (1982) *Juristische Analysen* 401.

Bradley, 'Healing Without Hurting the Troubled Mind' (1992) *12 New Scientist* 18.

Braithwaite, '*Cooper* and *Barnier*' (1981) *2 Supreme Court* [of Canada] *Law Review* 177.

Brand-Koolen, 'At the Government's Pleasure. Trends and Developments in the

Compulsory Treatment of Mentally Disturbed Offenders in the Netherlands' (1987) *International Journal of Law and Psychiatry* 339.

Burt, 'Of Mad Dogs and Scientists: The Perils of the "Criminal-Insane"' (1977) *123 University of Pennsylvania Law Review* 258.

Carney, 'Anachronisms of Our Criminal Insanity Laws', *Irish Times,* 13 January 1990.

Chiswick, 'Insanity in Bar of Trial in Scotland: A State Hospital Study' (1978) *132 British Journal of Psychiatry* 598.

—, 'Fitness to Stand Trial and Mutism and Deafness' in Bluglass and Bowden (eds.), *Principles and Practice of Forensic Psychiatry* (London, 1990).

Cooke, 'Being an Expert in Court' (1990) *The Psychologist* 216.

Cornils, 'Neuere Entwicklung der Kriminalpolitik in den nordishen Landern' (1987) *Zeitschrift für die gesamte Strafrechts Wissenschaft* 876.

Cowie and Slater, 'Genetic Studies in Schizophrenia' in Fleming (ed.), *Recent Progress in Psychiatry III* (London, 1959).

Crespi, 'Imputabilitã' in *Enciclopedia di Diritto XX* (Milan, 1970).

Crotty, 'The History of Insanity as a Defence to a Crime in English Criminal Law' (1924) *12 California Law Review* 105.

Crow, 'Monoamine Mechanisms in Chronic Schizophrenia: Post-mortem Neurochemical Findings' (1979) *134 British Journal of Psychiatry* 249.

—, 'Molecular Pathology of Schizophrenia: More Than One Disease Process?' (1980) *280 British Medical Journal* 66.

Cutler, 'A Review of the Statistical Evidence on the Association between Smoking and Lung Cancer' (1955) *50 Journal of the American Statistical Association* 267.

Davis et al, 'Dopamine in Schizophrenia: A Review and Reconceptualization' (1991) *148 American Journal of Psychiatry* 1474.

Dell, 'Diminished Responsibility Reconsidered' (1982) *Criminal Law Review* 809.

Diamond, 'Note' (1964) *25 Ohio State Law Journal* 1.

Dixon, 'A Legacy of Hadfield, M'Naghten and Maclean' (1957-8) *31 Australian Law Journal* 255.

Doll and Hill, 'Smoking and Carcinoma of the Lung: A Preliminary Report (1950) *2 British Medical Journal* 739.

—, 'A Study of the Aetiology of Carcinoma of the Lung (1952) *2 British Medical Journal* 1271.

—, 'The Mortality of Doctors in Relation to their Smoking Habits: a Preliminary Report' (1954) *1 British Medical Journal* 1451.

Emmins, 'Unfitness to Plead: Some Thoughts Prompted by Glenn Pearson's Case' (1986) *Criminal Law Review* 604.

Ennis and Litwack, 'Psychiatry and the Presumption of Expertise: Flipping Coins in the Courtroom' (1974) *62 California Law Review* 693.

Eicknoff, 'Die Benachteiligung des psychisch kranken Rechtsbrechers im Strafrecht' (1987) *Neue Zeitschrift für Strafrecht* 65.

Ferguson, 'Factors Affecting the Outcome of the Insanity Plea' (1984) *3 Medicine and Law* 287.

German and Singer, 'Punishing the Not Guilty: Hospitalization of Persons Acquitted by Reason of Insanity' (1976) *29 Rutgers Law Review* 1011.

Gert and Duggan, 'Free Will as the Ability to Will' in Fischer (ed.), *Moral Responsibility* (London, 1986).

Gibbens, 'Psychiatry and the Abnormal Offender' (1956) *Medico-Legal Journal* 24.

Grace, 'Phasic Versus Tonic Dopamine Release and the Modulation of Dopamine System Responsitivity: An Hypothesis for the Etiology of Schizophrenia' (1991) *41 Neuroscience* 1.

Gratz, 'Die Unterbringung geistig abnormer Rechtsbrecher—Ausbruch und Wirklichkeit' (1987) *Österreiche Zeitschrift der Justiz* 333.

Gray et al, 'The Neuropsychology of Schizophrenia' (1991) *14 Behaviour and Brain Science* 1.

Grey, 'The Psychological Basis of Introversion-Extraversion' (1970) *8 Behavior Research and Therapy* 249.

Griew, 'Another Nail for M'Naghten's Coffin?' (1984) *New Law Journal* 935.

Grubin, 'Unfit to Plead in England and Wales 1976-86: A Survey' (1991) *158 British Journal of Psychiatry* 277.

—, 'Regaining Fitness: Patients Found Unfit to Plead Who Return for Trial' (1991) *2 Journal of Forensic Psychiatry* 140.

Haracz, 'The Dopamine Hypothesis: An Overview of Studies with Schizophrenic Patients' (1982) *8 Schizophrenia Bulletin* 438.

Harding, 'Sane and Insane Automatism in Australia: Some Dilemmas, Developments and Suggested Reforms' (1981) *4 International Journal of Law and Psychiatry* 73.

Hare, 'A Research Scale for the Assessment of Psychopathy in Criminal Populations' (1980) *1 Personality and Individual Differences* 111.

Hayes, 'Diminished Responsibility: The Expert Witness' Viewpoint' in Meng Heong Yeo, *Partial Excuses to Murder* (Sydney, 1991).

Haynes, 'The Predictive Value of the Clinical Assessment for the Diagnosis, Prognosis and Treatment Response of Patients' in Webster, Aron and Hucker (eds.), *Dangerousness, Probability and Prediction: Psychiatry and Public Policy* (New York, 1985).

Heston, 'Psychiatric Disorders in Foster Home Reared Children of Schizophrenic Mothers' (1966) *112 British Journal of Psychiatry* 819.

Hrib, 'HP 236 and Schizophrenia' (1992) *35 Journal of Medicine and Chemistry* 2712.

Hunter and Bargen, 'Diminished Responsibility: Abnormal Minds, Abnormal Murderers and What the Doctor Said' in Meng Heong Yeo (ed.) *Partial Excuses to Murder* (Sydney 1991).

Iversen et al, 'Pathophysiology of Schizophrenia—Causal Role for Dopamine or Noradrenaline' (1983) *305 Nature* 577.

Kaplan, 'The Mad and the Bad: An Inquiry into the Disposition of the Criminally Insane' (1977) *2 Journal of Medicine and Philosophy* 244.

Kareklas, 'Griechenland' in Eser and Huber (eds.), *Entwicklungstendenzen in Europa* (Freiburg, 1988).

Keith, 'Some Observations on Diminished Responsibility' (1959) *Juridical Review* 109.

Kety et al, 'The Types and Prevalence of Mental Illness in the Biologic and Adoptive Families of Adopted Schizophrenics' in Rosenthal and Kety (eds.), *The Transmission of Schizophrenia* (Oxford, 1968).

—, 'The Biologic and Adoptive Families of Adopted Individuals Who Become Schizophrenic: Prevalence of Mental Illness and Other Characteristics' in

Wynne et al (eds.), *The Nature of Schizophrenia: New Approaches to Research and Treatment* (New York, 1978).

Klofas and Weisheit, 'Pleading Guilty But Mentally Ill: Adversarial Justice and Mental Health' (1986) *International Journal of Law and Psychiatry* 491.

Koskinen, 'Strafrechtsreform in Finland: Zielsetzung und Stand' in Eser and Cornils (eds.), *Neuere Tendenzen der Kriminalpolitik* (Freiburg, 1987).

Krümpelmann, 'Die Neugestaltung der Vorschriften über die Schuldfähigkeit durch das Zweite Strafrechtsreformgesetz vom 4 Juli 1969' (1976) *Zeitschrift für die gesamte Strafrechts Wissenschaft* 6.

Larkin and Collins, 'Fitness to Plead and Psychiatric Reports' (1989) *29 Medical Science and Law* 26.

Lozovsky et al, 'Modulation of Dopamine Receptor Supersensitivity by Chronic Insulin: Implications for Schizophrenia (1985) 343 *Brain Research* 190.

MacKay, 'Non-organic Automatism—Some Recent Developments (1980) *Criminal Law Review* 350.

Mackay, 'Post-Hinkley Insanity in the USA' (1988) *Criminal Law Review* 88.

—, 'The Decline of Disability in Relation to Trial' (1991) *Criminal Law Review* 87.

Maher, 'The Language of Schizophrenia: A Review and Interpretation' (1972) *120 British Journal of Psychiatry* 3.

Mandell, 'The Presumption of Innocence and the Canadian Bill of Rights: *Regina v. Appleby* (1972) *10 Osgoode Hall Law Journal* 450.

Martin, 'The Reliability of Psychiatric Diagnosis' in Webster, Aron and Hucker, eds. *Dangerousness, Probability and Prediction: Psychiatry and Public Policy* (New York, 1985).

Matheson, 'Norwegen' in Eser and Huber (eds.), *Entwicklungstendenzen in Europa* (Freiburg, 1988).

McAuley, 'The Action Component of *Actus Reus*' (1989) *23 Irish Jurist* 218.

McDowell, 'Time for Change', *Irish Independent,* 13 February 1991.

Melzer and Stahl, 'The Dopamine Hypothesis of Schizophrenia: A Review' (1976) *2 Schizophrenia Bulletin* 19.

Mestrovic and Cook, 'The Dangerousness Standard: What is it and how is it used?' (1986) *International Journal of Law and Psychiatry* 444.

Mewett, 'Section 16 [of the Canadian Criminal Code] and "Wrong"' (1976) *18 Criminal Law Quarterly* 413.

Meyer, 'Psychiatrische Diagnosen und ihre Bedeutung für die Schuldfähigkeit im Sinne der par: 20/21' (1976) *Zeitschrift für die gesamte Strafrecht Wissenschaft* 54.

Monaghan, 'The Psychiatrization of Criminal Behaviour: A Reply' (1973) *24 Hospital and Community Psychiatry* 105.

— and Splane, 'Psychological Approaches to Criminal Behaviour' in Bittner and Messenger (eds.), *The Criminology Yearbook* (Beverly Hills, 1980).

Morris, 'Acquittal by Reason of Insanity' in Monaghan and Steadman (eds.), *Mentally Disordered Offenders: Perspectives from Law and Social Science* (New York, 1983).

Morse, 'Crazy Behaviour, Morals and Science: An Analysis of Mental Health Law' (1978) *51 Southern California Law Review* 527.

—, 'Mentally Disordered Offenders' in *International Encyclopedia of Criminal Justice* (New York, 1983).

——, 'The Role of the Mental Health Expert' in *International Encyclopedia of Criminal Justice* (New York, 1983).

Mrozynsky, 'Krankheit—Hang—Schädliche Neigungen' (1985) *Goldhammers Archiv* 2.

Normand, 'Unfitness for Trial in Scotland: Proposed Adjudication of the Facts and the Right to Reprosecute' (1984) *7 International Journal of Law and Psychiatry* 415.

Note, 'Committment Following Acquittal by Reason of Insanity' (1968) *University of Pennsylvania Law Review* 924.

O'Hanlon, 'Not Guilty Because of Insanity' (1968) *3 Irish Jurist* 61.

Orchard, 'Insanity—A Psychiatrist's View of the Recent Rulings of the Supreme Court of Canada' (1981) *2 Supreme Court Law Review* 401.

Pagliaro, 'Colpevolezza e Responsibilità Obiettiva: Aspetti di Politica Criminale ed Elaborazione Dogmatica' (1988) *Rivista Italiana di Diritto e Procedura Penale* 389.

Pasewark, 'The Insanity Plea: A Review of the Research and Literature' (1982) *9 Journal of Psychiatry and Law* 357.

Pavey, 'Verbal Behaviour in Schizophrenia: A Review of Recent Studies' (1968) *70 Psychological Bulletin* 121.

Penrose, 'Mental Disease and Crime: Outline of a Comparative Study of European Statistics' (1939) *British Journal of Medical Psychology* 18.

Petrila, 'The Insanity Defence and Other Mental Health Dispositions in Missouri' (1982) *5 International Journal of Law and Psychiatry* 81.

Platt and Diamond, 'The Origins of the "Right and Wrong" Test of Criminal Responsibility and its Subsequent Development in the United States: An Historical Survey' (1966) *54 California Law Review* 1227.

Plaut, 'Punishment Versus Treatment of the Guilty But Mentally Ill' (1983) *Journal of Criminal Law and Criminology* 48.

Ponti et al, 'L'abolizione delle Prezunzioni di Pericolosità Sociale' (1987) *Rivista Italiana di Medicina Legale* 17.

Prevezer, 'Fitness to Plead and the Criminal Lunatics Act 1800' (1958) *Criminal Law Review* 144.

Probst, 'Die strafgerichtliche Behandlung geistig abnormer Rechtsbrecher aus kriminalpolitischer Sicht' in *AAVV Strafrechtliche Probleme der Gegenwart* (Ottenstein, 1981).

Rabkin, 'The Criminal Behaviour of Discharged Mental Patients: A Critical Appraisal of the Research' (1979) *86 Psychological Bulletin* 1.

Rasch, 'Die Zuordnung der psychiatrisch-psychologischen Diagnosen zu den vier psychischen Merkmalen der par 20 und 21 StGB' (1984) *Strafverteidiger* 265.

——, 'Die Prognose im Massregelnvollzug als Kalkuriertes Risiko' in *Festschrift Blau* (Berlin, 1985).

Ray, JJ and JAB, 'Some Apparent Advantages of Subclinical Psychopathy' (1982) *117 Journal of Social Psychology* 135.

Roxin, 'Schuldunfähigkeit Erwachsener im Urteil des Strafrecht' in *Festschift Spann* (Heidelberg, 1986).

Russo, 'Infirimità di Mente e Pericolosità Sociale' (1987) *Rivista Italiana di Medicina Legale* 736.

Schäffer, 'Belgien' in Eser and Huber (eds.), *Entwicklungstendenzen in Europa* (Freiburg, 1988).
Schmauk, 'Punishment, Arousal and Avoidance Learning in Sociopaths' (1970) *76 Journal of Abnormal Psychology* 325.
Schmitt, 'Die 'schwere andere seelische Abartigkeit in par. 20 und 21' (1980) *Zeitschrift für die gesamte Strafrechts Wissenschaft* 346.
Schulz, 'Probleme einer Revision des Allgemeinen Teils des Schweizerischen Strafgesezbuches' in *Festschrift Lackner* (Zürich, 1985).
Seeman, 'Analysis of Psychotic Language: A Review and Synthesis' (1970) *31 Diseases of the Nervous System* 92.
Shields and Slater, 'Genetic Studies' in Eyesenk (ed.), *Handbook of Abnormal Psychology* (London, 1960).
Steadman, 'Insanity Acquittals in New York State 1967-8' (1980) *American Journal of Psychiatry* 137.
Stephen, 'On the Policy of Maintaining the Limits at Present Imposed on the Criminal Responsibility of Madmen' in *Juridical Society Papers 1855-8* (London, 1883).
Sutherland and Gearty, 'Insanity and the European Court of Human Rights' (1992) *Criminal Law Review* 418.
Szasz, 'The Concept of Mental Illness' (1991) *The Lancet* 1574.

Taminga et al, 'Schizophrenia Symptoms Improve with Apomorphine' (1978) *200 Science* 567.
Torío Lopez, 'Las Fórmulas Legislativas sobre la Enfermedad Mental: Discusión del Concepto de "Enajenación"' in Torío Lopez (ed.), *Estudios Juridicos en Honor del Profesor Octavi Pérez-Vitoria* (Barcelona, 1983).
Verdun-Jones, 'The Insanity Defence since *Schwartz v. R*: First Steps along the Road towards the Rationalization of Canadian Policy?' (1979) *6 CR* (3d) 300.
—, 'The Evolution of the Defences of Insanity and Automatism in Canada from 1843 to 1979: A Saga of Judicial Reluctance to Sever the Umbilical Cord to the Mother Country' (1979) *14 British Columbia Law Review* 1.
White, 'The Criminal Procedure (Insanity and Unfitness to Plead) Act' (1992) *Criminal Law Review* 4.
Widom, 'A Methodology for Studying Non-institutionalised Psychopaths' in Hare and Schalling (eds.), *Psychopathic Behaviour* (New York, 1978).
Witter, 'Die Beurteilung der Schuldfähigkeit bei Belastungsreaktionen, Neurosen und Personlichkeitsstörungen am Beispiel der Affektdelikte' in Witter (ed.), *Die psychiatrische Sachverständige im Strafrecht* (Berlin, 1987).
—, 'Die Grundlagen für die Beurteilung der Schuldfähigkeit im Strafrecht' in —(ed.), *Die psychiatrische Sachverständige im Strafrecht* (Berlin, 1987).
Zilboorg, 'Misconceptions of Legal Insanity' (1939) *American Journal of Orthopsychiatry* 552.

BOOKS

*The following is a complete list of the works cited in the footnotes to the text. Unless otherwise indicated below, all references are to first editions.*


Addad and Benezech, *L'irresponsabilité Pénale des Handicapés Mentaux* (Paris, 1978).

Ancel et al, *Le Droit Pénal de Pays Scandinaves* (Paris, 1969).

Antilla and Joutson, trans. *The Finnish Penal Code* (London, 1987).

Antolisei, *Manuale di Diritto Penale* (Milan, 1989).

Arens, *Insanity Defence* (New York, 1974).

Archbold, *Criminal Pleading, Evidence and Practice,* 23rd. edn. (London, 1905).

Aristotle, *The Nichomachean Ethics,* trans. Thompson (London, 1955).

Aussel, *Les Délinquants Aliénés et Anormaux Mentaux* (Paris, 1966).

Backman et al, *Finnish Criminal Policy in Transition* (Helsinki, 1979).

Bandini et al, *Omicidio e Controllo Sociale* (Milan, 1983).

Baumann and Weber, *Strafrecht* (Bielefeld, 1985).

Beck, *Depression: Clinical, Experimental and Theoretical Aspects* (New York, 1967).

—, *Cognitive Therapy and the Emotional Disorders* (New York, 1976).

—, Rush, Shaw and Emery, *Cognitive Theories of Depression* (Pennsylvania, 1978).

Beran and Toomey (eds.) *Mentally Ill Offenders and the Criminal Justice System: Issues in Forensic Services* (New York, 1979).

Bertolino, *L'Imputabilità e il Vizio di Mente nel Sistema Penale* (Milan, 1990).

Bittner and Messenger (eds.), *The Criminology Yearbook* (Beverly Hills, 1980).

Blake (ed.), *Trials of Patrick Carraher* (Edinburgh, 1951).

Blakemore, *The Mind Machine* (London, 1990).

Bluglass and Bowden (eds.), *Principles and Practice of Forensic Psychiatry* (London, 1990).

Bracton, *De Legibus et Consuetudinibus Angliae,* ed. Woodbine (Oxford, 1915).

Brousolle, *Délinquance et Déviance* (Toulouse, 1978).

Brown, Farrier, Neal and Weisbrot, *Criminal Laws: Materials and Commentary on the Criminal Law of New South Wales* (Sydney, 1990).

Burchell et al., *South African Criminal Law and Procedure,* vol. 1 (Cape Town, 1983).

Cameron, *Personality Development and Psychopathology* (Boston, 1963).

Carbonell Mateu et al, *Enfermedad Mental y Delito: Aspectos Psichiatricos* (Valencia, 1987).

Cheang, *Criminal Law of Malaysia and Singapore* (Kuala Lumpur, 1990).

Christie et al., (eds.) *Scandinavian Studies in Criminology* (London, 1971).

Claridge, *Origins of Mental Illness* (Oxford, 1985).

Cobo del Rosal and Vives de Antón, *Derecho Penal* (Valencia 1984).

Córdoba Roda and Mourullo, *Comentarios al Codigo Penal* (Barcelona, 1976).

Costant, *Traité Élementaire de Droit Pénal* (Liege, 1965).

Cross, *The Golden Thread of English Criminal Law: The Burden of Proof* (Rede Lecture, 1976).

Cross and Jones, *An Introduction to Criminal Law,* 7th. edn. (London, 1972).

Culver and Gert, *Philosophy and Medicine* (London, 1982).

Davidson, *Essays on Actions and Events* (London, 1985).

Devesa, *Derecho Penal Español* (Madrid, 1986).

Doucet, *Précis de Droit Pénal Général* (Liege, 1965).
Duff, *Trials and Punishments* (Cambridge, 1991).
Eder and Rieder, *Die freiheitsentziehenden vorbeugenden Massnahmen* (Vienna, 1985).
Eser and Cornils (eds.), *Neuere Tendenzen der Kriminalpolitik* (Freiburg, 1987).
Eser and Huber (eds.), *Entwicklungstendenzen in Europa* (Freiburg, 1988).
Eyesenk (ed.), *Handbook of Abnormal Psychology* (London, 1960).
Fairfield and Fulbrook, *Trials of John Thomas Straffen* (London, 1954).
Fiandaca and Musco, *Diritto Penale, Parte Generale,* 2nd. edn. (Bologna, 1991).
Fingarette, *The Meaning of Criminal Insanity* (New York, 1972).
— and Hasse, *Mental Disabilities and Criminal Responsibility* (Berkeley, 1979).
Finkel, *Insanity on Trial: Perspectives on Law and Psychology* (New York, 1988).
Fioravanti, *Le Infermità Psichiche nella Jurisprudenza Penale* (Padua, 1988).
Fischer (ed.), *Moral Responsibility* (London, 1986).
Fleming (ed.), *Recent Progress in Psychiatry III* (London, 1959).
Friedman and Katz (eds.) *The Psychology of Depression: Contemporary Theory and Research* (Washington, 1974).
Gibson, *Homicide in England and Wales 1967-71* (Home Office Research Study No. 31, 1975).
Glatzel, *Forensische Psychiatrie* (Stuttgart, 1985).
Goldberg and Huxley, *Common Mental Disorders* (London, 1992).
Gordon, *The Criminal Law of Scotland,* 2nd. edn., (Edinburgh, 1978).
Gottesman and Shields, *Schizophrenia: The Epigenetic Puzzle* (Cambridge, 1982).
Grevi (ed.), *L'ordinamento Penitenzario Dopo la Riforma* (Padua, 1988).
Grey, *The Neuropsychology of Anxiety* (Oxford, 1982).
Gross, *The Psychological Society* (New York, 1978).
Hale, *Historia Placitorum Coronae 1* (London, 1736).
Hall, *General Principles of Criminal Law,* 2nd. edn. (New York, 1960).
Hare, *Psychopathy: Theory and Research* (New York, 1970).
Hare and Schalling (eds.), *Psychopathic Behaviour* (New York, 1978).
Hart, *Punishment and Responsibility* (Oxford, 1968).
Haslam, *Medical Jurisprudence as it Relates to Insanity According to the Law of England* (London, 1817).
Hippel, *Deutsches Strafrecht* (Berlin, 1925).
Hoffman, *Rationalization of Insanity: An Analysis of the Guilty But Mentally Ill Provision in Illinois* (Ann Arbor, 1987).
Johnson, *Criminal Law* (New York, 1985).
Kenny, *Outlines of Criminal Law,* 19th edn. (London, 1965).
—, *Cases on Criminal Law,* 4th. edn. (Cambridge, 1919).
Kraepelin, *Lectures in Clinical Psychiatry* (New York, 1968).
Kruger, *Kante van Imputasie in die Nederlandse en Suid-Afrikause Strafreg* (Lieden, 1972).
Langbein, *Torture and the Law of Proof* (Chicago, 1977).
Lolis and Mangakis (trans.), *The Greek Penal Code* (London, 1923).
Lopez-Rey, Crime: *An Analytical Appraisal* (London, 1979).
MacCormick, *HLA Hart* (London, 1981).
Maher, *Principles of Psychopathology: An Experimental Approach* (New York, 1966).
Mantovani, *Diritto Penale* (Padua, 1988).

Matthaeus, *De Criminibus ad lib. XLVII et XLVIII Dig. Commentarius* (Amsterdam, 1644).
Maurach-Zipf, *Strafrecht, Allg.* (Heidelberg, 1983).
Mayer-Gross et al, *Clinical Psychiatry* (London, 1960).
Mayerhoffer and Reider, *Das Österreichische Strafrecht* (Vienna, 1981).
McCord, W and J, *The Psychopath: An Essay on the Criminal Mind* (New York, 1964).
Meng Heong Yeo (ed.) *Partial Excuses to Murder* (Sydney 1991).
Merle and Vitu, *Traité de Droit Criminel* (Paris, 1987).
Mezger et al, *Das Ausländische Strafrecht der Gegenwart* (Berlin, 1959).
Mir Puig, *Derecho Penal* (Barcelona, 1984).
Monaghan, *The Clinical Prediction of Violent Behaviour* (Rockville, Md., 1981).
— and Steadman (eds.), *Mentally Disordered Offenders: Perspectives from Law and Social Science* (New York, 1983).
Morris, *Madness and the Criminal Law* (London, 1982).
Noll and Trechel, *Schweizerisches Strafrecht* (Zurich, 1986).
Oades, *Attention and Schizophrenia* (Boston, 1982).
Pagliaro, *Principi di Diritto Penale* (Milan, 1987).
Prichard, *On the Different Forms of Insanity in Relation to Jurisprudence* (London, 1842).
Radden, *Madness and Reason* (London, 1985).
Ray, *A Treatise on the Medical Jurisprudence of Insanity* (London 1839).
Robins, *Fools and Mad—A History of the Insane in Ireland* (Dublin, 1986).
Romano, *Commentario Sistematico del Codice Penale* (Rome, 1991).
Schuind, *Traité Pratique de Droit Criminel*, Bd. 1 (Bruxelles, 1980).
Schulz, *Schweizerisches Strafrecht* (Bern, 1989).
Schumann, *Psychisch kranke Rechtsbrecher* (Stuttgart, 1987).
Schwartz (ed.)., *Language and Cognition in Schizophrenia* (New York, 1978).
Simon and Aaranson, *The Insanity Defence: A Critical Assessment of Law and Policy in the Post-Hinkley Era* (New York, 1988).
Smith and Hogan, *Criminal Law,* 7th. edn., (London, 1992).
Steadman and Cocozza, *Careers of the Criminally Insane: Excessive Social Control of Deviance* (Boston, 1974).
Stefani et al, *Droit Pénal Général* (Paris, 1987).
Stephen, *History of the Criminal Law of England,* vol. II (London, 1883).
Stuart, *Canadian Criminal Law,* 2nd. edn. (Toronto, 1987).
Szasz, *Law, Liberty and Psychiatry,* 2nd. edn. (New York, 1989).
Taylor, *Principles of Medical Jurisprudence,* vol. 1, 11th. edn., (London, 1957).
Thornbury and Jacoby, *The Criminally Insane: A Community Follow-up of Mentally Ill Offenders* (Chicago, 1979).
Torío Lopez (ed.), *Estudios Jurídicos en Honor del Profesor Octavio Pérez-Vitoria* (Barcelona, 1983).
Trifter, *Österreichisches Strafrecht* (Vienna, 1985).
Van den Wyngaert, *Strafrecht en Procesrecht*, Boek 1 (Antwerp, 1991).
Waling, *Enstehung und Entwicklung des Niederlandisches Strafgesetzbuches,* Research Paper, Max Plank Institute (Freiburg, 1986).
Walker, *Crime and Insanity in England* (Edinburgh, 1968).
Webster, Aron and Hucker (eds.), *Dangerousness, Probability and Prediction:*

*Psychiatry and Public Policy* (New York, 1985).
Williams, *Criminal Law: The General Part,* 2nd. edn. (London, 1961).
—, *Textbook of Criminal Law* (London, 1978).
—, Katherine, *Textbook on Criminology* (Londom, 1991).
Winslade and Ross, *The Insanity Plea* (London, 1983).
Witter (ed.), *Die psychiatrische Sachverständige im Strafrecht* (Berlin, 1987)
Wootton, *Crime and the Criminal Law,* 2nd. edn. (London, 1981).
Wynne et al (eds.), *The Nature of Schizophrenia: New Approaches to Research and Treatment* (New York, 1978).
Ziskin, *Coping with Psychiatric Testimony,* 2nd ed. (New York, 1975).

## REPORTS AND DRAFTS

*The following is a complete list of the Reports, Drafts and Statements cited in the footnotes to the text. Where a Report has become identified with the chairperson of the committee responsible for producing it, the chairperson's name is given in square brackets.*

Advisory Council on the Penal System, *Sentences of Imprisonment* (HMSO,1978).
American Bar Association, *First Tentative Draft. Criminal Justice Mental Health Standards* (Washington, 1983).
American Psychiatric Association, *Glossary of Diagnostic and Statistical Manual,* 3rd. edn. (Boston, 1980).
American Psychiatric Association, *Diagnostic and Statistical Manual of Mental Disorders,* 3rd. edn. (Washington, 1980).
American Psychiatric Association, *Statement on the Insanity Defence* (Washington, 1982).
*Anteproyecto de Codigo Penal*; última versión, 30 Diciembre 1991).
Criminal Law Revision Committee, *Fourteenth Report: Offences Against the Person,* Cmnd. 7844 (London, 1980).
Law Commission, *Codification of the Criminal Law,* Law Commission Report Number 143.
*Report of the Royal Commission on Capital Punishment, 1949-53,* Cmnd. 8932 (London, 1953).
*Second Report of the Committee on Criminal Procedure in Scotland,* Cmnd. 6218 (London, 1957).
*Report of the Committee on Insanity and Crime,* Cmd. 2005 (London, 1924).
*Report of the Royal* [McRuer] *Commission on the Law of Insanity as a Defence in Criminal Cases* (Toronto, 1956).
*Report of the Committee on Mentally Abnormal Offenders* [The Butler Report], Cmnd. 6244 (London, 1975).
Report of the Canadian Law Commission. *Mental Disorder and the Criminal Process* (Ottawa, 1976).
World Health Organization, *Mental Disorders: Glossary and Guide to their Classification in Accordance with the Ninth Revision of the International Classification of Diseases* (WHO, 1978).
Third Interim Report of the Interdepartmental Committee [chaired by Mr Justice Henchy, then of the Supreme Court] on Mentally Ill and Maladjusted Persons. *Treatment and Care of Persons Suffering from Mental Disorder Who Appear*

*Before the Courts On Criminal Charges* (Dublin, 1978).
*Report of the Commission of Inquiry into the Responsibility of Mentally Deranged Persons* [the Rumpff Report] (Cape Town, 1967).
*Report(s) on Crime 1947-1991* [by the Garda Commissioner to the Minister for Justice] (Dublin, 1947-91).

# Table of Cases

# Table of Statutes

IRELAND



UNITED KINGDOM



MISCELLANEOUS

# Index